Christian Faith Perspectives in Leadership and Business

This book series is designed to integrate Christian faith-based perspectives into the field of leadership and business, widening its influence by taking a deeper look at its foundational roots. It is led by a team of experts from Regent University, recognized by the Coalition of Christian Colleges and Universities as the leader in servant leadership research and the first Christian University to integrate innovation, design thinking, and entrepreneurship courses in its Masters and Doctoral programs. Stemming from Regent's hallmark values of innovation and Christian faith-based perspectives, the series aims to put forth top-notch scholarship from current faculty, students, and alumni of Regent's School of Business & Leadership, allowing for both scholarly and practical aspects to be addressed while providing robust content and relevant material to readers. Each volume in the series will contribute to filling the void of a scholarly Christian-faith perspective on key aspects of organizational leadership and business such as Business and Innovation, Biblical Perspectives in Business and Leadership, and Servant Leadership. The series takes a unique approach to such broad-based and well-trodden disciplines as leadership, business, innovation, and entrepreneurship, positioning itself as a much-needed resource for students, academics, and leaders rooted in Christian-faith traditions.

More information about this series at
https://link.springer.com/bookseries/15425

Debra J. Dean · Robert B. Huizinga
Editors

Followership and Faith at Work

Biblical Perspectives

palgrave
macmillan

Editors
Debra J. Dean
Regent University
Colorado Springs, CO, USA

Robert B. Huizinga
North Saanich, BC, Canada

Christian Faith Perspectives in Leadership and Business
ISBN 978-3-030-90613-9 ISBN 978-3-030-90614-6 (eBook)
https://doi.org/10.1007/978-3-030-90614-6

This Palgrave Macmillan imprint is published by the registered company Springer Nature Switzerland AG
The registered company address is: Gewerbestrasse 11, 6330 Cham, Switzerland

Contents

Notes on Contributors

R. Mark Bell, Ph.D. is an Assistant Professor of Management at Wayland Baptist University and serves as a faculty member in WBU's Doctor of Management program. Mark holds an M.B.A. and a Ph.D. in Organizational Leadership. He spent 17 years working in management positions in the retail supermarket industry prior to his career in higher education which has included various academic leadership roles. Mark's research interests include effective followership, ineffective leadership, and healthy leadership. In addition to serving as a reviewer for a number of academic publications, Mark has published research articles in several peer-reviewed journals.

Christa Bonnet, Ph.D. is the founder of *The Difference Makers Africa NPO* focusing on the empowerment of female entrepreneurs. She fulfills a variety of roles including that of mother, social entrepreneur, facilitator, author, and consultant. She is an NLP Coach, SQ & Quantum Leadership Trainer, and Enterprise and Supplier Development (ESD) Consultant (South Africa). Her research interests include Christian leadership, spiritual formation, spiritual intelligence (SQ), and transformation. Christa graduated in 2020 at Regent University (Virginia Beach) with a Ph.D. in Organizational Leadership.

Jane Caulton, Ph.D. is an independent researcher, residing in Wake Forest, North Carolina. A retiree of the Library of Congress, Washington, DC, she holds a Master of Science in Strategic Human Resources and Organizational Development from Johns Hopkins University, Baltimore, MD. She received her Ph.D. in Organizational Leadership with a focus on Ecclesial Leadership from Regent University, Virginia Beach, Virginia. Dr. Caulton is an ordained minister of the Mount Calvary Holy Church of America International, and a member of the Society for Pentecostal Studies (SPS) and Celebration Church, Raleigh, NC. She has been published in Regent University's *Emerging Leadership Journeys* journal and SPS's *Pneuma* journal, among others.

Nestor L. Colls-Senaha, Ph.D. is retired from the U.S. Army after 23 years of service. He has a B.S. in Business Administration from the University of Central Florida, a M.A. in National Security and Strategic Studies from the Naval War College, and a Ph.D. in Organizational Leadership from Regent University. He serves as a part-time Adjunct Professor, Dissertation Chair, and Dissertation Committee member, at three universities where he teaches undergraduate, graduate, and doctorate level courses. He is married to Vicki and has five children (Nina, Erik, Jared, Ryan, and Terah), and three grandchildren (Bryan Jr., Penelope, and Hudson).

Debra J. Dean, Ph.D. is focused on research, publications, and speaking about integration of faith, followership, and respectful pluralism. She is an Adjunct Professor at several schools and has 25 years of corporate experience. She was awarded the 2020 Women of Influence by The Colorado Springs Business Journal, the 2020 Most Influential Business Consultancy CEO (USA) by Global CEO Excellence Awards, operational excellence leader with OPEX Week Business Transformation World Summit 2019, and awarded as top female leader with her previous global workplace. She has been included in Biltmore's Who's Who of Women Business Leaders, Continental Who's Who of National Business Leaders, and Who's Who Among University Students. She is married and has six amazing children and four wonderful grandchildren.

Joshua D. Henson is an Associate Professor of Leadership at Southeastern University. He is also the founder of Rediscover Oikos, LLC, a Christian leadership coaching and church consulting company. He holds a Ph.D. in Organizational Leadership from Regent University. He serves as a Ph.D. instructor in ecclesial leadership at Regent University and as the co-editor of the Journal of Biblical Perspectives in Leadership. He has published multiple articles and books including *Exegetical Analysis: A Practical Guide for Applying Biblical Research in the Social Sciences*, *Modern Metaphors of Christian Leadership*, and *Biblical Organizational Leadership*.

Robert B. Huizinga, Ph.D. is a senior executive with a global biotechnology company. Over his time in global drug development, he has been involved in the successful development of new medications in transplantation and autoimmune disease. He has published in top tier medical journals, continues to lecture extensively around the globe and is recognized as an expert in immunosuppression drug development from the preclinical to completed clinical programs. His most recent publications include the book *Organizational Metaphors: Faith as Key to Functional Organizations*. He is also a partner with EQUIP Leadership, teaching Christian leadership principles globally. Robert is an Adjunct Professor at The King's University in Edmonton Canada and has been married for 36 years with five children and seven grandchildren.

Omo N. Imoukhuede, Ph.D. a Nigerian immigrant to the USA, currently serves as the Resident Pastor at the CityLight International Assembly, Chicago south-side. In addition to his Pastoral calling, Pastor Omo broad experience covers areas in Leadership, Followership, Group Dynamics, Technology, Entrepreneurship, and Education. Omokhai seeks to inspire, encourage, and uplift individuals using various creative outlets like inspirational writings, trainings, and speaking. He is also the author of the book *Discovering Followership, Learn the Secrets of Walking Behind and still staying ahead*. Omokhai Imoukhuede is married to Osen who serves along with him at the CityLight International Church. They are blessed with four children Alina, Sophia, Hannah, and Jeremiah-Stephen

Nancy Nkirote Muriuki, Ph.D. is a consultant in leadership and governance and an adjunct lecturer at Pan Africa Christian University (PAC), Nairobi, Kenya. She is the founding director of Africa Success Enhancement Lab (ASEL) offering training on corruption prevention and good governance through servant leadership. Nancy spent over 25 years in other sectors before the current phase. Nancy holds a Ph.D. in Organizational Leadership from Regent University, USA, Master of Business Administration (MBA), a Bachelor of Commerce from the University of Nairobi and in 2020, completed a course for Doctoral Supervisors in African Universities from Stellenbosch University, South Africa. Her research interests include servant leadership, leaders' immunity to corruption and the role of followers in corruption prevention. Nancy is a member of the Institute of Certified Secretaries of Kenya (ICS), the Institute of Human Resources of Kenya, and the Greenleaf Centre for Servant Leadership, Seton Hall University. Nancy is married to Julius Muriuki and are blessed with four children.

Percy Opio, Ph.D. has over 20 years' experience in developing and leading successful teams in the ICT and Financial Services Industry. He is an Associate of The Leadership Group (K) Ltd. where he is a leadership development and strategy consultant. He is an adjunct lecturer at Pan Africa Christian University and Program Leader at International Leadership University, Kenya. Percy is also involved in developing technological and innovative solutions in healthcare and education. He is the author of *The Future of Banking in Kenya* (2015). He holds a Doctor of Strategic Leadership degree in Strategic Foresights from Regent University, a Master of Arts in Leadership degree from Pan Africa Christian University, and a Bachelor of Education degree from Moi University. He is an Associate Member of the Association of Professional Futurists. Percy has a passion for families and serves in the Marriage Outreach Ministry at the All Saints Cathedral, Nairobi.

Larry D. Phillips, Ph.D. has settled on a small farm in Upstate South Carolina with his wife Kim. Larry started his professional career with the United States Air Force in the Aircraft Maintenance Management field. His service included helping to operationalize the F-117 Stealth Fighter, serving in the first Gulf War and in many continental United States locations. Today Larry is a Director for Supply Chain Operations within the AdventHealth Health System. He holds a bachelor's degree from St. Leo University, a Master of Science degree from Troy University, and completed doctoral studies in Organizational Leadership at Regent University.

R. Lewis Steinhoff, Ph.D. is an Adjunct Professor with San Diego Christian College (SDCC) where he teaches graduate level organizational leadership, leadership behavior, and organizational communication. Dr. Steinhoff recently retired after 30+ years at the U.S. Department of Energy's National Nuclear Security Administration (NNSA) where he was Director of the Nuclear Weapon Acquisition Professional (NWAP) Certification Program. He also recently completed a two-year assignment at the U.S.A.F. Air War College as the NNSA Faculty Chair teaching and advising mid to senior level military officers and civilians on nuclear deterrence, leadership, and followership. He has a B.S. in Mechanical Engineering, a Master of Engineering Management from George Washington University, and a Ph.D. in Organizational Leadership from Regent University.

Boniface Toulassi, Ph.D. is Executive Director to *Bridge to Nations*. Boniface is a seasonal lecturer to International Leadership University-Kenya and the Global Academy for Transformational Leadership (GATL). Prior to that he was a visiting lecturer to The Advanced School of Administration and Management (ESAG), Faculty of Economic Sciences and Management (FASEG) in Togo, Noah Webster College in New Mexico, USA, and served as the deputy director of operations to the International Leadership Foundation in Florida, USA. His Radio and TV programs focus on the African culture and Christianity.

List of Figures

List of Tables

CHAPTER 1

Introduction

Debra J. Dean and Robert B. Huizinga

The sheep blindly follow the shepherd for the sheep know not what to do. Without a shepherd, the flock of sheep will follow each other. The act of unsighted followership is hard wired in their genetic code to unquestionably follow, even to their demise. Humans, on the other hand, are intelligent beings that follow more often than not. Although many say, "be a leader, not a follower" the reality is that everyone is a follower and there are more followers in this world than there are leaders. The humbling question is why there are not more books and classes on how

D. J. Dean (✉) · R. B. Huizinga
Regent University, Virginia Beach, VA, USA
e-mail: debrdea@regent.edu; drdebra@drdebradean.com

R. B. Huizinga
e-mail: rhuizinga@auriniapharma.com; robehui@mail.regent.edu

D. J. Dean
Regent University, Colorado Springs, CO, USA

R. B. Huizinga
North Saanich, BC, Canada

D. J. Dean and R. B. Huizinga (eds.), *Followership and Faith at Work*, Christian Faith Perspectives in Leadership and Business,
https://doi.org/10.1007/978-3-030-90614-6_1

to be a better follower since more people will spend more time following than they will leading.

To date, followership has been slow to arrive on the horizon of practical training material. However, scholarly pioneers such as Robert Kelley, Ira Chaleff, and Barbara Kellerman have led the way with the topic of followership. Kelley's first book on the topic was published in 1992. Ira Chaleff published the first version of the Courageous Follower in 2003. And Barbara Kellerman wrote her first followership book in 2008. Since then, there have been hundreds, if not thousands of scholars to follow. The purpose of these books on followership, along with the current book you are reading, is to help people to become better followers. To do that, it is helpful to know what type of follower a person is and what type of follower may best suit the situation at hand. In some cases, it is okay to be a bystander and in other cases, someone must stand up to be courageous. In this book, the types of followers will be defined as noted in the empirical literature by Kelley, Chaleff, and Kellerman. Additional followership styles will also be portrayed as followers of Jesus Christ are examined.

Most people agree that Jesus Christ is one of the best leaders of all times. He walked the earth 2000+ years ago and still has a following of people ready and willing to "deny himself and take up his cross" to follow the Lord of Lords and King of Kings (Matthew 16:24–26). In this book, 13 authors exegetically extract followership competencies from the disciples of Jesus Christ. As you will see, some followers were devoted and did give up everything they had to follow their Teacher and Master. One turned on their beloved leader to betray him. And, in some form or fashion, all had miraculous interventions that changed their lives forever.

Jesus Christ is not only a leader, but also a follower. As the Trinity, Jesus is one of three beings: God the Father, God the Son, and God the Holy Spirit. He came to serve and to love all people, knowing that in the end, he would be crucified on the cross. He endured terrible persecution while on earth. Luke 22: 39–46 gives a glimpse of Jesus praying, "Father, if you are willing, remove this cup from me. Nevertheless, not my will, but yours, be done." Jesus was more than capable to command an army of angels to take away the wrath and destroy the evil villains; however, He followed the plan and allowed the destruction of the temple to take place. He showed complete submission to the plan despite the risk. This book will look intimately at the lives of 14 followers of Jesus Christ. Disciples included in this book are Ananias, Andrew, Apollos, Aquilla, John, Judas, Jude, Mary of Magdala, Nathanael, Nicodemus, Peter, Philip, Priscilla, and Stephen. From each of their lives, careful attention was given to the way they followed Jesus Christ. The purpose of this book is to understand more about the followership types of the disciples in hopes to understand more of how we can be better followers in the twenty-first century.

Some may question why a book such as this is important. After all, it is more popular to be the leader than the follower. However, the reality is that most people spend more of their life following in some capacity than leading. And, of those that follow, they may be faced with situations where they need to risk it all for the sake of the cause or they may need to speak up courageously to stop the leader from making a horrible mistake. On one end of the spectrum are the leaders that clearly plan to do evil. On the other end of the spectrum are leaders that plan to do good, but may fall short or veer off the chosen path. In either situation, a good follower can call attention to the problem and correct the error quickly.

There are many evil leaders, those that plan to do harm to other human beings. However, these leaders did not act alone. They had followers, sometimes hundreds or thousands of followers that unquestionably did as they were told. These sheep-like followers were also intelligent beings; therefore, they must have known that what they were doing was wrong, yet they followed orders. The worse leaders in history include Mao Tse-Tung, the founding father of the People's Republic of China and Chairman of the Chinese Communist Party between 1949 and 1976. Under his reign, approximately 20 million people starved to death and 2–3 million people were killed by his regime. Joseph Stalin, known as one of the most evil dictators in history, ruled as a Soviet Union dictator from 1920 to 1953. During his control, more than 23 million people died. Adolf Hitler founded the Nazi party and served as Chancellor of Germany from 1933 to 1945. During that time, he brutally tortured 17 million people. It is the hope that this book will serve as an encouragement to followers around the globe to be courageous and challenge their leaders when choosing between good and evil.

Other leaders that likely started out good, but fell to greed and selfish ways include the likes of William Miller, known as 520% Miller in 1899 or Charles Ponzi in the 1920s. Modern day swindlers include Bernie Madoff who was arrested in 2008 with one of the largest Ponzi schemes in American history. Names such as Dick Fuld, Chairman and CEO of Lehman Brothers; Angelo Mozilo, Chairman and CEO of Countrywide Financial; Jimmy Cayne, CEO of Bear Stearns; Albert Dunlap, CEO of Sunbeam; and John Akers, President, CEO, and Chairman of IBM have all been on the Portfolio's Worst American CEOs of All Time list. Adding to the list of unscrupulous leaders are Robert Allen Stanford who was arrested in 2012 for his massive Ponzi scheme totaling $7 billion. He is now serving a 110-year sentence. WorldCom CEO Bernie Ebbers, known as the Telecom Cowboy, was convicted in 2005 for his accounting scandal.

Martin Frankel looted insurance companies to the tune of $200 million. He was caught in 1999 and convicted in 2004 for conspiracy, racketeering, securities fraud, and wire fraud. Unauthorized bonuses of $81 million lead to a conviction of Tyco International CEO, Leo Dennis Kozlowski in 2005. Enron leaders Kenneth Lay and Jeffrey Skilling are also known for mismanagement and dishonesty. Lay died before sentencing; however, Skilling spent 14 years in prison for conspiracy, securities fraud, false statement, and insider trading. More names include Markus Brown of Wirecard, John Stumpf of Wells Fargo, and Martin Winterkorn of Volkswagen. Each of these "bad guys" had followers that could have stood up and said something to have them change their ways. Perhaps some did try to change their ways. Perhaps some chose to turn and run to distance themselves from the unethical behavior. And perhaps it would not have made a difference if someone spoke up. The value of a good follower can never be discounted because good followers are needed for good businesses.

Aristotle declared, "He who cannot be a good follower cannot be a good leader." We are all followers. Synonyms of the word follower include esteemed roles of apostle, assistant, disciple, pupil, and subordinate. These, often termed, roles of second chair are necessary. However, the word follower usually conjures up a negative connotation. But why? Why are we told to be the leader, not the follower? What can be done to improve the image of the word follower? In the New King James version of the Bible, the word Lead appears 80 times; however, the word Follow appears 253 times. It is without a doubt that more attention needs to be given to followers than to leaders, especially in a time period where support roles (followers) have the ability to blow the whistle when leaders make unethical decisions.

Followership is an emerging topic originally pioneered by Ira Chaleff (2009), Barbara Kellerman (2008), and Robert Kelley (1992). The theory of followership flips the lens of leadership to examine the role of followers. It makes much sense to examine the roles of followers since the majority of the workforce (and the world) are followers, not in a formal position of power. Each of the pioneers took a stance in defining various types of followers and there have been instruments developed to assess the type of follower an employee is. This book expands the theory of followership to look at the faithful follower as a follower of Jesus. As more employees are integrating faith at work, this book will offer practical and theoretical guidance on how to be a better follower, defining the type of follower an employee is, and matching the type of follower a leader needs in various scenarios.

Faith at work, God at Work, His Way at Work, Marketplace Ministries, Spirit at Work, Spirituality in the Workplace, Theology of Work, and Workplace Spirituality are all phrases used to describe the application of religion to business. The earliest modern-day publication of this concept of taking God to work is likely Fortune Magazine. The October 1953 edition of Fortune Magazine included a 6-page article called *Businessmen on Their Knees*. In this article, Norton-Taylor included examples of employees at Alcoa, Blaw-Knox, Borg-Warner, Horne department store, Pittsburg Plate Glass, Sherwin Williams, and U.S. Steel who "put Christianity to work" (p. 140) and found that "religion is the best solution we have found to the problem of getting along with each other" (p. 141). In 2001, the cover of Fortune Magazine was titled *God & Business*. In that 11-page article, Gunther shared examples of employees at Blistex, Catalytica, Greyston Bakery, IBM, J.P. Morgan-Chase, LaSalle Bank, Pricewaterhouse, R.C. Wiley Home Furnishings, and Service Master. The author said that what he found were executives wrestling with questions such as "how can business promote family life, what is a just wage, [and] when are layoffs justified" (Gunther, 2001, p. 59). He also found that there was a yearning of business people to "find meaning in what they do" (Gunther, 2001, p. 80). Since these early popular press publications, there has been a movement of Faith at Work empirical research including Servant Leadership Theory (Greenleaf, 1970), Transcendental Leadership Theory (Cardona, 2000), and Spiritual Leadership Theory (Fry, 2003) where much of the research deliberates if religion and spirituality are synonymous. Nevertheless, for the sake of this chapter, understanding the followership styles of the disciples of Jesus is an attempt to integrate faith at work from a follower perspective.

References

Cardona, P. (2000). Transcendental leadership. *Leadership & Organization Development Journal, 21*(4), 201–207.

Chaleff, I. (2003). *Courageous follower*. Beret Koehler.

Chaleff, I. (2009). *The courageous follower: Standing up to & for our leaders*. Berrett-Koehler.

Fry, L. W. (2003). Toward a theory of spiritual leadership. *The Leadership Quarterly, 14*(6), 693–727.

Gunther, M. (2001). God & business. *Fortune Magazine*.

Greenleaf, R. K. (1970). *The servant as leader*. Greenleaf Center.

Kellerman, B. (2008). *Followership: How followers are creating change and changing leaders*. Harvard Business School Press.

Kelley, R. E. (1992). *The power of followership: How to create leaders people want to follow, and followers who lead themselves*. Doubleday/Currency.

Norton-Taylor, D. (1953). Businessmen on their knees. *Fortune Magazine*.

CHAPTER 2

Mary of Magdala: Faithful Follower

Debra J. Dean

Followership as an Art

There are a few pioneers of followership that are included in this chapter. The first is Robert Kelley (1992). He introduced the *Power of Followership* in an effort to "create leaders people want to follow and followers who lead themselves." Kelley's seminal work identified two dimensions and five basic styles of followership. The dimensions are provided below (Kelley, 2008, p. 7):

(1) Do they think for themselves? Are they independent critical thinkers? Or do they look to the leader to do the thinking for them?
(2) Are they actively engaged in creating positive energy for the organization? Or is there negative energy or passive involvement?

Kelley's five leadership styles include (a) the sheep, (b) the yes-people, (c) the alienated, (d) the pragmatics, and (e) the star followers. In 1997,

D. J. Dean (✉)
Regent University, Virginia Beach, VA, USA
e-mail: drdebra@drdebradean.com; debrdea@regent.edu

D. J. Dean and R. B. Huizinga (eds.), *Followership and Faith at Work*, Christian Faith Perspectives in Leadership and Business,
https://doi.org/10.1007/978-3-030-90614-6_2

Table 2.1 Followership typologies

Kelley	*Chaleff*	*Kellerman*
The sheep	Partner	Isolate
The yes people	Implementer	Bystander
The alienated	Individualist	Participant
The pragmatics	Resource	Activist
The star followers		Diehard

Ira Chaleff wrote *The Courageous Follower*. His book described four quadrants of support including (a) Partner: high support, high challenge; (b) Implementer: high support, low challenge; (c) Individualist: low support, high challenge; and (d) Resource: low support, low challenge. Below are the two critical dimensions of courageous followership (Chaleff, 2003, p. 40):

(1) The degree of support a follower gives a leader.
(2) The degree to which the follower is willing to challenge the leader's behavior or policies if these are endangering the organization's purpose or undermining its values.

The third pioneer of followership is Barbara Kellerman. In her 2008 book titled, *Followership: How Followers are Creating Change and Changing Leaders*, she divided followers by level of engagement. On one end of the spectrum, the follower is "doing absolutely nothing" and on the other end, they are "passionately committed and deeply involved" (Kellerman, 2008, p. 85). Her five types of followership are (a) isolate, (b) bystander, (c) participant, (d) activist, and (e) diehard.

As the journey of Mary Magdalene unravels over the subsequent pages, consider the type of follower she was to Jesus from the perspective of Kelley's, Chaleff's, and Kellerman's typologies as shown in Table 2.1 above and defined below.

Definition of Followership Types

The Sheep: Followers are passive and wait for the leader to think for them and motivate them. They do not think for themselves.

The Yes People: Followers have positive energy and always look to the leader for direction, thinking, and vision. They do not think for themselves.

The Alienated: Followers have negative energy and think for themselves. They will stand up to the boss to tell them why the plan is a bad idea.

The Pragmatics: Followers are wishy-washy. They sit on the fence and wait to see if the plan is good enough for them to join the effort.

The Star Followers: Followers have very positive energy and think for themselves. They are actively engaged. They will use critical thinking skills to decide if they agree or disagree with the leader and will voice their opinion.

The Partner: The follower offers vigorous support and is willing to question the leader about their behavior or policy. The partner is purpose driven, mission oriented, and a risk taker.

The Implementer: The follower is counted on heavily by the leader. They are the work horse that will do what is asked without question. However, they do not challenge the leader's behavior or policy. The implementer is dependable, supportive, and considerate.

The Individualist: The follower is less about support and more about challenging the leader or criticizing the plan. The individualist is confrontational, forthright, and self-assured.

The Resource: The follower does what they need to do to get by and nothing more. The resource is present, available, and uncommitted.

The Isolate: The follower is detached. They do not care, inquire, or respond to the leader in any way.

The Bystander: The follower observes but does not participate. They deliberately stand to the side, disengage, and withdraw from the group.

The Participant: The follower is actively engaged and will "put their money where their mouth is… to try and have an impact" (Kellerman, 2008, p. 92).

The Activist: The follower works hard and feels strongly (good or bad) about the leader.

The Diehard: The follower is all-consumed and prepared to die for the cause. They are deeply devoted to the leader.

The Introduction of Mary and Jesus

Mary Magdalene is first introduced in Galilee. This appears to be the initial encounter between Mary Magdalene and Jesus. The Sacred Text states:

> He went through every city and village, preaching and bringing the glad tidings of the kingdom of God. And the twelve *were* with Him, and certain women who had been healed of evil spirits and infirmities—Mary called Magdalene, out of whom had come seven demons, and Joanna the wife of Chuza, Herod's steward, and Susanna, and many others who provided Him from their substance. (Luke 8:1-4, NKJV)

The Bible tells us that she had seven demons. Seven means completeness or perfection. Some say she was totally possessed. Array et al. (2017) explain that her affliction could have included epilepsy or schizophrenia. Cargill et al. (2019) explains that it could have been schizophrenia, bipolar disorder, or Post-Traumatic Stress Disorder (PTSD). Whatever the infliction was, it was significant enough that it required a miracle to exorcise the demons from her being. Spangler calls her a "tortured soul whose mind has already descended into hell while her body lives on earth" (2015, p. 190) and wrote of Mary's dramatic before and after story where a "demon possessed woman becomes a devoted disciple" (pp. 189–198). While we do not know the details of her seven demons we know she had them and that she was liberated from the demons.

As a result of the freedom, Mary committed to following Jesus. Carson (1991) divulged a pattern where "the beneficiaries of the appearance are engulfed in human emotion (Mary, grief; the disciples, fear; Thomas, doubt). The risen Christ appears to them in the midst of their condition. As a result, their condition is transformed (Mary, mission; the disciples, gladness; Thomas, faith)" (p. 634). Jesus had blessed her immensely. He had changed her life, and as a result, she vowed to follow him. She became His student and viewed him as a teacher. Cargill et al. (2019) explain that she would have transformed from a social outcast to a follower of a great teacher and preacher. He said, she "goes from the outcast to the penthouse through a spiritual change" (Cargill et al., 2019).

Henry and Manser (2010, p. 1611) wrote that Mary Magdalene "owed all her strength and comfort to His power and goodness, which rescued her from the possession of seven demons (Mark 16–9), in gratitude for which she thought she could never do enough for him." At this point in her journey, Mary's followership style appears to be a Star Follower (actively engaged), a Partner (purpose driven, mission oriented, and risk taker), and a Participant (actively engaged and will put their money where their mouth is).

The Identity of Mary Magdalene

The history of Mary Magdalene is obscure. And, there is some confusion about events in the Bible and if they are related to Mary or not. Some believe this is because Mary was such a popular name of the time and it is confusing to know which Mary the scripture is talking about. To add to the confusion, there are several unnamed women that have been assumed as Mary Magdalene, too. Carroll (2006) explains that a Samaritan woman, an adulteress whom Pharisees took to Jesus for condemnation, Mary of Bethany, Mary the mother of James and Joseph, Mary the mother of Jesus, Mary the wife of Clopas, the sister of Martha and Lazarus, and the woman with the "bad name" who wipes the feet of Jesus with oil are all women that, at some point in history, have been confused with one another. To get a clear picture of who Mary of Magdala was, or who she was not, we will also examine some of the post-humus perversions below.

Was She a Prostitute?

Mary Magdalene was portrayed as a whore, prostitute, or harlot by Pope Gregory the Great in the sixth century. Apparently, Pope Gregory portrayed the several unnamed women as sinners and referred to them as one person: Mary Magdalene. However, nowhere in the Bible does it say that Mary Magdalene was a prostitute. It is assumed that Pope Gregory may have done this to portray a sinner as a role model. After all, it would be a great story to see such reformation. The fact is, however, that Mary Magdalene was not called a prostitute in the Bible; therefore, we cannot assume that was part of her identity.

In 1969, the Catholic Church attempted to clear her name and said she was not a prostitute and was "distinct from the sinful woman mentioned In the Gospel of Luke" (Bernstein & Scharf, 2019). In 2016, Pope Francis declared a major feast day for Mary Magdalene's witness of the resurrection. Scarrafia (2018) stated, "By doing this, he established the absolute equality of Mary Magdalene to the apostles, something that has never been done before and is also a point of no return." With this information, there is clearly no information in the Bible that points to Mary being a prostitute.

Was She Intimate with Jesus?

In 1945, Egyptian farmers near Nag Hammadi unearthed an ancient sealed jar with 13 leather bound books. The contents of the books comprised 52 mostly Gnostic treatises. Included were the Gospels of Thomas, Philip, and Truth. The Gospel of Philip included passages about Mary Magdalene and her relationship with Jesus. It was written that the three women that always walked with Jesus included His mother, His sister, and Mary Magdalene. There is also a passage referring to a kiss. However, it is important to note that in the days when Jesus and His disciples traveled together, they would all welcome each other with a kiss. Pope (2014) refers to the Holy Kiss as a greeting. It is shown in 1 Thessalonians 5:26, 2 Corinthians 13:12, Romans 16:16, and 1 Corinthians 16:20. Aray et al. (2017) explain that the newly discovered writings do not infer an intimate relationship between Jesus and Mary Magdalene any more than the closeness between friends of the other disciples.

Aray et al. (2017) expounded that Mary Magdalene has been portrayed by popular press media as the wife of Jesus and the mother of His child. *The DaVinci Code* by Dan Brown portrays Mary and Jesus as being intimate. And, some believe she fled to France after the ascension. According to Aray et al. (2017), Flavol stated the Basilica of Vezelay, Sanctuary of Sainte Marie-Madeleine became very popular after *The DaVinci Code* was written; however, the real Mary Magdalene is very different from what *The DaVinci Code* portrays. Brown (2003) wrote of Mary Magdalene in *The Da Vinci Code* as being Jewish, the wife of Jesus, and fleeing to Gaul after the crucifixion. According to Brown (2003), she gave birth to Jesus' daughter and her name is Sarah. However, Aray et al. (2017) explain that the facts are not available to support Brown's position. Welborn (2004) pointed out many errors in *The Da Vinci Code* related to Mary Magdalene explaining that Brown says Mary was of royal blood. That she was from the Tribe of Benjamin. That she was married to Jesus. And, that she gave birth to His child, moved to France, and was the "root of the Merovingian royal family." Welborn defends, Brown was an English teacher and "holds no advanced degrees in religion." With this information, there are no factual details that point to an intimate relationship between Jesus and Mary Magdalene.

Where is Her Body Buried?

It is unknown where her body is for sure. However, Lawlor (2015) suggests that Mary Magdalene's body had been buried by the 1st Bishop of Aix en Provence, with a sign that states, "Here lies the body of Mary Magdalene." The 1st Bishop of Aix was Maximin, presumably her good friend and one of the 72 disciples of Jesus. Some say that Mary was living in a cave for her last 30 years. And, some say she was John's wife. The cave was in the mountains of Sainte-Baume. Legend has it, when she knew she was dying, she went to her friend Maximin for communion and burial. In 1279, Mary Magdalene's body was discovered by Charles II of Anjou, King of Naples, Count of Provence and nephew of King Louis of France. According to Vattayil (2019), when Charles II opened her marble tomb, a "wonderful smell of perfume filled the air." The jawbone was missing from the tomb, but a "small piece of skin attached to her skull in the spot where Jesus touched her after His Resurrection" was still alive. The piece of skin is called "noli me tangere" or the "touch me not" skin and is carefully sealed in a glass vase. She was not originally buried in a marble tomb; however, a note in her sarcophagus read,

> The year of the birth of the Lord 710, the sixth day of December, at night and very secretly, under the reign of the very pious Eudes, King of the Franks, during the time of the ravages of the treacherous nation of Saracens, the body of the dear and venerable St. Mary Magdalene was, for fear of the said treacherous nation, moved from her alabaster tomb to the marble tomb, after having removed the body of Cedonius because it was more hidden.

Assumingly, her missing jawbone was reunited with the body in 1295. Today, her skull is located in a golden reliquary, which weighs 880 pounds. It is located in the Basilica of St. Maximin and carried through the streets during Mary Magdalene Feast Week. Caution is recommended as it is unknown if the skull or the bones are, in fact, those of Mary Magdalene.

According to Brown, the author of *The Davinci Code*, the bones of Mary Magdalene with the exception of her skull are buried beneath the glass pyramid at the Louvre, La Pyramide Inversee. Welborn (2004) refutes this claim saying they are not among the many things buried beneath the pyramid. According to National Geographic, her body is buried "in a medieval town in the south of France" in "a crypt tucked beneath a basilica" (Gibbens, 2017). However, Gibbens points out that remains of Mary Magdalene have been claimed "in at least five other regions." The information about her final resting place is rather complicated and it is difficult to say with certainty exactly where her body was buried or if it remains in the original resting place.

The Gospel of Mary of Magdala

This chapter would not be complete without the mention of the Gospel of Mary. Warner (2019) explained that the Gospel of Mary is considered heretical because it "is not listed in any early list of canonical texts and dates far too late to have been written by an eyewitness to the life of Jesus." The manuscript is dated mid or late second century. According to the Bergersen (1994), her gospel was found "in the late nineteenth century somewhere near Akhmim in upper Egypt. It was purchased in Cairo in 1896 by a German scholar, Dr. Carl Reinhardt, and then taken to Berlin." King (2003) explained that fewer than "eight pages of the ancient papyrus text survive[d]." The surviving pages appear to record a dialogue between Jesus and the disciples where he teaches, and they are free to interact with questions in an informal manner. Chapter 5 appears to be a dialogue between Andrew, Mary, and Peter where Mary stood up and spoke to the disciples. It is not clear from this excerpt if this is Mary of Magdala or another Mary. Warner (2019) wrote that "scholars disagree about the identity of Mary within the text." Therefore, it is not clear if this document is authentic or not. However, for the sake of exhausting all written accounts, a couple of samples are provided. According to Bergersen (1994), Chapter 5 reads,

> Then Mary stood up, greeted them all, and said to her brethren, do not weep and do not grieve nor be irresolute, for His grace will be entirely with you and will protect you. But rather, let us praise His greatness, for He has prepared us and made us into Men. When Mary said this, she turned their hearts to the Good, and they began to discuss the words of the Savior. Peter said to Mary, Sister we know that the Savior loved you more than the rest of woman. Tell us the words of the Savior which you remember which you know, but we do not, nor have we heard them. Mary answered and said, what is hidden from you I will proclaim to you. And she began to speak to them these words: I, she said, I saw the Lord in a vision, and I said to Him, Lord I saw you today in a vision. He answered and said to me, blessed are you that you did not waver at the sight of Me.

> For where the mind is there is the treasure. I said to Him, Lord, how does he who sees the vision see it, through the soul or through the spirit? The Savior answered and said, He does not see through the soul nor through the spirit, but the mind that is between the two that is what sees the vision and it is [...]

And, Chapter 9 states,

> When Mary had said this, she fell silent, since it was to this point that the Savior had spoken with her. But Andrew answered and said to the brethren, say what you wish to say about what she has said. I at least do not believe that the Savior said this. For certainly these teachings are strange ideas. Peter answered and spoke concerning these same things. He questioned them about the Savior: Did He really speak privately with a woman and not openly to us? Are we to turn about and all listen to her? Did He prefer her to us? Then Mary wept and said to Peter, My brother Peter, what do you think? Do you think that I have thought this up myself in my heart, or that I am lying about the Savior? Levi answered and said to Peter, Peter you have always been hot tempered. Now I see you contending against the woman like the adversaries. But if the Savior made her worthy, who are you indeed to reject her? Surely the Savior knows her very well. That is why He loved her more than us. Rather let us be ashamed and put on the perfect Man, and separate as He commanded us and preach the gospel, not laying down any other rule or other law beyond what the Savior said. And when they heard this, they began to go forth to proclaim and to preach.

Warner (2019), using his detective skills, proclaims these samples from the eight surviving papyrus pages "fails the test" when examined with criteria used to establish eyewitness reliability. He wrote "it is a legendary fabrication written by an author who altered the story of Jesus to suit the purposes of his or her religious community." Therefore, they will not be used in this chapter to exegetically examine Mary of Magdala and her following of Jesus Christ.

Just the Facts

Deuteronomy 4:2 reminds us to "not add to the word which I am commanding you, nor take away from it, so that you may keep the commandments." For the purpose of this chapter, the focus will be on what we know for sure. Welborn (2004) pointed to Mary Magdalene in saying she was demon possessed and healed. She was present at the crucifixion. She was present at the tomb. And she was sent by Jesus to announce the Good News to the other disciples. Mary Magdalene was born in Israel.

Sacred Text

The scripture related to Mary Magdalene includes the following: Matthew 27:55–61 and 28:1–10; Mark 15:40–47 and 16:1–20; Luke 8:1–4, 23:49–56, and 24:1–53; and John 19:25–27 and 20:1–31. Using the New King James Version, she is mentioned fourteen times in the gospels. In eight of those instances, she is listed with other women and her name tops the list. In the one instance where her name does not top the list it is because she is alongside Jesus' mother and aunt (John 19:25). In the five times she is mentioned alone, it is in connection with Jesus' death and resurrection (Mark 16:9, John 20:1, 11, 16, 18).

The gospels of Matthew, Mark, Luke, and John are the texts where her name is mentioned. To understand more about her authors, this section will examine who the author was and how many times he mentioned her name. Matthew, tax collector and publican, wrote the name of Mary Magdalene three times. He did not have a direct quote from her. Mark, an evangelist, wrote the name Mary Magdalene four times. Only one time did "they" say something. It was not clear if Mary spoke the 14 words, but the question was, "Who will roll away the stone from the door of the tomb for us?" Luke, a doctor, wrote the name of Mary Magdalene two times. He did not have any direct quotation from her. Distinctively, only the Gospel of Luke provides the details of Jesus and Mary with the seven demons. And, while Luke provided this one detail, he was the one author that mentioned her name the least. John, a fisherman, wrote the name Mary twice and Mary Magdalene three times. He also had four direct quotations totaling 58 words from Mary Magdalene in John 20:1–31 as shown below:

- "They have taken away the Lord out of the tomb and we do not know where they have laid Him."
- "Because they have taken away my Lord, and I do not know where they have laid Him."
- "Sir, if You have carried Him away, tell me where You have laid Him, and I will take Him away."
- "Rabboni!"

It is not known why Luke included the information about the demons and why John included more words than the other authors. However, it is important to know more about the authors to try and understand their lens with which they write from. Aray et al. (2017) stated that the gospels were probably written 30–70 years after Jesus' death. It is believed that Mark's gospel was the first, followed by Matthew, Luke, and finally John. According to McDowell (2013), it is believed that Mark died in Alexandria Egypt. His death involved His body being dragged by horses. Matthew died as a Martyr in Ethiopia, possibly by a sword. Luke was hung in Greece. And, John faced much persecution, including being boiled in oil; however, he died peacefully in Ephesus. As a matter of logistics, John's Tomb at the Basilica of St. John is approximately 1800 miles away from Mary of Magdala's presumed resting place in the French town named Saint Maximin la Sainte Baume. It seems inconvenient for them to have been married and die so far apart from one another. The disciples obviously scattered throughout the region and perhaps their memories of the events themselves, the importance of the events, and the details of the events were different based on the authors different perspectives and the lens with which they experienced the events themselves. Nevertheless, from an exegetical perspective, we only know what was written and can only assume the author's point-of-reference. This chapter continues with what we do know of Mary Magdalene as fact.

Her Hometown

Today, the city of Magdala proudly claims to be the hometown of Mary Magdalene and is located on the shores of Galilee. This first-century town was an important fishing community. The name Magdala means *tower* in Hebrew and *Tower of Fishes* in Aramaic. In Greek, the word means *fish preserved by salting or drying*. It is the place where they processed fish and exported them to the Mediterranean world.

Her Name

In the time period when Jesus and Mary met and walked the earth together, men nor women had surnames. People were usually identified by their relatives and women were usually associated with their father or husband. In this case, Mary was never called Mary, Jesus' wife. She was also not called Mary, daughter of anyone. It is believed that she was never married or widowed, thus reinforcing the idea that she and Jesus were not intimate. Instead, she had a proper title of a prominent woman from the city of Magdala. It is interesting that Mary of Magdala is the only woman that took the name of their town. This unconventional female name may infer her status in the town.

The initial passage of Mary Magdalene in scripture follows:

> He went through every city and village, preaching and bringing the glad tidings of the kingdom of God. And the twelve *were* with Him, and certain women who had been healed of evil spirits and infirmities—Mary called Magdalene, out of whom had come seven demons, and Joanna the wife of Chuza, Herod's steward, and Susanna, and many others who provided Him from their substance. (Luke 8:1-4, NKJV)

At the end of the introductory passage, several other women were introduced including Joanna, Susanna, and unnamed women. The last sentence states that they provided for them out of their own resources. Aray et al. (2017) explain that women of that time period did not inherit wealth. They were maintained by their fathers and/or husbands. However, there were times when fathers provided property for their daughters and that is possibly the form of wealth that Mary Magdalene had. Nevertheless, it is also important to note that Jesus and His followers had humble needs; therefore, it is possible that it would not take much to provide for their substance.

This passage in Luke reveals more about Mary Magdalene and the other women such as their status in the town. These women were likely prominent figures, well-to-do, and respectable. It appears Mary had time and money. This would have been uncommon since women in that time period were not able to own property, were not trusted as reliable witnesses, and were usually looked at as being unable to provide for themselves, much less anyone else.

In summary, we know that Mary Magdalene was demon possessed and healed. She was present at the crucifixion. She was present at the tomb. And she was sent by Jesus to announce the Good News to the other disciples. Mary Magdalene was born in Israel. This is all that we know for sure and will be the basis for the remaining text in this chapter.

The Journey to the Cross

The date is unknown as to when Jesus and Mary Magdalene met; however, the Bible records that she was with Jesus when her demons were cast out. She was also with Jesus as he endured crucifixion, died, was buried, and rose from the dead. One can imagine there was a period of time, possibly months or years, that Jesus taught Mary among the other disciples.

Cargill et al. (2019) explain that Mary really came to the forefront of the disciples as the crucifixion unfolded. Cargill et al. (2019) states that the women had a lot more freedom than the male disciples because they were not under the same cloud of suspicion as the men; therefore, the women could move in and fill the void. However, Mary would have known there was still risk for her following Jesus to Calvary.

Aray et al. (2017) explain that prior to Mary's birth, there was political activity, violence, Roman revolts, and Roman oppression in Galilee. The Galilean rebels had moved into caves above Magdala and Herod the Great, appointed as *King of the Jews* by the Roman Senate, was determined to get rid of the rebels. Mary of Magdala probably heard these stories as she grew up. She probably knew of the story recorded by Josephus where Herod tricked the cave dwellers by lowering his soldiers in cradles to attack the families. In one story, the family included a father, mother, and seven sons. Instead of submitting to the Roman authority, the father threw down each son and his wife from the cave. Ultimately, the father also jumped to his death.

In the time of the crucifixion, it was also not uncommon for a person to be accused as guilty by association. If family members were grieving at the cross, they could just as well be punished. The male disciples were afraid they would be executed as well. Mary was well aware of the danger involved with following Jesus and decided it was worth the risk to follow Christ. At this point, her followership type emerged from Star Follower (actively engaged), Partner (purpose driven, mission oriented, and risk taker), and Participant (actively engaged and will put their money where their mouth is) to also include Activist (works hard and feels strongly about the leader), and Diehard (all-consumed, prepared to die for the cause, deeply devoted to the leader).

Spangler (2015, p. 197) proclaims that Mary Magdalene was "the most prominent witness of Jesus' death, burial, and resurrection" and "though most of the disciples fled once Jesus was arrested and tried, Mary and the other women were with him at the crucifixion." Spangler proclaims that for Mary Magdalene, "as a woman who remained faithful to Jesus throughout His crucifixion, death, burial, and resurrection, she is a model of what it means to follow Jesus."

To say that Jesus endured a painful death would be a huge understatement. The anguish, pain, suffering, taunting, and mocking would have been unbearable for any human being to witness, let alone those that knew him and loved him. Henry and Manser explain that "when good people are suffering greatly, they must not think it strange if some of their best friends are reluctant to be with them" (2010, p. 1558). However, Mary Magdalene was with him, as were some other women including Mary the mother of James (aka Mary the wife of Clopas).

As Jesus carried the cross to Golgotha, he spoke directly to the women. In Luke 23:28, Jesus said, "Daughters of Jerusalem, do not weep for Me, but weep for yourselves and for your children." Cargill et al. (2019) explain that Jesus was "predicting the coming destruction of Jerusalem and the fact that in the future there will be much more serious things for them to lament over." Mary of Magdala did not waiver in her following of Jesus. She had the courage to see her discipleship through till the end.

Henry and Manser (2010) explained that as Jesus journeyed to the cross, the women were unable to physically care for him. "They were there watching. When they were prohibited from carrying out any other task of love to him, they looked with a look of love toward him." It was a sorrowful look. We may well imagine how it cut them to the heart to see him in that amount of torment. Let us have the eye of faith, so that we may see Christ, and him crucified (1 Cor 2:2) and let us be moved by the great love with which he loved us. Yet it was no more than a look; they saw him, but they could not help him. "When Christ was suffering, even His best friends were merely spectators and onlookers" (Henry & Manser, 2010, p. 1558).

The Crucifixion

Mary Magdalene took a leading role at the crucifixion. While John was there, it appears that Mary was the leader for the followers of Jesus Christ. Aray et al. (2017) note the most significant moment is when she is with Christ on the cross. The other apostles left because they were afraid, but she stayed by His side. She took a significant risk as it was dangerous to be at the crucifixion, to show grief, and to be associated with the person being crucified. Cargill et al. (2019) continued in saying that "of all the people that knew Jesus, Mary Magdalene had the courage to see her discipleship through to the end. Even though it is painful, she doesn't skirt her responsibilities." Mary Magdalene was not only emerging as the leader of the women, she was also comforting Mary, the mother of Jesus.

The Burial

It was uncommon to have a crucified body taken down for a proper burial. Most bodies were left on the cross to rot. In fact, Golgotha means "the place of the skull" because skulls were left lying around. Mary Magdalene not only followed the body to the tomb, but she accompanied Jesus' mother and sister to wash and anoint the body. This act, presumably, was a very private moment as the women cared for Jesus after His death and speaks to the unconditional love she has for her savior. This uncommon act reinforces the followership styles Star Follower (actively engaged), Partner (purpose driven, mission oriented, and risk taker), Participant (actively engaged and will put their money where their mouth is), Activist (works hard and feels strongly about the leader), and Diehard (all-consumed, prepared to die for the cause, deeply devoted to the leader).

The Empty Tomb

It appears that Mary Magdalene was Jesus' most devoted follower and she supported Him wholeheartedly despite the cost. Cargill et al. (2019) shared that "Jesus trusted her the most."

Mary was not alone when she went to the tomb. However, Carson (1991) writes, "she figures prominently in the resurrection accounts" (p. 616). Mary and the other women were courageous when she went to the tomb. Mark 16 details that "when the Sabbath was over, Mary Magdalene, Mary the mother of James, and Salome brought spices so that they could go and anoint Jesus' dead body." John 20 records that it was "early on the first day of the week, while it was still dark." Luke 24 notes that "the women took the spices they had prepared and went to the tomb." He then explains that when they returned from the tomb, "Mary Magdalene, Joanna, and Mary the mother of James; also the other women with them were telling these things to the apostles." Matthew 28: 5–8 explains that "the angel said to the women" and the "women hurried away from the tomb, afraid yet filled with joy, and ran to tell His disciples."

The Resurrection

Henry and Manser (2010) state that Jesus "appeared to Mary Magdalene, to her first, in the garden, which out of whom he had cast seven devils, and she loved much (Luke 7:47). Christ did her the honor of making her the first who saw him after His resurrection. The closer we are to Christ, the sooner we may expect to see him, and the more we may expect to see of him" (p. 1613). Mary had been faithful each step of the way. She was present at the crucifixion. She was present at the tomb. And she was sent by Jesus to announce the Good News to the other disciples. Perhaps Mary was being repaid on earth for what she had done for Jesus, as noted in Matthew 16:27, "For the Son of Man is going to come in the glory of His Father with His angels and will then repay every person according to his deeds." After the death, burial, and resurrection, Jesus appeared first to Mary Magdalene (Matthew 28:9–10, Mark 16:9, John 20:19).

The Ascension

Acts 9–12 accounts for Jesus' ascension to heaven. There is no specific mention of Mary Magdalene; however, the Sacred Text does state "they were gazing intently into the sky while He was going." John 14:3 records Jesus' promise as saying, "when I go and prepare a place for you, I will come again and will take you to myself, that where I am you may be also." This beautiful promise is a testimony of the unconditional love Jesus has for His followers and His promise of eternal life.

Swiftly Forgotten

After Jesus' death, burial, and resurrection, there is not any other mention of Mary Magdalene in the Bible. She just disappears. Mary played such a significant role in Jesus' life and it is interesting that the Sacred Text does not have more scripture about her after His ascension to Heaven. She is, however, known as the beginning of Christianity. She simply obeyed the commandment of Jesus to "go quickly and tell… that He is risen from the dead, and indeed He is going before you into Galilee; there you will see Him." She clearly obeyed the command to go and tell the others. And, as a result, Christianity spread "through a multitude of humble, ordinary believers whose names have been long forgotten" (McKenzie, 2010).

Conclusion

Mary of Magdala emerged as Star Follower (actively engaged), Partner (purpose driven, mission oriented, and risk taker), Participant (actively engaged and will put their money where their mouth is), Activist (works hard and feels strongly about the leader), and Diehard (all-consumed, prepared to die for the cause, deeply devoted to the leader). She is acclaimed to be the start of Christianity and one of the most important people in the entire new testament (Cargill et al., 2019). There is so little known about her, but so much that can be inferred. She is the founder of Christianity. Without her carrying the message from Jesus' resurrected body to the others, the Good News may have never been shared. She was with Jesus when he died on the cross, was buried, and resurrected on the 3rd day. She was a faithful follower at the right place and at the right time. It's the only thing we know for sure.

She had her fair share of demons while on earth; however, after her death, Mary Magdalene has continued to have her fair share of trials and tribulations. She may be the most misunderstood woman in the Bible. She has had a tarnished reputation since the sixth century and if what we read about her burial and exhumation of her body is true, she has had her fair share of problems posthumously. She was wrongly accused of prostitution by a Catholic Pope. And, she has had a "foul stigma" attached to her name for centuries; however, she has supporters that claim she is the only woman of the Bible that "superseded Mary (the mother of Jesus) in her devotion to the Master" (BibleGateway, n.d.).

In addition to followership styles of Star Follower (actively engaged), Partner (purpose driven, mission oriented, and risk taker), Participant (actively engaged and will put their money where their mouth is), Activist (works hard and feels strongly about the leader), and Diehard (all-consumed, prepared to die for the cause, deeply devoted to the leader), I propose new followership styles for Mary of Magdala to include servant follower, devoted follower, and faithful follower.

Chapter Takeaways

Much can be learned from this chapter. The first is that an ideal follower of Christ may involve many of the same characteristics of Mary Magdalene. And, the second is a potential new followership style known as the Servant Followership Style.

Kelley (2008) wrote that the Star Followers are referred to as the "right-hand person" or the "go-to person" and exude characteristics of thinking for themselves, being very active, having positive energy, and independent evaluation of the leader's decisions. If they agree with the leader, they offer full support. If they do not agree, they will challenge the leader and offer constructive options. Kelley (2008) referred to the Star Follower as leaders in disguise.

Chaleff (2003) refers to the Partner as a follower offering vigorous support; yet willing to challenge the leader. The Partner displays the following attitudes and behaviors: complements leader's perspectives, confronts sensitive issues, cultivates relationships, focuses on strengths and growth, holds self and others accountable, mission oriented, peer relations with authority, purpose driven, and risk taker.

Kellerman (2008) wrote of the Participant as one that "puts their money where their mouth is" and for Mary of Magdala, she did just that. Luke 9:23 quotes Jesus in saying, "if any man will come after me, let him deny himself, and take up his cross daily, and follow me." From the scripture that includes Mary of Magdala, it appears she did just that. She invested time and money in following and supporting the Jesus movement.

The Activist is another one of Kellerman's followership styles and Mary of Magdala seems to use this style too. Kellerman wrote that the Activist feels "strongly about their leaders and they act accordingly. They are eager, energetic, and engaged" (2008, p. 92).

The Diehard is also shown as Mary Magdalene's followership style. In her following of Jesus, Mary of Magdala risked it all. Kellerman explains that,

> Diehards are as their name implies -- prepared to die if necessary for their cause… are deeply devoted to their leaders… are defined by their dedication, including their willingness to risk life and limb. Being a Diehard is all-consuming. It is who you are. It determines what you do.

The final followership style proposed in this chapter is Servant Follower. Mary clearly showed devotion and faithfulness. The Servant Leadership Theory was coined by Robert Greenleaf in 1970 and his 1977 book epitomizes servant leaders as one that serves first, noting the best way to know if you are successful as a servant leader is to look at your followers and ask the following questions:

> Do those served grow as persons? Do they, while being served, become healthier, wiser, freer, more autonomous, more likely themselves to become servants? And, what is the effect on the least privileged in society? Will they benefit or at least not be further deprived?

In flipping the servant leadership theory over to become servant followership theory, we can see how Mary served Jesus and the other disciples. She was faithful, devoted, exhibited many of the constructs shown in servant leadership assessments such as agapao love, altruism, empowerment, humility, trust, and vision from the Servant Leadership Assessment Index by Dennis and Bocarnea (2005). She also displayed servant leadership characteristics of voluntary subordination, authentic self, conventional relationship, responsible morality, transcendental spirituality, and transforming influence as measured by the Servant Leadership Behavior Scale by Senjaya, Sarros, and Santora (2008). And, Mary of Magdala also showed altruistic calling, emotional healing, wisdom, persuasive mapping, and organizational stewardship as measured by the Servant Leadership Questionnaire by Barbuto and Wheeler (2006). Finally, her character traits also appear to include emotional healing, creating value for the community, conceptual skills, empowering, helping subordinates grow and succeed, putting subordinates first, and behaving ethically as measured by the Servant Leadership Scale (Liden et al., 2015).

Reflective Questions

In closing out this chapter, the following questions are presented as a way to reflect on this text, initiate critical thinking, and take action.

1. Can I remove the distractions and misinformation about Mary of Magdala and focus entirely on just the facts?
2. Am I able to relate to Mary of Magdala and her journey with Jesus Christ? If so, in what ways am I similar and in what ways am I different?
3. What behaviors of Mary Magdalene do I want to include in my followership style of Jesus Christ?
4. How can I transfer this followership style into a daily practice with other leaders in my life?
5. What have I learned about Mary of Magdala that I would like to know more about?

References

Aray, R., Banai, M., De Boer, E., Ehrman, B., Flavol, V., Ilan, T., Langfur, S., Michelet, T., Ravotti, J., Riches, S., & Tabor, J. (2017). *Why did the Church hate Mary Magdalene?: Secrets of the cross: Timeline*. Retrieved December 13, 2020, from https://youtu.be/51VXjm5itcg

Barbuto, J. E., & Wheeler, D. W. (2016 [2006]). Scale development and construct clarification of servant leadership. *Group & Organization Management, 31*(3), 300–326. https://doi.org/10.1177/1059601106287091

Bergersen, T. (1994). *The gospel of Mary*. Retrieved December 27, 2020, from http://gnosis.org/library/marygosp.htm

Bernstein, A., & Scharf, I. (2019, April 1). *Mary Magdalene was not a prostitute, scholars say. This is what she really was*. Retrieved December 14, 2020, from https://www.independent.co.uk/news/world/middle-east/mary-magdalene-feminism-metoo-jesus-disciples-apostle-christianity-judaism-pope-francis-vatican-a8281731.html

Brown, D. (2003). The da vinci code. Doubleday.

Cargill, R., Cleveland, C., Curry, M., Dubois, J., Goodacre, M., Lewis, N., Majeski, K., Martin, J., Montefiore, S., Morris, J., Moss, O., Moss,C., Peppard, M., Smith, S., Sparks, S., & Witherington, B. (2019). *Mary Magdalene: The Crucifixion*. A&E Networks (Firm) and Infobase (Directors).

Carroll, J. (2006). *Who was Mary Magdalene?* Retrieved December 13, 2020, from https://www.smithsonianmag.com/history/who-was-mary-magdalene-119565482/

Carson, D. A. (1991). *The Gospel according to John*. Eerdmans Publishing.

Chaleff, I. (1997). The courageous follower: Standing up to and for our leaders. *NASSP Bulletin, 81*(586), 119–119. https://doi.org/10.1177/019263659708158616

Chaleff, I. (2003). *The Courageous follower: Standing up to & for our leaders* (2nd ed.). Berrett-Koehler.

Dennis, R. S., & Bocarnea, M. (2005). Development of the servant leadership assessment instrument. *Leadership & Organization Development Journal, 26*(8), 600–615. https://doi.org/10.1108/01437730510633692

Gibbens, S. (2017). *Is this the face of Mary Magdalene?* Retrieved December 13, 2020, from https://www.nationalgeographic.com/news/2017/09/mary-magdalene-face-skull-france-video-spd/

Greenleaf, R. (1977). *Servant leadership: A journey into the nature of legitimate power and greatness—25th Anniversary Edition* (Kindle). Paulist.

Henry, M., & Manser, M. H. (2010). *The new Matthew Henry Commentary: The classic work with updated language*. Grand Rapids, Zondervan.

Kellerman, B. (2008). *Followership: How followers are creating change and changing leaders*. Harvard Business School Press.

Kelley, R. (1992). *The power of followership:How to create leaders people want to follow, and followers who lead themselves*. Doubleday/Currency.
Kelley, R. (2008). Rethinking followership. In R. Riggio, I. Chaleff & J. Lipman-Blumen (Eds.), *The art of followership: How great followers create great leaders and organizations* (pp. 5–15). Jossey-Bass.
King, K. (2003). *The Gospel of Mary of Magdala: Jesus and the first woman Apostle*. Retrieved December 28, 2020, from http://www.gnosis.org/library/GMary-King-Intro.html
Lawlor, P. (2015). *Skull of Mary Magdalene*. Retrieved December 13, 2020, from http://www.magdalenepublishing.org/skull-mary-magdalene/
Liden, R. C., Wayne, S. J., Meuser, J. D., Hu, J., Wu, J., & Liao, C. (2015). Servant leadership: Validation of a short form of the SL-28. *The Leadership Quarterly, 26*(2), 254–269. https://doi.org/10.1016/j.leaqua.2014.12.002
McDowell, S. (2013). *Did the Apostles really die as Martyrs for their faith?* Retrieved December 13, 2020, from http://magazine.biola.edu/article/13-fall/did-the-apostles-really-die-as-martyrs-for-their-f/
McKenzie, T. (2010). *How did Christianity spread?* Retrieved December 28, 2020, from https://www.christianity.com/jesus/early-church-history/early-churches/how-did-christianity-spread.html
Pope, K. (2014, May 01). *Greet one another with a holy kiss*. Retrieved December 14, 2020, from https://focusmagazine.org/greet-one-another-with-a-holy-kiss.php
Scarrafia, L. (2018). Editor of Women Church world monthly magazine. In A. Bernstein & I. Scharf. Mary quite contrary; 'prostitute' magdalene reimagined as wealthy supporter of jesus. *The Calgary sun*.
Sendjaya, S., Sarros, J. C., & Santora, J. C. (2008). Defining and measuring servant leadership behaviour in organizations. *Journal of Management Studies, 45*(2), 402–424. https://doi.org/10.1111/j.1467-6486.2007.00761.x
Spangler, A. (2015). *Wicked women of the Bible*. Grand Rapids, Zondervan.
Vattayil, X. (2019). *Saint-Maximin-la-Sainte-Baume, France—The Shrine of Mary Magadalene*. Retrieved December 13, 2020, from https://www.afcmmedia.org/Shrines-04.html
Warner, J. (2019). *Why shouldn't we trust the non-canonical "Gospel of Mary"?* Retrieved December 28, 2020, from https://coldcasechristianity.com/writings/why-shouldnt-we-trust-the-non-canonical-gospel-of-mary/
Welborn, A. (2004). *The Da Vinci Code: The facts behind the fiction*. Retrieved December 13, 2020, from https://www.catholiceducation.org/en/controversy/common-misconceptions/the-da-vinci-code-the-facts-behind-the-fiction.html

CHAPTER 3

"Follow Me!": The Story of Followership Through the Eyes of the Apostle Peter

Christa Bonnet and Joshua D. Henson

According to Jerry (2013), "Better followers begets better leaders" (p. 345). It is said that there is no leadership without followership (Uhl-Bien et al., 2014); that is the other side of the leadership coin (Ekundayo, 2010). There are certainly many more followers in the world than leaders and many leaders in organizations who themselves are followers (Collinson, 2006). Bastardoz and Van Vugt (2019) wrote that the term "followership" is arguably the default setting in people's brains, and many people are more likely to be followers than leaders. Furthermore, human history has been guided by the impact of followers (Bastardoz & Van Vugt, 2019) and this specifically true in the history of the Christian faith.

C. Bonnet (✉) · J. D. Henson
Regent University, Virginia Beach, VA, USA
e-mail: christa@thedifferencemakers.org.za

J. D. Henson
e-mail: joshhen@regent.edu

D. J. Dean and R. B. Huizinga (eds.), *Followership and Faith at Work*, Christian Faith Perspectives in Leadership and Business,
https://doi.org/10.1007/978-3-030-90614-6_3

Followership is the essential calling of all believers as Jesus invited His disciples to "Follow me" (*English Standard Version*, 2001/2016, Matt. 4:19). In order to empower people, leadership has to be more than titles and positions, and it has to reflect Jesus in every way (Sanderson, 2017). Christian leaders can learn a lot from Jesus' example as teacher and apply it in their succession planning, mentoring, and skills development to empower followers (Bonnet, 2020). Jesus' empowerment style as a leader was an expression of the relationship that he developed with his followers (Wilkins, 2017). Following the call of Shamir (2007), there is a need to "reverse the lens" and focus, not only on the leadership of Jesus but the followership of His Disciples. An exploration of the followership of Jesus' disciples cannot be complete without an examination of the Apostle Peter as he is distinguished as the spokesman of the Twelve and his words and actions often serve to speak for the entire group (France, 2007; Henson, 2016). The call to discipleship is also a call to followership as followership focuses on the symbiotic relationship between leader and follower (Atterson, 2020). Therefore, the purpose of this chapter is to explore followership through the lens of the Apostle Peter.

Peter as Exemplar of Followership

According to Leung (2001), character development is a significant element in studying and interpreting biblical characters. This is especially true in the case of the Apostle Peter as an exemplar and dynamic character in Scripture narratives. Peter is portrayed as a character of contrasts and ambivalence who changes his spiritual formation and heart transformation in becoming an influential Christian leader. The leadership transformation of Peter under the supervision of Jesus took him through some crucibles on his spiritual formation journey (George, 2003). Firstly, Jesus allowed Satan to sift Peter like wheat (Luke 22:31–32); secondly, Peter's restorative process happened (John 21:15–17); and lastly, Peter was tested again before launching him toward his cross-cultural missionary journey to the Gentiles (Acts 10:9–16). In the process of refinement through his crucibles, Peter's self-confidence was tempered and replaced with his total dependence on God (Mathew, 2017).

Peter also had the honor and responsibility as chosen Jesus' principal helper who collated Jesus' disheartened followers after Jesus' crucifixion to form them into a Christian community (Grant, 1995). This was a difficult task and required a Christian leader and mentor whose heart was transformed, a who was a follower of Christ who was spiritually mature and able to exercise extraordinary influence and have bespoke communication skills.

Peter's spiritual formation journey from a disciple with an untransformed heart to an influential apostle with a transformed heart is a story of courage of a man who assumed the responsibility and took up the challenge to become the pioneer and leader of the first-century church to serve God's flock. Not only did Peter take ownership of his own spiritual formation process, but he became a spiritual mentor of others' spiritual transformation processes as well later in his ministry.

Throughout Scripture, Peter is known as a courageous man who was not scared to take moral action to stand for God's vision and Jesus' mission when needed. Without Peter's work after the crucifixion, and without Peter, there would have been no Christian Church, neither in the subsequent centuries nor today (Leung, 2001). The Apostle Peter is an effective exemplar of followership in that the New Testament records his development from his initial call in Matthew 4 to his restored call in John 21. Further, the New Testament recorded his actions and behaviors as a follower and leader as well as his advice for future followers. Using Chaleff's (2009) model of *exemplary followership*, the life of Peter, as recorded in the Scriptures, provides insight into followership from the perspective of a restored disciple whose heart was transformed by the Holy Spirit to do God's work.

Leadership and Its Link to Followership Theory

The leader–follower relationship is a form of covenant, which often is not explicitly expressed, in which followership lives in the shadow of leadership (Bligh, 2011). Uhl-Bien et al. (2014) posited that an understanding of leadership is incomplete without an understanding of followership through the identification of followership constructs, which then should be placed in the context of followership theory. Followership continues to be a field of study in the larger field of leadership (Martin, 2015; Northouse, 2019). According to Larsson and Nielsen (2017), researchers typically portray followership as a safe alternative to leadership identity. In terms of recent theoretical developments, Epitropaki et al. (2013) wrote that categorization theory has offered significant insights into the cognitive structure of leadership and followership and the process of which Implicit Leadership Theories (ILT) and Implicit Followership Theories

(IFT) impact leadership and followership perceptions in applied settings. Uhl-Bien et al. (2014) identified followership theory as the study of the nature and impact of followers and following in the leadership process. For the purpose of this chapter the reference of Uhl-Bien et al. (2014) in terms of followership theory is used as the reference base of Peter as follower of Christ.

According to Crossman and Crossman (2011), despite growing attention in professional and academic literature, a commonly accepted definition of followership does not exist. Kellerman (2008) defined followers as "subordinates who have less power, authority, and influence than do their superiors and who therefore usually, but not invariably, fall into line" (p. xix). Uhl-Bien and Pillai (2007) referred to it as some form of deference to a leader, stating that, "If leadership involves actively influencing others, then followers involves allowing oneself to be influenced" (p. 196). Further, as a follower, a person voluntarily submit to the ideas and inspirational example of the leader (Alvesson & Blom, 2017). However, Fineman (2002) stated that both leaders and followers are bound together in a complex emotional web and thus interdependent. This was evident in the case between Jesus as leader and Peter as follower in this chapter.

Baniissa and Alattari (2019) wrote that, "Leaders are often portrayed as the element that 'makes or breaks'. By contrast, a follower's role is understated or neglected. Followers are treated as 'silent or passive participants'" (p. 117). Conventionally, the labels follower and followership have been viewed as terms conveying images of passivity, deference, obedience, and submission to leaders (Hoption et al., 2012). This image of followers is misconceived (Burak & Bashur, 2013). However, there is a growing recognition that proactive, participatory, empowered followership styles are feasible and desirable (De Zilwa, 2014, 2016; eCuncha et al., 2013; Kellerman, 2013; Uhl-Bien et al., 2014). An increasing number of writers argue that followers are integral to the leadership process (Marion & Uhl-Bien, 2001), and that exemplary, courageous and star followers are a precondition for successful organizations (Kelley, 1992, 1998; Chaleff, 2009). This latter aspect forms the foundation of the discussion in this chapter.

Alvesson and Blom (2017) posited that leadership is about relating to and influencing people's hearts and minds—i.e., managing their meanings. The process of leadership and followership identity development must be seen as a dance and an ongoing process of the social construction of the leader and follower identity as co-constructs that merge, develop and shaped through ongoing social interactions (Epitropaki et al., 2017). This suggests that the leadership and followership area is a broader class of phenomena than previously conceptualized (Piettraszewski, 2019). In alignment, Alipour et al. (2017) posited that, in order to understand leadership and followership perceptions more holistically, insight into the dynamics in relevant contexts is needed.

Followership According to Kelley, Chaleff, and Kellerman

According to Smith (1997), followers are people with wants and desires of their own. According to the theory of reasoned action (Ajzen, 1991), an individual's beliefs and attitudes interact with context to influence behavior. This means that a follower need to believe that the context will allow them to act on their beliefs and their feelings of responsibility and their sense of power to act to stand up for what is morally right (Carsten & Uhl-Bien, 2013). In understanding how Jesus (leader) empowered Peter (follower) it is important to have a better understanding of the expectations of typical followers.

Berlew (1974) listed a number of interesting expectations of followers—e.g., people wanting a chance to: (a) be tested and make it on their own; (b) take part in a social experiment; (c) do something well; and (d) change the way things are. Smith (1997) noted that the modern follower seeks a sense of personal worthiness, longing for self-actualization and identity, meaning in life, having a reason for existence on earth, and leaving a legacy behind. Gardner (1995) calls these followers "believers" (pp. 23–35).

For the purpose of this chapter, three authors—Kelley (1992, 1998), Chaleff (2009), and Kellerman (2008)—who have written extensively on followership in the organizational leadership context—were discussed in the context of identification which type of follower the Apostle Peter was.

Kelley (1992, 1998) identified five follower typologies: (a) *alienated followers* refer to those who think freely and critically, but do not participate in teams in their organization, value independent thinking and are not active in engagements; (b) *exemplary followers* who perform well in all aspects and work independent from the leader or group; (c) *conformist followers* who are content to take orders from their leaders and are not independent thinkers; (d) *passive followers* allow their leaders to think on their behalf, score low on independent thinking and need micromanagement; and (e) *pragmatic followers* who question their leader's decisions, are not too critical, and score mid-range in terms of independent thinking and engagement.

Kelley (1992, 1998) highlighted that exemplary followers display active involvement, critical thinking, independence, and a positive disposition to achieve their organization's vision. These followers are often referred as the "go-to person" or the "right-hand person" through which positive followership are enabled. Such individuals demonstrate initiative and facilitate the needs and interests of peers, leaders, and the organization, and exhibit the courage required to go beyond what they are asked for in accordance with organizational objectives (Kelley, 2008). They offer their help when they notice a need and get morally involved (Van den Abeele & Legrand, 2013). Special characteristics of such followers include: (a) leveraging their strengths to complement weaknesses of their leaders; (b) they approach everything with a critical mindset and make forthright statements that may challenge or criticize their leaders' decisions if it clash with their beliefs or organizational goals; (c) they subscribe to organizational goals, voluntarily cooperate and join in activities that support the cause—even if they are not directly responsible for the execution; and (d) they have a challenging spirit, seek new improvements, take on new challenges, and provide new insights to leaders (Kelley, 1992, 1998). Tee et al. (2013) proposed that followers themselves take the responsibility to moderate the influence of leaders through unified group-level emotions, shared identity, and collective action toward leaders.

Kellerman's (2008) typology classifies followers into five categories based on their levels of engagement: (a) *isolates* detached from their leaders and remain uninterested, unmotivated and keep a low profile; (b) *bystanders* make a conscious decision to watch, observe, and disengage from both the team and the leader—they follow passively and let events unfold with little participation and accept control from their leader with ease; (c) *participants* care about their organization and are engaged in some way if they agree with the leader's views and vision; (d) *activists* are eager, energetic, and feel strongly for or against their leaders or group—they are engaged individuals working for their leaders or the cause; (e) *diehards* displays high levels of engagement and are prepared to die for what they stand for or their beliefs (whether an individual, idea or both).

The Apostle Peter as follower did not fit the profile of the first four categories; however, he was a true diehard (in a mature way) follower of Jesus Christ after he was restored to ministry in John 21 and his heart was transformed by the Holy Spirit later—this was evident from his own upside down crucifixion as death.

Chaleff's (2009) typology is based on the level of their participation and the assurance to followers that they can courageously stand up if their leaders are either good or bad and can challenge them when needed. Chaleff's (2009) typology includes four categories: (a) *implementers* get the work done; (b) *partners* support their leaders, but challenge them when not agreeing with them; (c) *individualists* speak their truth and withhold their support from people in authority with the consequence of marginalization; (d) *resources* do what is expected from them and not much more. The Apostle Peter as follower did not fit the profile of the first four categories; rather, he is what Chaleff (2009) referred to as a *courageous* follower who assumes responsibility, serves his leader (Jesus) and team (fellow disciples), challenges them when needed, and takes a stand for what is morally right. The *courageous followers* in Chaleff's (2009) followership typology endeavor to make followers active partners who continuously scan and monitor the environment, and their leader's needs, while feeling empowered to speak to and influence the hierarchy. Courageous actions at the root of the interaction of the leader–follower dynamics include the courage to assume responsibility for themselves and the organization without any expectation that the leader or organization will provide security, opportunities for growth or require permission to initiate improvements (Dalcher, 2018). They participate fully in transformation and change processes (Crossman & Crossman, 2011).

Jesus Empowered Peter as Follower

According to Sanderson (2017), real leaders seek to empower others and not themselves—like Jesus did with his disciples as his followers. Jesus understood the human reality that leaders cannot be everything to everyone, therefore, he empowered the chosen people around him to use and develop their God-given talents to the best fulfillment of their higher purpose and in the service of God's mission. The Apostle Peter was one of the chosen followers Jesus empowered. Jesus' actions offer insights into his empowerment strategies such as developing his disciples' confidence and self-efficacy, challenging their values and beliefs, and equipping them with the skills needed for their ministries and leadership path (Hoehl, 2008).

Concepts having similar meanings as empowerment occurs in literature such as delegation of authority, motivation, self-efficacy, job enrichment, employee ownership, autonomy, self-determination, self-control, self-influence, high-involvement, and participative leadership (Lee & Koh, 2001). In terms of follower confidence and self-efficacy, empowerment can improve follower perceptions of self-efficacy (Choi, 2006). Specific strategies for strengthening follower-efficacy include placing followers in settings that are conducive to success (Choi, 2006; Pigg, 2002; Zhu et al., 2004), encouraging sharing of information, knowledge, and resources as well as participative management (Kizilos, 1990; Pigg, 2002), and removing obstacles to create success and powerlessness (Zhu et al., 2004).

In terms of the Petrine Four-Vector Model of Empowerment (Bonnet, 2020), the first principle referred to *empowering the follower*, which referred to both Jesus and Peter's method of equipping followers to empower them to lead God's flock, which included their competency, ability, agency, and performance as the key elements. In her study on Peter's transformation as disciple, Bonnet (2020) referred to the following characteristics related to this principle of empowerment—i.e., asking difficult questions, confidence, consequences, delegation, empowering others, insight and understanding, trust, self-awareness, teaching, self-efficacy, clear directives, boundaries, challenging beliefs, Christlike characteristics, emotional intelligence, guidance, renewed mindset, spiritual maturity, performance feedback, and visionary leadership.

It is important that effective Christian leaders allow their people to experiment with the process of change in order for them to begin to anticipate its effects (Buzzell, 2013). Furthermore, God's change proposal to Peter was well prepared (Acts 10:1–7, 19–23, 30–33). God anticipated Peter's reservations and questions, and in doing so, He had the necessary evidence ready to support His answers to Peter's questions and objections. When introducing change, Christian leaders should be prepared to answer difficult questions that might arise (Buzzell, 2013). God did not ask, instruct, or forced Peter to implement the change; rather He invited Peter to participate in improving what he already loved doing. This allowed Peter to see the advantages of the new over the old (Acts 10:34). God also demonstrated early in the subtle change management process the benefits that the new focus would produce through the

Holy Spirit coming upon all who heard Peter's words when they were converted and saved (Acts 10:44–46).

Christian leaders will not accomplish their highest potential until they learn to empower others, however, they also start out as followers themselves. It was this deposit of God's grace in the life of Peter that caused him to become *the rock* on which Christ's church ultimately was built. When Peter's heart was ready and eager, the Holy Spirit's work became fruitful in his heart. Jesus invites Christian leaders every day to open their hearts to allow the Holy Spirit to work in their lives as the Spirit of God's love wants to awake this same divine love in their minds and hearts to make it real—like it did with Peter (see Rom. 5:5). It is key for Christian leaders to ensure that, in their own spiritual formation journey, they acquire experiential learning like Peter did, so that, when God's calling came to serve on a larger and more complex platform, as courageous followers they would be ready and could answer "Yes, God, pick me, as I am ready to serve as you take me to the next and higher level of challenges!"

Peter as Follower of Christ

Peter started out as a fisherman and went through an intense spiritual formation journey under Jesus' mentorship and leadership before he made the transition to a disciple. In terms of Kelley's (1992, 1998) followership typology Peter is an *exemplary follower*. This is also known as a *star follower* or and *effective follower*. As a *courageous follower* under Chaleff's (2009) followership typology Peter had the courage to assume responsibility, serve, challenge, participate in transformation, and take moral action. Kelley (1992) and Kellerman (2008) concurred that the antecedent to courageous or effective followership is a relationship between the follower (in this case Peter) and the leader (in this case Jesus) that is based on mutual trust.

However, Peter as follower experienced this both from an untransformed heart prior to his restoration in John 21 as well as from a transformed heart after his restoration to ministry (Bonnet, 2020). Kelley (1998) wrote that an *exemplary* or *star follower* should exhibit the skill of independent critical thinking from a maturity point of view. Peter could only exhibit that characteristic when his heart was transformed by the

Holy Spirit. Such a follower brings positive energy into their commitments and carry their roles that influences the team morale and collective energy. Peter ticked those boxes.

Table 3.1 compares the followership typologies as per Chaleff's (2009), Kelley (1992, 1998), and Kellerman (2008) as discussed earlier in this chapter. For the purpose of the discussion the focus will be on Peter as a combined *courageous follower* (Chaleff, 2009) and *exemplary follower* (Kelley, 1992, 1998) and their followership typologies.

In his earlier years as disciple and follower of Jesus, Peter exercised little constraint, and his answers, solutions, decisions, and speech were evidently coming from an untransformed mind and heart. At times, Peter's behavior was perceived as insensitive, inconsiderate, selfish, brash, impulsive, and many times immature. Like many great leaders, Peter survived himself, and as a result he is an excellent exemplar and role model to learn from. With Jesus' guidance, Peter's fertile and active mind matured, and his renewed mind reflected the mind of Christ as it started thinking renewed thoughts, dwelling on new things, and had new understanding (Capill, 2014).

Table 3.1 Comparison of followership typologies

Followership category	*Not applicable to Peter*	*Untransformed heart*	*Transformed heart*
Chaleff	• Individualistic	• Implementer • Partner • Resource	Courageous follower (assume responsibility, serve, challenge, participate in transformation, take moral action)
Kelley	• Alienated • Passive • Conformist • Pragmatic	Exemplary follower (Not-mature)	Exemplary follower (Mature)
Kellerman	• Isolates • Bystander • Participants	• Activist (Not-mature) • Diehard (Not-mature)	• Activist (Mature) • Diehard (Mature)

Peter the Courageous and Effective Follower of Christ

The following examples can be applied by both Christian leaders and followers daily in the workplace.

Voluntarily Submission

Being a follower to a leader entails voluntarily submission (Alvesson & Blom, 2017). Jesus saw love as the key element in representing him to the world (John 13:35), and Peter carried this emphasis further in his ministry as Christian leader with love as a significant theme throughout the letter of 1 Peter 2. Peter knew that love was a vital way through which Christian leaders could show the world their holiness, even in times of trials, to be representatives of Christ in the world as exemplars of God's love. Peter as a disciple of Jesus, and later as an Apostle, was a faithful follower and voluntarily followed Jesus and later ministered his God's Word and vision as leader of the first-century church.

Peter's fierce loyalty to Jesus and his deep love for Christ was an undeniable followership trait (Mark 14:29; Luke 8:45, 51; 9:20, 28, 33; 12:41; 18:28; 22:8). The Bible urged accountability of Christian leaders and followers as every person one day will be accountable to God of their whole life and their talents. In John 21 Peter was given the accountability and responsibility of taking care of Christ' lambs, feed his sheep and look after their well-being and spiritual formation process. As follower of Jesus, Peter took that responsibility and commitment seriously. As Christian leaders and followers we also should put others before ourselves, receive them with graciousness and care for their well-being like Peter did.

A Basket Full of Followership Traits

In their study in terms of Integrated Followership Theories (IFT)'s, Junker and Van Dick (2014) referred to the typical and ideal follower as effective, which they described as interested in work, thorough, an independent thinker, productive, a team player, loyal, performance-orientated, building good relationships, positively influencing the culture, contributing to follower happiness and well-being, work well together with others, being a collaborator, and being qualified for the job at hand. Peter fitted all the aforesaid criteria in the context of discipleship as the "work at hand" of the disciples as the team of followers under the leadership of Jesus focused on God's business.

Carsten et al. (2010) stated that, as follower Peter falls within the "more dynamic and courageous role of followership in which they see themselves more as partners in the relationship or even co-leaders" (p. 545). The transformed Peter as follower, as one of the three disciples in Jesus' inner circle of trust, become his partners in a way and these three disciples as followers trusted each another. In John 13 Peter learned a valuable lesson that, as cross-cultural leaders, and followers of Christ, they should be willing to be challenged in their beliefs, open to learn from other cultures, and make decisions that are best for the greater good in alignment with God's Will (Bonnet, 2020; Lauren & Henson, 2021*)*.

Peter displayed other important follower attitudes as social constructs (i.e., the beliefs about the personal qualities and behaviors that makes followers effective). For example, Peter was both a leader and team player among his fellow disciples. He also showed a willingness to cooperate with others and was known for his collective effort to ensure success when his fellow fishermen had to haul in the catch of 153 fish that day to the shore (John 21). A collected effort and strength was needed to bring the catch on board and to shore. Peter as follower took initiative easily and his behavior was proactive when he had to identify, confront, and solve problems or issues, or recognize or act on initiatives without deferring to Jesus as his leader at times. This became evident more and more after Jesus' resurrection when the Holy Spirit anointed Peter (John 21) and he was restored by Jesus to ministry.

Self-Efficacy and Motivation

Peter displayed evident follower traits such as extraversion (Schyns & Felfe, 2006) as well as self-efficacy and motivation (Dvir & Shamir, 2003). Mathew (2017) reminded that Peter's calling brought a sense of direction like no other motivation ever could have done as his calling was ultimately connected to Jesus Christ—his leader who provided the inner drive and sustained endurance to face challenges.

Acts 3:1–26 demonstrated that: "*Demonstration plus Proclamation = Credibility*" (Maxwell, 2007, p. 1347). This lesson could be seen in Peter being the most improved team player and turned-around follower of Jesus. Peter—the same man who promised to follow Jesus even if it meant his own death as a result, cowered in fear and denied Jesus three times—later spoke the name of Christ with great power and authority without any fear of the consequences. The transformed follower used his authority properly by caring and guiding others without any expectation or without using reward or punishment as a motivator (Crowther, 2012). As a follower who became a leader later himself, the Apostle Peter imitated Jesus' empowering leadership and supportive approach. This is described well by Carsten et al. (2010) as "providing autonomy and encouragement to followers and sharing information to build efficacy and strengthening follower performance" (p. 549).

Flexible, Open, and Adaptive

As a follower Peter was flexible and open to new ideas or experiences and was willing to adapt to and be malleable. Peter was the bridge-man who did more than any other follower of Jesus to pioneer diversity and inclusion in the first-century church and to hold together the diversity of first-century Christianity (Dunn, 1977). Further, according to Buzzell (2013), effective leaders know the importance of creating an environment in which followers are allowed to make mistakes but could still progress. From Scripture it is evident that Peter experienced this truth first-hand (Bonnet, 2020). After having denied Jesus three times, this former fisherman probably assumed that his service for Christ was ended, and Peter knew that he betrayed Jesus and that God would not entrust him with further responsibilities. Not only did Jesus forgave Peter, Jesus used him in a powerful way after his forgiveness and restoration (John 21). If there is one truth that Peter's amazing turnaround illustrated, it was the fact that God allowed His followers room to make mistakes and fail, then permitted them to get back up and still be used by Him (Buzzell, 2013).

Integrity and a Moral Rock

Another follower trait as social construct that Peter was known for was his integrity. Jesus taught Peter and the disciples habits of true holiness, which Bruce (1983) called the "lessons in religious integrity" (p. 68). Without this spiritual nourishment on the spiritual formation journey believers would wither and die and retreat to their old ways of sin (Faulhaber, 2007). As follower of Jesus, Peter learned the lesson that, through suffering integrity and trust are developed as important ingredients of Christian leadership (Bonnet, 2020).

From Jesus' empowerment approach with his disciples, it is evident that Jesus called his followers to teach them the Scriptures while he discipled them in his ways of godly living (e.g., teaching them and showing them how to pray, how to forgive, and how to serve one another with humility), and by giving them moral instruction (MacArthur, 2007). Jesus called Peter to enter the process of gathering people and rescuing them from the danger of a fallen world. God's Word would became Peter's master toolset instead of boats and nets (Block, 1996).

As follower of Christ, Peter's adherence to moral and ethical principles never wavered. He was also dependable and responsible. His word was his bond. His fellow fishermen and disciples, and Jesus as his mentor and leader, knew that Peter was worthy of being trusted and capable of being depended on. He was an honest man with a sound moral character—he was the *rock* that Jesus saw next to the Sea of Galilee when he was still just Simon the fisherman. Jesus saw the future rock on which his church would be built in him at that early stage already.

Morally, Peter's outlook matured as he accepted the moral freedom both Jews and Gentiles could enjoy cross-culturally through their diversity in Christ's love. In terms of the characteristic of self-transcendent wholeness in the *Updated Petrine Model based on the Nine Characteristics in the Fortosis (2001) Spiritual Formation Stage Model (SFSM)*—(see Bonnet, 2020)—the Apostle Peter later developed self-transcendence for the sake of others, he then had a thorough biblical knowledge and wisdom, and had a universal moral framework as a confronter of public and private injustice as a moral rock and follower of Christ.

Peter's Strengths/character Traits as a Follower

The following three strengths have been identified from the Apostle Peter as an effective follower of Jesus from the period during which his heart was transformed:

1. Peter mastered the concept of self-management. As underlined by both Chaleff (2009) and Kelley (1992, 1998), Peter as courageous and exemplary follower was able to work without close supervision and could anticipate his leader's needs. He took responsibility and ownership for it. He walked his talk. The Apostle Peter was an exemplar of the required level of engagement in followership.

2. Peter was an independent and critical thinker using his knowledge, skills, morals, ethics, and beliefs in support of Jesus' mission and God's vision. Peter could be considered an active critical thinker who gave voice to his opinions in a considered and powerful way as a skillful communicator rather than keeping them to himself.
3. Riggio et al. (2008) distinguished exemplary followers as actively engaged and adopting work attitudes such as "I am a steward of the business" (p. 130). Peter as follower of Christ was indeed as steward of God's business. With God as the Chief Executive Officer (CEO), the transformed Peter had the necessary job skills for the leadership role Jesus called him to fill, which he skillfully applied through understanding commitments and delegating to their team, using his organizational skills and values as listed as requirements by Kelley (1992) for exemplary followers.

Chapter Takeaways

Northouse (2019) wrote that it is normally the leadership abilities, and not the followership activities, that are being requested by organizations from people applying for jobs. When reflecting on Peter as leader in his ministry, it is important to reflect on his strengths as a follower while with Jesus. This is important as leaders and followers together create the leadership relationship, and Uhl-Bien et al. (2014) reminded that, without an understanding of the process of following, an understanding of leadership is incomplete.

The Apostle Peter as a follower of Christ learned the hard way in the approximately three and a half tough years of his spiritual formation journey with Jesus, that only a focus on Christ's mission and self-discipline as a Christian follower and leader in the end could provide the foundation for solid Christian leadership (Maxwell, 2007). In the end, God transformed Peter from an impetuous, loud influence to a thoughtful, humble, and effective follower and leader that stood as an exemplar in contemporary Christian leadership more than 2000 later (Maxwell, 2007).

Reflective Questions

1. How can leaders empower followers to be courageous and effective followers? What lessons can be learned from the relationship between Jesus and Peter?
2. Followership involves voluntary submission. What are the factors that contribute to a follower's willingness to voluntarily submit to leadership?
3. What is the Jesus-Disciple-Model of followership (being a steward of God's business as follower)? How do we reintroduce it into contemporary organizational leadership and contemporary research?
4. The reference to *transformation* in Chaleff's exemplary follower seems too broadly defined in a world speaking of transformation, diversity and inclusion, and empowerment in overlapping terms and terminologies. How can this term be redefined in terms of followership theory to ensure clarity and a contribution to the literature in organizational leadership?

References

Ajzen, I. (1991). The theory of planned behavior. *Organizational Behavior and Human Decision Processes, 40*(2), 179–211. https://doi.org/10.1016/0749-5978(91)90020-T

Alipour, K. K., Mohammed, S., & Martinez, P. N. (2017). Incorporating temporarily into implicit leadership and followership theories and followership theories: Exploring inconsistencies between time-based expectations and actual behaviors. *The Leadership Quarterly, 28*, 300–316.

Alvesson, M., & Blom, M. (2017). Beyond leadership and followership: Working with a variety of modes of organizing. *Organizational Dynamics, 48*, 28–37.

Atterson, M. L. (2020). Christian leaders as mentors: The challenge of emerging leaders. In J. D. Henson (Ed.), *Modern metaphors of Christian leadership: Exploring Christian leadership in a contemporary organizational context* (pp. 261–274). Palgrave Macmillan.

Baniissa, E., & Alattari, A. (2019). Followership styles and their relationship with leadership styles of academic leaders as perceived by faculty members at Universities of Northern Jordan. *Jordan Journal of Educational Sciences, 16*(1), 117–128.

Bastardoz, N., & Van Vugt, M. (2019). The nature of followership: Evolutionary analysis and review. *The Leadership Quarterly, 30*, 81–95.

Berlew, D. (1974). Leadership and organizational excitement. *California Management Review, 17*(2), 23.

Bligh, M. C. (2011). Followership and follower-centered approaches. In *SAGE Handbook of Leadership* (pp. 425–436). Sage.

Block, D. L. (1996). *Luke: The NIV application commentary*. Zondervan.

Bonnet, C. M. (2020). *Leading from a transformed heart: A content analysis of biblical pivotal moments in the life of the Apostle Peter* (Publication No. 27836374) (Published doctoral dissertation). ProQuest Dissertation Publishing.

Bruce, F. F. (1983). *The Gospel of John: Introduction, exposition, and notes*. Eerdmans Publishing.

Burak, O., & Bashur, M. R. (2013). Followership, leadership, and social influence. *The Leadership Quarterly, 24*, 919–934.

Buzzell, S. (2013). *NIV leadership Bible* (Updated ed.). Zondervan.

Capill, M. (2014). *The heart is the target: Preaching practical application from every text*. P&R Publishing.

Carsten, M. K., & Uhl-Bien, M. (2013). Ethical leadership: An examination of followership beliefs and crimes of obedience. *Journal of Leadership & Organizational Studies, 20*(1), 49–61.

Carsten, M. K., Uhl-Bien, M., West, B. J., Patera, J. L., & McGregor, R. (2010). Exploring social constructions of followership: A qualitative study. *The Leadership Quarterly, 21*, 543–562.

Chaleff, I. (2009). *The courageous follower: Standing up to and for our leaders*. Berrett-Koehler Publishers.

Choi, S. J. (2006). *A new heart to know the Lord: Rhetorical analysis of Jeremiah 21–24* (Unpublished doctoral dissertation). University of Gloucestershire.

Collinson, D. (2006). Rethinking followership: A post-structuralist analysist of follower identities. *The Leadership Quarterly, 17*, 179–189.

Crossman, B., & Crossman, J. (2011). Conceptualising followership—A review of literature. *Leadership, 7*(4), 481–497.

Crowther, S. S. (2012). *An examination of leadership principles in 1 Peter in comparison to authentic and kenotic models of leadership* (Publication No. 3515407) (Published doctoral dissertation). ProQuest Dissertation Publishing.

Dalcher, D. (2018, October). Advances in project management series: The leadership imperative and the essence of followership. *PM World Journal, 7*(10), 1–15.

De Zilwa, D. (2014). A new conceptual framework for authentic followership. In L. Lapierre & M. Carsten (Eds.), *Followership: What it is, and why do people follow?* Emerald Group Publishing.

De Zilwa, D. (2016). The strengths and capacities of authentic followership. *Leadership & Organizational Journal, 37*(3), 310–324.

Dunn, J. D. G. (1977). *Unity and diversity in the New Testament: An inquiry into the character of earliest Christianity*. Westminster.

Dvir, T., & Shamir, B. (2003). Follower development characteristics as predicting transformational leadership: A longitudinal field study. *The Leadership Quarterly, 14*(3), 327–344.

eCuncha, M., Rego, A., Clegg, S., & Neves, P. (2013). The case for transcendent followership. *Leadership, 9*(1), 87–106.

Ekundayo, J. (2010, Fall). Tine to focus on followers: Looking at the other side of the leadership 'coin'. *Academic Leadership: The Online Journal, 8*(4), Article 78.

Epitropaki, O., Sy, T., Martin, R., Tram-Quon, S., & Topakas, A. (2013). Implicit leadership and followership theories "in the wild": Taking stock of information processing approaches to leadership and followership in organizational settings. *The Leadership Quarterly, 24*, 858–881.

Epitropaki, O., Kark, R., Mainemelis, C., & Lord, R. G. (2017). Leadership and followership identity processes. *The Leadership Quarterly, 28*, 104–129.

Faulhaber, J. (2007). The role of tribulation and virtue in creativity: A sacred texture analysis of 1 Peter. *Journal of Biblical Perspectives in Leadership, 1*(2), 135–147.

Fineman, S. (2002) *Emotions in organizations* (2nd ed.). Sage.

Fortosis, S. (2001). Theological foundations for a stage model of spiritual formation. *Religious Education, 96*(1), 49–63.

France, R. T. (2007). *The Gospel of Matthew*. Eerdmans Publishing.

Gardner, H. (1995). *Leading minds: An anatomy of leadership*. Basic Books.

George, B. (2003). *Authentic leadership: Rediscovering the secrets to creating lasting value*. Jossey-Bass.

Grant, M. (1995). *Saint Peter: A bibliography*. Scribner.

Henson, J. D. (2016). Cognitive dissonance, value congruence and ethics in the life of Peter. In B. E. Winston & K. Patterson (Eds.), *Ethics: The Old Testament, the New Testament, and contemporary application*. CreateSpace Independent Publishing Platform. ISBN 13: 9781535184731.

Hoehl, S. (2008). Empowered by Jesus: A research proposal for an exploration of Jesus' empowerment approach in John 21:1–25. *Journal of Applied Christian Leadership, 2*(2), 5–17.

Hoption, C., Christie, A., & Barling, J. (2012). Submitting to the follower label. *Zeitschrift fur Psychologie, 220*(4), 221–230.

Jerry, R. H. (2013) *Leadership and followership* (Vol. 44, pp. 345–354). University of Florida Levin College of Law, Faculty Scholarship Repository.

Junker, N. M., & Van Dick, R. (2014). Implicit theories in organizational settings: A systematic review and research agenda of implicit leadership and followership theories. *The Leadership Quarterly, 25*, 1154–1173.

Kellerman, B. (2008). *Followership: How followers are creating change and changing leaders*. Harvard Business School Press.

Kellerman, B. (2013). Leading questions: The end of leadership. *Leadership, 9*(1), 135–139.

Kelley, R. (1992). *The power of followership: How to create leaders people want to follow and follower who lead them themselves*. Broadway Business.

Kelley, R. (1998). Followership in a leadership world. In L. Spears (Ed.), *Insights on leadership: Service, stewardship, spirit, and servant-leadership*. Wiley.

Kelley, R. (2008). Rethinking followership. In R. E. Riggio, I. Chaleff, & J. Lipman-Blumen (Eds.), *The art of followership—How great followers create great leaders and organizations*. Jossey-Bass.

Kizilos, P. (1990). Crazy about empowerment? *Training, 50*, 47–56.

Larsson, M. F., & Nielsen, M. F. (2017). The risky path to a followership identity: From abstract concept to situated reality. *International Journal of Business Communication*. https://doi.org/10.1177/2329488417735648

Lauren, K., & Henson, J. D. (2021). Jesus as humble servant. In J. D. Henson (Ed.), *Biblical organizational leadership: An exploration of contemporary leadership through the lens Jesus's leadership in the Gospel of John* (pp. 105–120). Palgrave Macmillan.

Lee, M., & Koh, J. (2001). Is empowerment really a new concept? *The International Journal of Human Resource Management, 12*(4), 684–695.

Leung, D. C.-Y. (2001). *Peter in the fourth gospel: Character development and reader empathy* (Publication No. 3002965) (Published doctoral dissertation). ProQuest Dissertation Publishing.

MacArthur, J. F. (2007). *Luke: The Savior of the world*. Moody Press.

Marion, R., & Uhl-Bien, M. (2001). Leadership in complex organizations. *The Leadership Quarterly, 12*(4), 389–418.

Martin, R. (2015, October–December). A review of the literature of the followership since 2008: The importance of relationships and emotional intelligence. *Sage Open*, 1–9. https://doi.org/10.1177/2158244015608421

Mathew, S. (2017). *Apostle Peter's cross-cultural leadership in Christian missions to the Gentiles: A socio-rhetorical analysis of Acts 10:1-11:18* (Publication No. 10747526) (Published doctoral dissertation). ProQuest Dissertation Publishing.

Maxwell, J. C. (2007). *The Maxwell leadership Bible* (Rev. and Updated ed.). Thomas Nelson Publishers.

Northouse, P. G. (2019). *Leadership: Theory and practice* (8th ed.). Sage.

Piettraszewski, D. (2019). The evolution of leadership: Leadership and followership as a solution to the problem of creating and executing successful coordination and cooperation enterprises. *The Leadership Quarterly*. https://doi.org/10.1016/j.leaqua.2019.05.006

Pigg, K. E. (2002). Three faces of empowerment: Expanding the theory of empowerment in community development. *Journal of the Community Development Society, 33*(1), 107–123.

Riggio, E. R., Chaleff, I., & Lipman-Blumen, J. (2008). *The art of followership: How great followership create great leaders and organizations*. Jossey-Bass.

Sanderson, R. (2017). *Love to lead: How love empowers leadership*. Leadership Revolution LLC.

Schyns, B., & Felfe, J. (2006). The personality of followers and its effect on the perception of leadership: An overview, a study, and a research agenda. *Small Group Research, 37*(50), 522–539.

Shamir, B. (2007). *From passive recipients to active co-producers: Followers' roles in the leadership process*. Information Age Publishers.

Smith, R. M. (1997, November 19–23). *Defining leadership through followership: Concepts for approaching leadership development*. Paper presented at The National Communication Association Convention, Chicago, IL. School of Arts and Sciences, University of Tennessee at Martin, TN.

Tee, E. Y. J., Paulsen, P., & Ashkanasy, N. M. (2013). Revisiting followership through a social identity perspective: The role of collective follower emotion and action. *The Leadership Quarterly, 24*, 902–918.

Uhl-Bien, M., & Pillai, R. (2007). The romance of leadership and the social construction of followership. In B. Shamir, R. Pillai, M. Bligh, & M. Uhl-Bien (Eds.), *Follower-centered perspectives on leadership: A tribute to the memory of James R. Meindl* (pp. 187–210). Information Age Publishers.

Uhl-Bien, M., Riggio, R. E., Lowe, K. B., & Carsten, M. K. (2014). Followership theory: A review and research agenda. *The Leadership Quarterly, 25*, 83–104.

Van den Abeele, A., & Legrand, M. (2013). *The desirability to develop followership—A discussion on three perspectives*. Linnaeus University.

Wilkins, M. J. (2017). Peter's theology of discipleship to the crucified Messiah (1 Peter 2: 2:18–25). *SBJT, 21*(3), 53–75.

Zhu, W., May, D. R., & Avolio, B. J. (2004). The impact of ethical leadership behavior on employee outcomes: The roles of psychological empowerment and authenticity. *Journal of Leadership & Organizational Studies, 11*(1), 16–26.

CHAPTER 4

Come, See, Do: Igniting the Spark that Energizes Followers

Jane Caulton

Introduction

Nearly two thousand years ago, an itinerant Jewish preacher introduced a new religious practice, which became known as "The Way" (Edwards & Edwards, 1997). The concept sparked a movement that grew into what is commonly known as the Christian church, thus making it one of humanity's oldest organizations. This organization has outlasted civilizations as it has continued to grow through two millennia, in spite of the fact that its founder was executed before it was ever fully established. The Center for Global Christianity reported that more than 2.4 billion people—one third of the world's population—are followers (Zurlo et al., 2019). Christianity exists in many forms, and can be found on all continents and in most countries, even in secret communities (Edwards & Edwards, 1997; Oosthuizen & Lategan, 2015). One segment, The Movement International,

J. Caulton (✉)
Regent University, Virginia Beach, VA, USA
e-mail: janicau@mail.regent.edu

D. J. Dean and R. B. Huizinga (eds.), *Followership and Faith at Work*, Christian Faith Perspectives in Leadership and Business,
https://doi.org/10.1007/978-3-030-90614-6_4

is busily at work establishing churches in areas that do not have access to technological innovations such as the Internet or television (http://www.themovementintl.org/). Many of these places can only be reached on foot traveling across tough terrain. Like The Movement's ancient predecessors, its followers establish churches in homes, disciple new members, and empower these converts to do the same. As a result, The Movement International has won thousands of souls and established many churches in approximately seven nations.

The Movement International's blueprint for operation was established by the organization's founder, Jesus Christ, and instituted by twelve men traveling from Israel to Samaria and the rest of the world according to Jesus' command (Acts 1:8). These men fought determinedly to complete their assignment of spreading the gospel, as their leader had directed. Thus, without such followers, "The Way" would have been just another chapter in Jewish history. This perspective of followership leads me to consider the research question, "What can contemporary leaders learn from observing the followers of Christ and how can they apply such lessons in their operations?" This chapter will consider this question through a socio-rhetorical analysis of Matthew, Chapter 10, highlighting Jesus' leadership style and its effect as represented by the Apostle Philip. Philip, viewed from the Gospel of John, was one of the first disciples that Jesus called and is always listed in the top five (McDowell, 2015; Zavada, 2020). He was noted as curious, faithful, and outspoken, whereby his character provides a model for the followership theories of Chaleff (2009), Kelley (1988), and Kellerman (2007). Examining the apostle's response to Jesus' leadership is applicable for developing like-minded followers, the efficacy of which is manifest through contemporary organizations such as The Movement International, which are yet following Christ's instructions to spread the gospel.

Literature Review

Leadership Theory

Followership is a product of leadership; for without followers, one cannot be a leader. It is important, however, to note that leadership and management are not one and the same. Rost (1991) emphasizes that "leadership and management are not synonymous terms, [*sic*]one can be a leader without being a manager ... Conversely one can manage without leading" (Rost, 1991, p. 101). While both are decision-making roles, leaders must make the critical decisions that provide organizational direction and their major power is influence. Leaders provide the vision for the mission while managers execute it. Thus, leaders engage interactively with others to bring about change. Their techniques are persuasive rather than coercive, personal rather than mechanical. They engage their followers and enable them to see themselves as important in organizational goals.

Follower-centric leadership is practiced by those who wish to empower their subordinates. Such leaders "treat employees as the most valuable organizational assets, investing available resources in them" (Maslennikova, 2007, p. 3). They treat their staffs as equals and involve them in the decision-making process. Favorable perceptions of leaders determine leader effectiveness (Yukl, 2006). Those who practice encouraging their workers through praise, rewards, and support are most likely to receive high approval. They are considered follower-centric because they are concerned about the development of their people; their leadership style may be charismatic, servant, or transformational.

Charismatic leadership theory is one of the earliest reverse-pyramid (leaders at the bottom) theories. Prior to these, most theories emphasized the importance of the leader. But in 1947, sociologist Max Weber used the term "charisma"[1] to describe follower response to a favorable perception of their leaders. Over the years, the theory has been developed through empirical studies but leaders who espouse change from the current status and are unconventional in their processes are generally considered as charismatic. These leaders demonstrate self-sacrificing behavior and inspire support through emotional appeal. Klein and House (1995) posited that charisma resides in the leader–follower relationship, rather than the person. They described charisma as "a fire that ignites followers' energy and commitment, producing results above and beyond the call of duty" (p. 183). It has three elements: spark, flammable material, and oxygen. The leaders provide the spark in their articulation of vision, communication of confidence in the follower's ability to excel, and the projection of a collective identity over an individual one. Doing so in the proper environment (oxygen) ignites the flammable material (spark) of follower engagement, consciousness, and commitment.

[1] The term comes from the Greek, meaning "divinely inspired gift" (Yukl, 267).

The resulting fire—charisma—charges the organizational environment, resulting in success.

Robert Greenleaf also associated organizational success with follower engagement (Washington et al., 2014). In 1977, he proposed the servant leadership theory that emphasized the value of people, authenticity, and community. He proposed that leaders should place interest in the good of all over the good in themselves and should see themselves as servants of followers rather than followers as their servants. He advocated that followers should be seen as constituents and that power should be shared with them. Greenleaf stressed the importance of developing followers: "The new ethic requires that growth of those who do the work is the primary aim, and the workers then see to it the customer is served and that the ink on the bottom line is black. It is their game" (Greenleaf, 1977, p. 121). Such action strengthens and allows followers to participate in decision-making as paramount to increasing organizational quality. Practicing servant leadership, according to Greenleaf, ensures corporate growth.

Corporate growth is also the goal of transformational leadership, a theory introduced by James McGregor Burns in 1978 (Yukl, 2006). This follower-centric approach also highlighted empowering followers and increasing their ability to make decisions independently. Yukl said "transformational leadership appeals to the moral values of followers in an attempt to raise their consciousness about ethical issues and to mobilize their energy and resources to reform institutions" (p. 267). Burns opined that increasing follower awareness of the significance of their roles improves performance and that providing incentives is more effective than coercive tactics, such as penalizing (Yukl).

Transformational leaders are considered change agents who focus on revitalizing, creating new vision, and normalizing change (Morse, 1996). Transformational leaders operate in four dimensions of follower interaction (Bass & Avolio, 1994). They serve as role models (idealized influence), they motivate and inspire others (inspirational motivation), they stimulate creativity and innovation (intellectual stimulation), and they are attentive to the professional developmental needs of their constituents (individualized consideration). These efforts create a relationship that nourishes the intrinsic needs of followers while promoting a growth environment that is profitable for the total organizational community.

Followership Theory

Followership is an innate projection of nature, which craves order (Kellerman, 2008). Order produces results with minimal conflict and is most clearly seen in the animal kingdom, where hierarchies are natural. This social order enables groups to work together, in which someone leads and others follow. Kellerman said "the virtues of ranking include the efficient division of labor, the stability of the group organization, and the maintenance of order" (p. 52). Therefore, most people agree to follow a leader, who may be selected by a group or self-appointed.

People have been bred to embrace leadership from the womb, where they enter into a preset hierarchy headed by their parents (Kellerman, 2008). This arrangement provides comfort, security, and stability. Humans then learn that acquiescing to authority benefits them. Kellerman said "(a) leaders provide individuals with safety, security, and a sense of order; (b) leaders provide individuals with a group, a community, to which they can belong; and (c) leaders provide individuals with someone who does the collective work" (p. 56). Thus, the leader–follower relationship is beneficial collectively as well as individually; groups can more efficiently accomplish a purpose and are more effective with leaders. Everyone does not follow willingly but some resist leadership for a variety of reasons, which can cause variance and stall efforts (Kellerman, 2008). However, those followers can be brought back into alignment by their fellow followers. "Followers" said Kellerman, "model their behavior on others similar to themselves" for the same reasons that they follow leaders: the need for stability, security, order, meaning, and belonging (p. 56).

Followers may be better understood by their roles rather than their positions (Kellerman, 2007). Traditionally, followers are perceived as those who report to someone who has more authority, power, or influence. They execute assignments and relay results to those who have the power to make decisions. Kellerman said "they may comply so as not to put money or stature at risk" (p. 2). However, with the technological and cultural changes of the twenty-first century where the boundaries of work space have been altered by virtual spaces and teams spanning the globe, followership can be perceived differently. These workers now have the power to make decisions quickly in the service of customers on behalf of their organizations. The workplace is an environment where knowledge has become more important than position; and therefore, followers are deciding what is necessary to achieve organizational goals.

Followership has thus become a subject worthy of attention as companies now realize that their success or failure depends on the character and behavior of their representatives at the bottom of the chain as well as the top. Kellerman (2007) proposed that the best means of assessing the value of followers is to consider their levels of engagement. The author proposes that they will fall into one of five categories: isolates, bystanders, participants, activists, and diehards. The most dangerous of these to an organization are the first two—the isolates and the bystanders. These two groups of people evidence no investment in the organization, its mission, or its leaders. Their primary focus is personal survival. Isolates have separated their interests from day-to-day issues and events while bystanders are aware but determined not to participate. They do not report problems, but wait to see what will happen. These two groups are like speed bumps in the road; they slow down growth and innovation through the absence of contribution.

On the other hand, the last three—participants, activists, and diehards—are jewels in the organizational crown. They are the ones who keep the company moving forward and their leaders looking good. The difference in the three is the level of their investment, with participants having the lowest and diehards having the highest. Each of these followers will take steps they feel necessary for organizational advancement; however, if they disagree with or disapprove of their leaders, they can become a problem as they may become saboteurs rather than supporters—and that can have negative outcomes. Companies seeking growth must ensure that its front line is strong, so leaders must periodically observe the character, behavior, and contributions of followers and consider how best to encourage and improve their activities (Kellerman, 2007). Suggestions for incentivizing range from appealing assignments to increased responsibilities with monetary rewards and/or compensation.

Organizations that embrace the creative abilities of their followers effectively and efficiently combat stagnancy (Jaussi et al., 2008). They value their employees as individuals and allow them to shape and pursue ideas that promote and expand the organizational good. Jaussi et al. (2008) explained "creative organizations are extremely people-centric, and they recognize that creativity is an essentially human endeavor. They understand that ideas originate in individuals, and groups of individuals shape, develop, and lead new ideas to fruition" (p. 292). As a result, such organizations are continually evolving as they allow their followers to take them to new heights. Organizations must allow followers to function as individuals who have different interests, different degrees of abilities, and different degrees of passion. All followers will not operate in the same way, but all have something to contribute to the mission.

Kelley (1988) defined effective followers as "enthusiastic, intelligent, and self-reliant" participants in pursuit of an organizational goal while in a subordinate position (p. 3). Though these people may value their positions and may even find them virtuous, their motivations and perceptions vary as some find satisfaction in supporting a person or a goal, others in the context of a role, and still others as a means of personal achievement. Kelley theorized that follower behavior can be identified by their ability to think critically and independently and their pattern of engagement ranges from passive to active. Five patterns emerged from Kelley's theory: sheep, yes people, alienated followers, survivors, and effective followers.

Sheep are the least engaged followers who perform their tasks and wait for their next assignment (Kelley, 1988). They are not likely to take initiative, but will most likely do the work. "Yes" people look to their leaders for inspiration and direction. They do not veer from the leader's vision and may be servile in their performance, which does not advance the agency. Alienated followers can be described as passive-aggressive as they have their own opinions but do not engage. They are cynical but not oppositional; they have disengaged. Survivors are those who go along to get along while effective followers are the organization's most valuable employees. They are energetic, motivated, interested, and participative. Kelley said "effective followers are well-balanced and responsible adults who can succeed without strong leadership" (p. 4). These followers are star performers who work in partnership with leaders in advancing the organization. Star performers are those who manage themselves well; are committed to the organization, purpose, principles, and others. They build their competence and focus their efforts for maximum impact and are courageous, honest, and credible. They are mature and able to handle delegation with efficiency, effectiveness, and aplomb. They can be depended on to accomplish their assignments and support the organizational mission.

Followers have a responsibility to their organizations to assertively respond to leadership (Chaleff, 2004). The organization best prospers when all ideas are brought to the table and properly aired. Conversely, the organization suffers when followers bow to the will of leaders in the interest of self-preservation. Chaleff said "Those who work most closely with the leader, the senior 'followers' if you will, need to assume responsibility for keeping their relationship with the leader honest, authentic and courageous. 'Yes men' need not apply" (p. 1). Followers must avoid personal survival games and be willing to participate in helping the organization to accomplish its goals and execute its mission. On the other side, leaders must create environments where follower contribution is welcome. Such environments are shaped by integrity, respect, open communication, and interest in the common good which breeds self-confidence, information sharing, and strong morale.

Both leaders and followers need to take time to examine their goals and motives. They must ask themselves the hard questions about the reasons for their choices, which will bring about transformative action. Chaleff (2004) posited that "at the heart of all transformation of relationships lies transformation of ourselves. This is both where we have the most power to create change and the most reluctance to confront the need for it" (p. 2). When both leaders and followers engage in self-improvement, the organization prospers.

Though the role of follower is often diminished by society's focus on the leader, organizational success is the responsibility of both leaders and followers (Chaleff, 2009). The stronger a follower is the stronger the leader will be; therefore, the follower has a responsibility to the leader and to the organization. To be effective, followers must be aware of and accept their power, appreciate their leaders, and understand and counteract the seductiveness of power. This type of followership takes courage (Chaleff, 2009). Courageous followers, according to Chaleff, are those who assume responsibility, serve, participate in transformation, speak to leadership, and take moral action.

Followers assume responsibility when they take the organizational mission and vision as their own. Chaleff (2009) said "courageous followers discover or create opportunities to fulfill their potential and maximize their value to the organization" (p. 6). They serve by using their strengths to support their leaders by ensuring that they can perform their roles without distraction. And sometimes doing so, means that followers must sometimes challenge policies and behaviors that do not support organizational integrity. Chaleff said "they are willing to stand up, to stand out, to risk rejection, to initiate conflict in order to examine the actions of the leader and group when appropriate" (p. 7). In this way followers participate in transformation, as well as working with leadership and championing the recommendations for change. They do not shrivel in the process or become divisive. When necessary, they take moral action by making tough calls according to their convictions. In such situations, morally conscious followers must be prepared to determine their own conscience and choose a direction that may lead away from the group or organization, which requires a high level of maturity.

The maturity of followers often determines the level of leadership interaction (Hersey et al., 1979). The less mature a follower is the less courage will be demonstrated and more interaction with leaders will be required. Follower maturity may fall into one of four basic categories of maturity: low, moderate, moderate to high, and high, and may be managed accordingly (Hersey et al., 1979). Attention, however, must be paid to follower disposition or readiness, (Hersey & Blanchard, 1997). Readiness may be categorized as (a) able and willing (confident), (b) able but unwilling (insecure), (c) unable but willing or confident (deficient), and (d) unable and unwilling or insecure. The first category of follower maturity, low maturity, indicates a need for more guidance, requiring leaders to maintain a high-task/low-relationship behavior engaging one-way communication in order to define activities and expectations. At the second category of follower maturity, moderate maturity, followers may be prepared but insecure and thus, require more direction. Leaders engage in a high-task/high-relationship involving two-way communication to provide support and build confidence. The third level of maturity allows leaders to engage a high-relationship/low-task leader strategy, wherein leaders may relax communication as followers are willing to accomplish goals. Finally, the high-maturity follower can be trusted to accomplish goals with little interaction with the leader. The leader may delegate assignments with confidence of effective efficiency. Thus, understanding the follower's maturity level assists leaders in determining the level of required interaction.

Follower maturity level, of course, determine their attitudes and behaviors, which are often shaped by environmental influences, including conscience, culture, peers, roles, world events, and language of followership (Kelley, 2008). Each area yields a plethora of possibilities for consideration, such as what cultures may shape sheep, what qualities allow people to serve as followers, and how does leadership shape the leader–follower relationship. Kelley posited that much is to be learned from the study of followership and such study may shape better leaders.

Method: Socio-Rhetorical Analysis

To explore the research question "What can contemporary leaders learn from observing the followers of Christ and how can they apply such lessons in their operations," I will use socio-rhetorical analysis, which allows the examination of scripture from a variety of positions and allows the investigation and creation of picturesque themes to inform audiences. Robbins (1996) theorized that the substance of a biblical text extends beyond the words on the page to a consideration of the rich textile formed by all the elements of life, including language, culture, and social relationships. Through socio-rhetorical interpretation, readers can view the biblical manuscript under five textural lenses: inner texture, intertexture, social and cultural texture, ideological texture, and sacred texture (Robbins, 1996). Inner texture is concerned with the texts as intended by authors and experienced by readers, whether implied or actual. Intertexture considers the relationship of the texts to other disciplines, social and cultural texture considers the relationships of the characters to each other and their society, ideological texture considers the relationship of voices to the power structures of their period, and of course, the sacred texture considers the relationship of the text to God (Henson, 2014; Huizinga, 2016; Oginde, 2011). An interpreter may examine a text through one or multiple textures, depending on how rich a project is undertaken.

Making a case for the necessity of leadership, Henson (2014) conducted a thorough intertexture analysis of the book of Titus. He explored all four sub textures of intertexture—oral-scribal, historical, social, and cultural—to land upon some interesting observations about Paul's perspective on leadership. This study found that leaders are the pivotal element in group dynamics. In times of conflict and opposition, groups look to the leader for solutions. Leaders, however, must deal with their own internal conflicts as Henson found that leaders often manifest a dual nature wherein the human propensity for behavior struggles with the spiritual tendency for good. As leaders mature, they lean more toward their spiritual nature as they engage the process of becoming authentic leaders. Henson said "Paul elevated honesty, sincerity, and authenticity as characteristics of godly ecclesial leaders" (p. 199). Authentic leaders must be self-aware, moral, transparent in their relationships, and able to make decisions objectively.

Oginde (2011) teased out the requirements of good Christian leadership using socio-rhetorical analysis of the first seven verses of 1 Timothy 3.

He concluded that leadership requires willingness, discipline, and demonstration. Explaining that leaders should have a higher concern for others than themselves and be willing to make sacrificial decisions, Oginde said leaders must "be disciplined in character, maintaining high moral standards. This leadership is identified with a commitment to self-control and mastery of passions; and practicing restraint where money, wine, or violent temper is concerned" (p. 30). These characteristics, he opined, are the minimal requirements for successful leadership.

Huizinga (2016) conducted a socio-rhetorical examination of the biblical book 1 Peter to explore the value of humility in leaders. Using sociological intertexture, he explained that Peter encouraged the first-century church to maintain humility and longsuffering and he used historical intertexture to show that their conversion had brought them into the family of God. Through ideological intertexture, Huizinga noted that Jesus' predisposition for humility presented an example for the new Christians to follow and that humility places one "under God's direct protection, not God's judgment" (p. 37). Leaders who embrace humility strengthen their positions as they are more inclined to acknowledge, recognize, and celebrate other organizational contributors. They are more concerned about their organizations than themselves and are therefore more in tune to their abilities and achievements. They acknowledge their mistakes, are open to new ideas, and a greater appreciation for the world (Huizinga).

Veiss (2018) used an intertextual analysis of 2 Timothy 3:10–17 to determine the strategy Paul used to develop his follower, Timothy. She found that the text demonstrated modeling as the most influential method of change. Paul followed Jesus' positive-modeling example and advised Timothy to do the same. Veiss said "positive modeling is further informed by Paul's ability to show Timothy virtuous living, model fortitude, practice sound teaching, and serve through benevolent deeds" (p. 164). Her findings align with contemporary followership theory, which are also demonstrated in Christ's relationship with his followers.

Method

Intertexture Analysis: The Leadership of Jesus as Demonstrated in Matthew 10

Jesus had surely and carefully prepared the disciples for rejection and persecution (McDowell, 2015). Following him would be costly, as they would be rejected, persecuted, and eventually killed. In Matthew 10:24–25, Jesus emphasized

> The disciple is not above his master, nor the servant above his lord. It is enough for the disciple that he be as his master, and the servant as his lord. If they have called the master of the house Beelzebub, how much more shall they call them of his household?

Yet, he also told them that their work was important for building the kingdom (Henry, 1708–1714). Having been with Jesus a while, the disciples had seen the gospel in action. They had listened to his teaching, saw him heal people, raise the dead, and cast out demons; and now in Matthew, Chapter 10, their Master was giving them the opportunity to demonstrate their understanding of their call (Henry, 1708–1714; Maxwell, 2002).

Matthew 10 begins with the identification and ordination of the Twelve, as they are often called in scripture:

> Simon, who is called Peter, and Andrew his brother; James the son of Zebedee, and John his brother; Philip, and Bartholomew; Thomas, and Matthew the publican; James the son of Alphaeus, and Lebbaeus, whose surname was Thaddaeus; Simon the Canaanite, and Judas Iscariot, who also betrayed him. (Matthew 10:2–4)

He did not call them as a group but recognized each individually, signifying personal responsibility for their response to His call. Henry (1708–1714) noted that this commission drew them closer into the Lord's confidence as they now shared His ministry, as well as His life.

In Matthew 10:5–42, Jesus then commissioned them to use their gifts, defined their assignment, set clear objectives, and presented a clear message (Maxwell, 2002). He provided guidance for engaging with others, while instilling confidence by assuring them of their ability to complete the mission. He cautioned them to be wise but to avoid offending others, even as he warns them that their journey will not be easy. They will endure hardships, persecution, and threats to their lives, yet they will know what to say at the right time. He tells them not to be afraid and assures them that they have his support and can depend on His presence. In Mark's account (6:7–11), He then sends them out in pairs; Barnes (1847–1885) explained that "this was a kind arrangement, that each one might have a companion, and that thus they might visit more places and accomplish more labor than if they were all together." The Master carefully and compassionately crafted and executed the apostles' first assignment. Thus, Matthew, Chapter 10, demonstrates that Jesus took a follower-centric approach in leading the disciples (Chang, 2013; Maslennikova, 2007; Maxwell, 2002).

Three follower-centric styles are easily identified in the chapter: charismatic, servant leadership, and transformational leadership. As a charismatic leader, Jesus endeared himself to the apostles by spending time with them and creating personal bonds. He was unconventional in choosing the apostles on two levels: (1) followers normally chose the rabbi that they would follow and (2) disciples were trained in the scriptures from their youth (Greenwold, 2007; McDowell, 2015). Jesus chose his followers and empowered them by building relationships and commissioning them to carry out His work, though they had little formal training, if any. He communicated a vision for a cultural and spiritual change. His practice of empowering his followers, developing his disciples, and sharing power is also characteristic of servant leadership. Servant leaders seek the best for all, which Jesus excelled at in all facets of His life. His practice of providing counsel and guidance to the disciples in executing their mission was demonstrative of transformational leadership. He modeled the vision, instilled confidence, and provided his disciples an opportunity to use their training (Table 4.1).

Intertexture Analysis: The Call and Service of the Apostle Philip; Preparation for Service

Though the term "disciple" in Christendom is most closely associated with the followers of Jesus, it was customary for Jewish rabbis to have followers (Bivin, 1988; Daugherty, 2013). Even the prophet Isaiah, references his "disciples" (*limmûd* in Hebrew, meaning "instructed") in Isaiah 8:6 (Strong, 1996, p. 413). In first century, A.D., those disciples were totally committed to the person whom they chose to follow (Bivin, 1988;

Table 4.1 Leadership style of Jesus according to theory

Pericope	*Action*	*Leadership style*
Matthew 10:1–4	Identifies and empowers followers Builds relationship with followers Presents a collective identity	Charismatic Transformational
Matthew 10:5	Commissions followers to serve Articulates vision Provides opportunity to serve	Servant Transformational
Matthew 10:6–14	Instructs them on execution Explains handling acceptance and rejection Provides clear instruction	Servant Charismatic
Matthew 10:16–23	Warns that they will suffer but God will be with them Shares power Provides a clear vision	Servant Charismatic Transformational
Matthew 10:24	Admonishes followers to emulate their leader Provides a model for service	Charismatic leadership Servant

Daugherty, 2013). The teaching of their sage was more important than anything, including family. Bivin (1988) explained that "this form of discipleship was a unique feature of ancient Jewish society" (para. 3). Studying was the priority and the teacher was to be held in the esteem of a father, and unless the natural father was a scholar, the rabbi was to be given higher regard (Bivin, 1988; Daugherty, 2013). Disciples were apprenticed to their sage, and expected to emulate them. This sentiment was marked even by Jesus, who admonished that following him meant leaving family and possessions (Luke 9:61; Luke 14:28–33).

John 1:43–48 presents the call and conformance of the disciple who would become known as the Apostle Philip. Jesus had been baptized by John in Bethbara and called Philip to discipleship as he left the area for Galilee (McDowell, 2015). Philip did not flinch at his call but recognized Jesus as the Messiah for whom Israel had been waiting. Philip was not new to discipleship but had been a follower of John the Baptist (McDowell, 2015; Zavada, 2020). He may even had been at the baptism of the Lord and witnessed the Holy Spirit commission him as the Son of God. The disciple quickly emulated his master, bringing his friend Nathanael along. At Nathanael's reluctance, Philip challenged him, "Come and see"

(John 1:46; McDowell, 2015). Nathanael did and Jesus received him, thus becoming Philip's first recruit in the new kingdom.

Philip's eagerness to share truth with others landed him in the auspicious group of twelve who would follow Jesus through his ascension (Matthew 10:2–4; Luke 6:13–15). Always listed in the fifth position when the apostles are named, Philip may have had leadership responsibilities within the group (McDowell, 2015). His decisive recruitment of Nathanael is the first indication of his desire to emulate his sage. As a member of the twelve, he often learns at the feet of Jesus (Mathew 10:2–4; Mark 3:17–19; Luke 6:13–15). Gentz (1986) describes the apostle's followership of Christ as ideal, thus aligning him with Kelley's (1988) description of a star performer and Kellerman's model of a die-hard follower. Philip's commitment to Christ never dimmed, even when he failed to understand the divinity of his sage. Jesus explained that by knowing him, the apostles had known the Father. Philip challenged, "Lord, show us the Father, and it sufficeth us" (John 14:8). McDowell explained that

> Having determined in his thinking that the Father of whom Jesus spoke must be the Ultimate Absolute, Philip demanded that he and his associates might see him. Philip was materialistic; apparently abstractions meant little to him. Nevertheless, he had a deep desire to experience God for himself. (p. 195)

Philip certainly does not fit Kelley's description of a "yes" man, as scripture demonstrates that the disciple shared his opinions openly and honestly. In John 6:7, Philip responded frankly to Jesus' inquiry about acquiring food for the multitude that had come to learn from the Master: "we don't have the resources." McDowell (2015) noted "Philip perceives the problem entirely on a human level, hopelessly wondering how they could produce the means to feed all the people" (p. 194). Chaleff (2009)'s model identifies Philip as a courageous follower as he demonstrated courage in speaking frankly to his leader, but servitude in remaining with him and learning how the task could be accomplished through faith. Though Philip's name does not appear in many gospel stories, Acts 1:13 names him among the apostles who met in the Upper Room after Christ's ascension, showing that his level of commitment held study.

Table 4.2 Followership style of Philip according to theoretical models

Pericope	*Action*	*Model*
John 1:43–48 John 12:20–22	Witness to Nathanael Assistance to Greek seekers of Christ	Star performer (Kelley, 1988) Enthusiastic Self-confident Intelligent Diehard (Kellerman, 2007) Highly invested Supportive of leader and the mission Courageous Follower (Chaleff, 2004) Participates in transformation
John 6:7	Advises leader of insufficient funds	Courageous Follower (Chaleff, 2004)
John 14:8–9	Requests accountability from Jesus	Makes tough call Morally conscious

According to church tradition, Philip was the missionary who carried the gospel to Greece, Syria, and Phrygia, which aligns him with Kelley's description of an effective follower (Nelson, 2016). The earliest traditions, according to Nelson, point to him being martyred in Hierapolis, whereupon he would fit Kellerman's (2007) die-hard model. (McDowell [2015] questions whether the apostle has not been confused with Philip the Evangelist, appointed as a deacon in Acts 6 and who figures prominently in the rest of the book.) Undoubtedly, however, the Apostle Philip traveled Asia preaching the gospel as he was a witness of Christ's resurrection, his response to Jesus demonstrates a missionary mindset, and he was willing to bear the consequences of his call to follow the Master (Nelson, 2016; RCL Bensiger Saints Resource, 2020; Zavada, 2020) (Table 4.2).

Conclusion: Application to Contemporary Workplace

An organization's leader determines the direction of the organization. The leader's vision sets the paradigm of operations for those who follow. Jesus demonstrated the importance of sharing that vision with followers and his onboarding process set the foundation for kingdom organizational operations. Turner (2013) said "he was able to deploy the Apostles to effective service because they ultimately desired nothing more than building this new form of organization" (p. 5). His follower-centric approach ignited a spark in His followers, the Apostles, that has been transmitted through the ages.

Followers like the Apostle Philip therefore committed their lives to spreading the gospel. Though unlearned, they responded to the charisma of Jesus, accepting His call, receiving the vision, and carrying out the mission. They were so inspired by their connection with Jesus that they continued even after separating from him. And they did it the way that Jesus did. Consider the instructions of the Apostle Paul in writing the Philippian church: "The things which you learned and received and heard and saw in me, these do, and the God of peace will be with you" (Philippians 4:9). The work initiated by the followers of Jesus is still carried on today.

Believers in Christ can be found on every continent. The message Christ taught is echoed in pulpits around the globe in a plethora of languages and new converts are won every day. Most amazing, followers of Christ still carry the gospel into the hinterlands where technology does not reach. One such group is headquartered in the United States, but operating in Asia and Northern Africa. Established in September 2015, the Movement has 100,000 people in 5,000 churches in nine nations (Ryan Brubaker, personal communication, 8/26/20; The Movement International, http://www.themovementintl.org).

Converts come into the local church established by The Movement International, which meets in a believer's home, where they are trained to take the gospel to surrounding villages and locales. Lisa Brubaker, Director of Operations, said "our church planters started 10 new house churches in different unreached villages that are now filled with over 250 former Hindus and Buddhists that are being discipled in their new faith every day. In just 6-months, almost 50,000 people have heard the Gospel for the first time, and we doubled the amount [*sic*] of churches and Christians in that district" (Personal communication, July 8, 2020). Just as Christ ignited His followers' spark and lit the fire that fueled the spread of the gospel, The Movement International is using the same follower-centric approach of building relationships, providing guidance and training, and giving followers opportunity to perform. As a result, follower energy is ignited by the leader's vision, empowerment, and confidence in them.

These are the practices handed down through the generations that have enabled Christianity to outlive empires and they provide a framework for contemporary leaders. The follower-centric approach used by Christ is applicable in today's society. It involves knowing your followers, understanding their strengths and weaknesses, developing their skills and talents, giving them an opportunity to perform, building their confidence, and rewarding their efforts. Followers then experience the pleasure of belonging, a sense of security, and the benefit of stability which creates, as the Apostle Philip demonstrates, passion and loyalty which promotes organizational prosperity.

Five Chapter Takeaways

1. Followers play a major role in organizational success.
2. Followers operate in a variety of roles with just as many characters, aspirations, and dispositions.
3. Successful leaders maintain an acute awareness of their followers' level of engagement and incentivize appropriately.
4. Jesus sets a model as a follower-centric leader while the Apostle Philip represents organizational benefits of such leadership.
5. Follower-centric leadership produces successful organizations.

Five Reflective Questions

1. This chapter presents three theories of organizational followers. How are they alike? How do they differ?
2. Describe leadership's responsibility to followers. What results will it breed?
3. What theories support follower-centric leadership? What is their organizational application?
4. How do successful leaders conduct themselves? Highlight the operative characteristics.
5. Describe the follower-centric leadership characteristics found in Matthew 10. How might you apply them in your workplace?

References

Barnes, A. (1847–1885). *Barnes' noted on the Bible*. Retrieved from Studylight.org. http://biblehub.com/commentaries/hebrews/11-21.htm

Bass, B. M., & Avolio, B. J. (1994). Improving organizational effectiveness through transformational leadership. In G. R. Hickman (Ed.), *Leading organizations: Perspectives for a new era* (pp. 135–140). Sage.

Bivin, D. (1988). Jesus' education. *Jerusalem Perspective*, 14–15. https://www.jerusalemperspective.com/555/

Chaleff, I. (2004). *Courageous followers, courageous leaders: New relationships for learning and performance—Ideas for leaders*. https://www.courageousfollower.net/wp-content/uploads/Courageous-Followers.pdf

Chaleff, I. (2009). *The courageous follower: Standing up and for our leaders* (3rd ed.). Berrett-Kohlers Publishers. https://www.bkconnection.com/static/The_Courageous_Follower_3rd_EXCERPT.pdf

Chang, P. (2013). The consummated harvest of Jesus' follower-centric approach in the last chapter of the Gospel according to John. *Journal of Biblical Perspectives in Leadership, 5*(1), 115–141. https://www.regent.edu/acad/global/publications/jbpl/vol5no1/7chang.pdf

Daugherty, J. (2013). *Discipleship is Jewish*. Heart of God Israel, a ministry of Heart of God International. https://heartofgodisrael.org/messianic-messages/discipleship-is-jewish/

Edwards, G., & Edwards, D. L. (1997). *Christianity: First 2000 years: The first two thousand years*. Orbis Books.

Gentz, W. H. (1986). *The dictionary of Bible and religion*. Abingdon.

Greenwold, D. (2007). *Being a first-century disciple*. Bible.org. https://bible.org/article/being-first-century-disciple

Greenleaf, R. K. (1977). Servant leadership in business. In G. R. Hickman (Ed.), *Leading organizations: Perspectives for a new era* (pp. 115–129). Sage.

Henry, M. (1708–1714). *Matthew Henry commentary on the whole Bible (complete)*. BibleStudyTools.com. http://www.biblestudytools.com/commentaries/matthew-henry-complete

Henson, J. D. (2014). Getting God's house in order: An intertexture analysis of Titus. *The Journal of Biblical Perspectives in Leadership, 6*(1), 176–200. https://www.regent.edu/acad/global/publications/jbpl/vol6no1/12Henson.pdf

Hersey, P., & Blanchard, K. H. (1997). Situational leadership. *Dean's Forum, 12*(2), 5. https://citeseerx.ist.psu.edu/viewdoc/download?doi=10.1.1.201.4096&rep=rep1&type=pdf#page=4

Hersey, P., Blanchard, K. H., & Natemeyer, W. E. (1979). Situational leadership, perception, and the impact of power. *Group & Organization Studies, 4*(4), 418–428. https://doi.org/10.1177/105960117900400404

Huizinga, R. B. (2016). An understanding of humility-based leadership impacting organizational climate. *Emerging Leadership Journeys, 9*(1), 34–44. https://www.regent.edu/acad/global/publications/elj/vol9iss1/2ELJ-Huizinga.pdf

Jaussi, K. S., Stefanovich, A., & Devlin, P. G. (2008). Effective followership for creativity and innovation: A range of colors and dimensions. In R. E. Riggio, I. Chaleff, & J. Lipman-Blumen (Eds.), *Art of followership: How great followers create great leaders and organizations* (pp. 291–307). Jossey-Bass. https://b-ok.cc/book/697418/b703c7#:~:text=The%20Art%20of%20Followership%3A%20How%20Great%20Followers%20Create,play%20and%20their%20often%20complex%20relationship%20to%20leaders

Kellerman, B. (2007). What every leader needs to know about followers. *Harvard Business Review, 85*(12). http://thebusinessleadership.academy/wp-content/uploads/2017/03/What-Every-Leaders-Need-to-Know-About-Followers.pdf

Kellerman, B. (2008). *Followership: How followers are creating change and changing leaders*. Harvard School Press.

Kelley, R. E. (1988). In praise of followers. *Harvard Business Review Case Services*, 142–148. https://www.kquattrin.com/uploads/2/5/8/7/25876455/kelley_1988.pdf

Kelley, R. E. (2008). Rethinking followership. In R. E. Riggio, I. Chaleff, & J. Lipman-Blumen (Eds.), *Art of followership: How great followers create great leaders and organizations* (pp. 5–16). Jossey-Bass. https://b-ok.cc/book/697418/b703c7#:~:text=The%20Art%20of%20Followership%3A%20How%20Great%20Followers%20Create,play%20and%20their%20often%20complex%20relationship%20to%20leaders

Klein, K. J., & House, R. J. (1995). On fire: Charismatic leadership and levels of analysis. *The Leadership Quarterly, 6*(2), 183–198. http://www.management.wharton.upenn.edu/klein/documents/Klein_House_1995.pdf

Maslennikova, L. (2007). Leader-centered versus follower-centered leadership styles. *Leadership Advance Online*, 14. https://www.regent.edu/acad/global/publications/lao/issue_11/pdf/maslennikova.pdf

Maxwell, J. C. (2002). *Maxwell leadership Bible*. Maxwell Motivation Inc.

McDowell, S. (2015). *The fate of the Apostles: Examining the martyrdom accounts of the closest followers of Jesus*. Ashgate Publishing. https://doi.org/10.4324/9781315558196

Morse, M. (1996). *The relationship of wisdom to transformational leadership: Illustrated by the historical Jesus* (Dissertation). George Fox University. https://digitalcommons.georgefox.edu/cgi/viewcontent.cgi?article=1047&context=gfes

Nelson, R. (2016). Who was Philip the Apostle? *The Beginner's Guide*. https://overviewbible.com/philip-the-apostle

Oginde, D. A. (2011). Antecedents of Christian leadership: A socio-rhetorical analysis of 1 Timothy 3: 1–7. *Journal of Biblical Perspectives in Leadership, 3*(2), 23–31. https://www.regent.edu/acad/global/publications/jbpl/vol3no2/JBPL_Vol3No2_Oginde_pp23-31.pdf

Oosthuizen, A. J., & Lategan, L. O. K. (2015). "Managing the household of God": The contribution from management sciences to the sustainability of the church as an organization. *Stellenbosch Theological Journal, 1*(2), 551–568.

RCL Bensiger Saints Resource. (2020). *Philip the Apostle*. http://saintsresource.com/philip-the-apostle

Robbins, V. K. (1996). *The tapestry of early Christian discourse: Rhetoric, society, and ideology*. Psychology Press.

Rost, J. C. (1991). Leadership and management. In G. R. Hickman (Ed.), *Leading organizations: Perspectives for a new era* (pp. 97–114). Sage.

Strong, J. (1996). *The new Strong's complete dictionary of Bible words*. Nelson Reference & Electronic Publishing.

Turner, C. K. (2013). *Prototypical Jesus? A discussion of followership development from John 6*. https://www.regent.edu/acad/global/publications/lao/issue_23/turner1.pdf

Veiss, S. D. (2018). Follower development: Paul's charge to Timothy. *Journal of Biblical Perspectives in Leadership, 8*(1), 150–167. https://www.regent.edu/acad/global/publications/jbpl/vol8no1/Vol8Iss1_JBPL_12_Veiss.pdf

Washington, R. R., Sutton, C. D., & Sauser, W. I., Jr. (2014). How distinct is servant leadership theory? Empirical comparisons with competing theories. *Journal of Leadership, Accountability & Ethics, 11*(1). https://studydaddy.com/attachment/98472/How+Distinct+is+Servant+Leadership+Theory+Empirical+Comparisons+with+Competing+Theories.pdf

Yukl, G. (2006). *Leadership in organizations*. Prentice Hall.

Zavada, J. (2020, February 11). *Philip the Apostle—Follower of Jesus Christ*. https://www.learnreligions.com/philip-the-apostle-follower-of-jesus-701070

Zurlo, G. A., Johnson, T. M., & Crossing, P. F. (2019). Status of global Christianity, 2015. In the context of 1900–2050. *International Bulletin of Missionary Research, 39*(1), 29. https://www.gordonconwell.edu/center-for-global-christianity/wp-content/uploads/sites/13/2020/01/Status-of-Global-Christianity-2020.pdf

CHAPTER 5

Implicit Followership Traditions in the New Testament: Priscilla, Aquila, and Apollos

Larry D. Phillips

Introduction

Through the last two decades of the twentieth century, scandalous corporate operations brought forth an era of new research in leadership. Still, a gap exists between the examination of desired leadership characteristics and the study of followership. Leadership effectiveness is often examined through organization outcomes or influence on followers; however, investigation of follower identity, implicit leader image of follower development, or the notion of follower mission awareness is scarce. The leadership question thus looms that without follower action toward the organization's mission is leadership present. There is an absolute value to this discussion through the interpretation of the works of biblical New Testament authors and the characterization of first-century citizens of the early Church. This chapter introduces followership identity through

L. D. Phillips (✉)
Regent University, Virginia Beach, VA, USA
e-mail: larrphi@mail.regent.edu

D. J. Dean and R. B. Huizinga (eds.), *Followership and Faith at Work*, Christian Faith Perspectives in Leadership and Business,
https://doi.org/10.1007/978-3-030-90614-6_5

the activity of Priscilla, Aquila, and Apollos bringing to life Paul's early church planting. According to Robbins (1996a), the texts as language integrates society, culture, ideology, and religion. Social Rhetorical Exploration convictions of the text from different angles, as introduced by Robbins, help develop beliefs and values through a social and cultural texture perspective.

Herein is presented a hermeneutical investigation, first of Priscilla and Aquila, then Priscilla's interaction with Apollos, and lastly, traditions of the early Christian Church are connected through emerging followership theory and thought for reflection and reaction. This chapter examines the concept of followership useful within the context of organizational mission. The organization's mission statement is a concise statement of purpose—the organization's reason for existence—and is valuable in achieving shared purpose at every level of organizational leadership. New Testament Christ-followers Priscilla, Aquila, and Apollos align under the leadership of the Apostle Paul to bring the Gospel promise for eternal life to Jew and Greek alike. Priscilla and Aquila, the tent maker couple, emerge as leaders of an ecclesial community out of Rome, following Claudius' likely banishment (Acts 18:2) of chief Jewish leaders in 49 CE. Arriving in Corinth ahead of Paul, traveling from Athens and being of the same trade, they collaborated, eventually traveling together to Ephesus. In Ephesus, Priscilla and Aquila met Apollos, a Jew born in Alexandria. Unlike Priscilla and Aquila, who were known as evangelists (see Acts 18:26) and protectors and fellow workers of Paul, Apollos appears with the art of rhetoric and very much an individualist (Meeks, 2003). Together Aquila and Priscilla, the teachers; Apollos, the orator; and Paul, a preacher of the Gospel, combine as a knowledgeable team with a shared mission to extend the Gospel message.

Ideological Texture

For the reader of the biblical text, considering the world in which the test is written is beneficial. In Paul's letters to Corinth, he would have considered the trauma of the significant destruction by Rome and the eventual re-foundation of Corinth as a Roman colony, which beseeches the question as to which characterization of Corinth Paul addressed, the Greek or the Roman (Alexander & Green, 1995). According to Alexander and Green, the tendency to treat biblical text as a special kind of literature is averse to the literary contexts that shape the New Testament.

Paul would have known the convictions of the Church he founded and Luke, likewise, of the Church he investigated. Paul and Luke would have considered Rome's destruction of Corinth and the reformation together with the persuasive strategies of first-century philosophers and orators in their letter writing, consequently developing text, which is the literary context within history. Robbins (1996b) argues that ideological analysis addresses the social, cultural, and individual location and perspective of writers and readers. Ideological criticism seeks out the way of life situations by connecting the flesh with the ideas and theology of the text (DeSilva, 2004). Through ideological intertextual analysis and interpretation, the shape of the history and the diverse culture of Rome, Corinth, and Ephesus are revealed. We glean insight concerning individual interaction of the time. The readers of Luke's Acts were knowers, and as such, according to Castelli (2004), being a holder of knowledge is considered a valuable commodity or desirable characteristic of life. Priscilla, Aquila, and Apollos are included in Paul's team of knowledge workers advancing two primary Christian organization mission and objectives; promoting the advent of the Holy Spirit through baptism and transmission of the gospel of Jesus Christ.

The primary focus of ideological texture is people (Robbins, 1996b). Robbins argues social location as a central component of ideology, suggesting one's social location is the rhetorical context through which one views the world, constructs reality, or interprets biblical texts. An ideological analysis examines the biases, opinions, preferences, and stereotypes of a writer and reader of a text. The three interests of ideological texture include (Robbins, 1996a):

- The writer is the beginning place for analysis and interpretation
- The analysis and interpretation of the text by others
- The inclusion of one or more other texts.

The focus of ideology extends beyond the individual actor within the text and includes one text's interaction with another text. Robbins suggests ideologies are shaped by specific views of realities shared by the group. Dvorak (2007) contends that text forms cognitive and affective dimensions and includes an ideological dimension through an evoked emotional response that fulfills a social function. According to Dvorak, text evokes an emotional response and performs social functions. DeSilva

(2004) reasons early Christians were deeply steeped in Greco-Roman and Hellenistic Jewish traditions. According to DeSilva, the New Testament text looked to influence history and social relations; therefore, NT text is a rich vault of information for discovering everyday life, how relationships unfold and grow, and social-scientific analysis. Hogg (2001) supposes the collective identity of the group and social solidarity is a central significance of the household of the early Christian movement, thus a lens through which text is analyzed. Using Robbin's (1996a) guidelines for texture analysis, this chapter explores Luke's writings of Aquila, Priscilla, and Apollos through ideological analysis.

Apostle Paul Called to Lead First-Century Christian Followers

"So, being sent out by the Holy Spirit, they went down to Seleucia; and from there they sailed to Cyprus" (Acts 13:4, New Revised Standard Version). From what may be the D-Day calling for Barnabas and Paul, from heaven when "Another angel came out of the temple, calling with a loud voice to the one who sat on the cloud, 'Use your sickle and reap, for the hour to reap has come because the harvest of the earth is fully ripe'" (Rev. 14:15) as if to show the blessedness of the faithful and servants of God (Henry, 1991). With the needs of their heart being the same, Barnabas and Paul are separated from among disciples and, on the command of the Holy Spirit, are sent out to bear Christ's name and a way to the Gentiles (Acts 9:15). Hence, according to Henry, these disciples are given a discharge from their current service and filled with the Spirit (see Acts 14:26) sent out (i.e., given their mission) to break up the fallow ground.

Scripture traces Paul's path, crossing paths with rival teachers whose ulterior mission is to pervert the gospel (Gal. 1:6). Paul and Barnabas seek to preserve the integrity of the covenant through the perpetuation of circumcision and Torah observance on the converts (DeSilva, 2004). The rituals of the Torah observance reflected truth and embodied a culture, purpose, and values for the followers; therefore, these evolve as a social identity even if contrary to faith in Christ and spiritual transformation introduced by Paul. The parallel accounts of Acts 22:6–21 and 26:12–23 and what Moessner (1986) argues develop out the larger Christological-historical pattern of Luke's narrative of Christ's glory when the light flashed on the road to Damascus through which Young (2015) suggests; Paul is called to guide Christ-followers' faith. Paul is called to transform society. Through conversion, the values of a Christian transform and a new order from God are set in place for community within a social context. Through Christian conversion the supernatural transforming work of the Holy Spirit is exhibited (Mott, 1982). In mission then, according to Mott, a new order for life through community support is required.

Robbins (1996a) maintains people are the primary subject of ideological analysis and interpretation, with the issue being the social, cultural, and individual location. The interpreter's interest in ideology is not satisfied by the mere examination of one individual. Instead, we examine the ideology concerns of respective presuppositions, dispositions, and values in common with other people. The previous perspectives of the world are shaped by the group's shared views of reality. A review of social location is called for to understand the ideological culture of the text.

From Text to Context the Social Location of Luke's Acts 18 Community

Social location narrows the scope of context and reveals the social system position, reflecting the worldview (Robbins & Neyrey, 1991). In other words, the social location shows the conditions and perception of how things work and fit together to determine what is real. According to Robbins (1996b), the social location is the rhetorical context for how the world is viewed, how reality is constructed, and how the biblical texts are interpreted. Moxnes (1994) suggests the text communicates between the implied reader and empirical audience, linking the social and cultural society providing meaningful relation to their world. The community situation of Lukan Acts included gentile Christian, Jewish Christian, and a mixture of these; thus, the narrative of the text, according to Moxnes (1994), "must correlate to the social context of the Mediterranean world in antiquity" (p. 380).

Acts 18:1 describes that Paul has transitioned from Athens to Corinth and found a sure Jew named Aquila because Claudius had exiled all Jews from Rome. Eusebius on church history writes Claudius had banished the Jews from Rome as Paul completed his journey from Jerusalem (Maier, 1999). Keller (2010), in contrast, proposes a total expulsion of the Jew estimated to have been forty to fifty thousand Judeans and complete removal, a difficult, if possible, at all undertaking. Keller suggests Luke's narrative "...because Claudius had ordered all Jews to leave Rome" (Acts

18:2) as typical Lukan "rhetorical hyperbole" (p. 9). Keller introduces Leon (1995) and suggests Claudius likely banned chief Jewish leaders of a dispute that arose in 49 CE. This exile is essential to note. It indicates that a displaced Aquila and his wife Priscilla from Rome arrived in Asia Minor, not as mere converted Jews, but have arrived in Corinth with credentials in the early Christian movement. Luke enlightens the reader to hostilities toward the Jewish people and perhaps radical in their actions leading to expulsion; however, we do not find that Paul experienced hostilities while in Athens. Henry (1991) describes Corinth as a rich and splendid city of Achaia others, such as Keller (2010), describes Corinth attracting people of all kinds and a place teeming with the opportunity with promise for a keen eye to make contacts with new Christian converts.

DeSilva (2004) suggests Paul undertakes a common thought approach toward faith in the gospel of Christ Jesus and the power of spirituality through the body of the Church. DeSilva argues it was the culture and ethic of the ancient household Paul sought in the churches he founded. It was an ethic of relationship characterized by the harmony that Paul employed to dispute the speeches of the sophist (i.e., use of rhetoric and philosophy), which greatly influenced citizens of bustling centers such as Corinth. According to DeSilva (2004), Paul repudiated prevalent Hellenistic societal, cultural norms. For Paul, the proclamation that "Christ sent me to preach the gospel" rather than the impressiveness of voice, gesture, or vocabulary the philosophers used must serve the message. The use of any worldly means to gain conviction would be to undermine the transformative power of God. Paul's mission involved heuristic constructs, which emerged as converts were won on the grace of God through faith in Christ, so, in sum, Robbins and Neyrey (1991) argue the social location in the heuristic sense refers to a social location of thought.

Followership—Paul's Workers in Christ

Presenting the accomplishments of Paul through the second half of his narrative, Luke introduces Priscilla and her husband Aquila in the context of Paul's second missionary journey and within the framework of his first trip to Corinth (Keller, 2010).

> 1 After this, Paul left Athens and went to Corinth. 2 There, he found a Jew named Aquila, a native of Pontus, who had recently come from Italy with

> his wife Priscilla because Claudius had ordered all Jews to leave Rome. Paul went to see them, [3]and, because he was of the same trade, he stayed with them, and they worked together—by trade, they were tentmakers. (Acts 18:1–3, NRSV)

Concerning the intellectual, rhetorical culture of the first century, Walker (2008) suggests Luke's gentilic affiliation of Aquila with Pontus (Acts 18:2) invokes the possibility of heresy connecting Aquila to the shared origin of Marcion. The inclusion of Pontus in the descriptive account of Aquila suggests that Luke's portrayal of Aquila and Priscilla interweaves text with his anti-Marcionite agenda. Aquila, the converted Jew of Pontus, shared national affiliation with Marcion, who claimed Paul the only true apostle of Jesus Christ while yet juxtaposing a perverted notion of two gods to Christianity's Jesus as the creator. Marcion and Paul preached at opposite ends of the spectrum concerning salvation through the resurrected Christ.

Keller (2010) positions Luke's introduction within the context of Paul's exit from Athens with mixed results having been scoffed (Acts 17:34) as others joined him in becoming believers or responded as Felix had in disbelief (Acts 24:25). After living eighteen months in Corinth (Acts 18:11), Paul departs with Priscilla and Aquila from Corinth and travels to Ephesus (Acts 18:18–19), then moving on after rebuffing the couple's plea for him to remain longer, Priscilla and Aquila are trusted to persevere without his company. While caring for the Church in Ephesus, Priscilla and Aquila meet Apollos, a native of Alexandria, one who is well versed in the scripture, an eloquent man instructed in the way of the Lord with enthusiasm for the accurate teaching of the things concerning Jesus, though knowing only the baptism of John (Acts 18:24–25). Speaking boldly within the synagogue, Priscilla and Aquila heard him, took him aside, and explained the way of God more accurately (Acts 18:26).

Scholars (e.g., Den Dulk, 2020; Walker, 2008) frequently note Alexandria, Apollos' origin, as a learning center, which contrasts with Aquila's origin as a native of Pontus (Acts 18:2). Much of Priscilla and Aquila is speculation; according to Keller (2010), Aquila might have been born a free man, slave, or freed slave of a Roman Acilian family. It is there he may have met Priscilla, quite possibly, like Aquila, who could have been a free woman, slave, or daughter of a freedman. Luke includes little else of Aquila's origin; however, Pontus is a vital narrative point. Pontus might be divergent of Apollo's orientation connected with Alexandria, the epic center for learning. Conversely, Pontus is regarded best as inconsequential (Den Dulk, 2020).

The Missionary Couple: The Social Location of Aquila and Priscilla

There is no evidence that Luke was acquainted with Aquila and Priscilla, but Luke does introduce the pair to his readers as a married couple (Acts 18:2). There has been considerable attention given to the order of introduction either by Luke in Acts or the letters of Paul, with each presenting Priscilla (Prisca) first when referring to the couple in Corinth (Walker, 2008). Marriage in the Hellenistic society created provision for the future through offspring and inheritance, having little to do with companionship, but was an arranged affair with a promise of an honorable future (DeSilva 2004). Keller (2010) postulates that as nascent Jesus believers from a diverse stratum, often unable to enter a legal marriage, enter a spiritual marriage to live together without joining a physical union. Rordorf (1969) contrasts Keller referring to the Christian society as uncritically accepting of social structures and adherence to culture concerning marriage in the early Church. Horrell (2016) brings forward the challenge of NT authors to construct positive group-identities of Christ-followers that are non-ethnic as trans-ethnic having to address the trans-ethnic Judaism and non-ethnic Christianity. However, custom or act brought Aquila and Priscilla to marriage; this couple shared life in companionship with faith in Christ.

From Luke's Acts, it is inferred the pair lived a missionary life in the faith of Jesus Christ not only in developing trade skills as tent makers, affording their simplified nomadic lifestyle. We know little from Luke concerning Aquila and Priscilla's life before Corinth, but their mission to support Paul is evidenced. First, in their expulsion from Rome and their willingness to move on with Paul to Ephesus (Acts 18:1, 18:18). Priscilla and Aquila demonstrated a faith that pre-dates Paul and brought what Frye et al. (2007) referred to as the "whole self" (p. 244) to the workplace.

According to Kelley (1988), "followership dominates our lives, but not our thinking…" (p. 3). In other words, even as leaders, we are active as followers; whether we report to a boss, a board, or a committee, we all function as followers. Kelley presents four follower types, which operate on two underlying behavioral dimensions: the degree to which followers exercise independent critical thinking and the other regarding a passive-active scale. Along these dimensions, Kelley identifies four follower types: Alienated, those who think critically but may not act in carrying out the role and maybe disengaged at a time; Conformist, who follow established order, are not in the habit of questioning the boss, are engaged but lack independent thinking; Pragmatist, they occasionally question the boss, stick to the middle of the road and often are attuned to the political shifts of the organization; and Exemplary, take the initiative and are critical thinkers. As followers Aquila and Priscilla conform to Kelley's (1992) depiction of active and fully engaged exemplary followers.

Gentleman Scholar the Social Location of Apollos

The narrative of Acts 18:24 presents many ways of Apollos: Apollos is a Jew, an eloquent man from Alexandria, well versed in the scriptures, and instructed in the way of the Lord. Smith (1915) suggests Apollos, a disciple of the Baptist, who likely baptized the twelve disciples in Ephesus. Apollos being "instructed in the Way of the Lord" (Acts 18:25) refers to the Messianic prophecies of the Old Testament yet in need of further instruction (Smith, 1915). Keller (2010) points out Acts 18:26 as Priscilla and Aquila's only evangelistic activity recorded by Luke recording "He began to speak boldly in the synagogue; but when Priscilla and Aquila heard him, they took him aside and explained the Way of God to him more accurately." Apollos' knowledge of "the way" was not flawless. Smith (1915) suggests, may be indicative of a lack of circulation, as some scholars of Paul's letters advocate. Thus, it is conceivable that Apollos' training included instruction from a disciple ignorant at the time of the Apostolic rule of Baptism.

Hart (1905) argues there was perhaps no more excellent speaker than Apollos, describing him on a continuum between learned and eloquent. As a historian should, Luke asserts Apollos as "...instructed in the Way of the Lord..." (Acts 18:24), which Hart (1905) promotes, is the general practice teaching of Apollos. Having been taught by the Baptist (Acts 18:25), and unlike Paul, brought to teaching Christ Jesus by the flash of light, Apollos thought there might be work, and having his mind so inclined by God, with friendly encouragement, he went as inclined to Ephesus (Henry, 1991). Keller (2010) argues that Apollos is no ordinary convert; instead, he is "... well versed in the scriptures" (Acts18:24), thus demonstrating sufficiently knowledgeable to teach—trusted enough to be left with Aquila and Priscilla. When he wished to move on to Achaia, these believers first encouraged him and then sent forward a recommendation he be received with a welcome (Acts 18:27), showing by the scriptures that the Messiah is Jesus.

Apollos' success comes through his leadership skill in humility and vulnerability enough to learn and with emotional intelligence to hear Priscilla's teaching. Chaleff (1998) postulates that many great organizations fail for lacking in courage and skill to address dysfunctional behavior. As Barton (1924) suggests, Apollos comes into Corinth with a force of character and far more intellectual influence than Paul in teaching the Corinthians. Apollos understood Paul's overarching vision to develop followers in Christ among Jew and Gentile through grace and faith in salvation through Christ's resurrection. As Chaleff (1998) proposes, courage as a follower is beneficial at any organizational level to accept the teaching and carry forward learning. Or, as Kelley (1992) argues, if people lead, the leaders will follow. As a fully engaged follower of the faith in Christ Jesus, Apollos may have exhibited a conformist attitude before his encounter with Priscilla and Aquila (Acts 18:26). This meeting led him to exemplary follower behavior, as well.

Shared Vision and the Integration of Faith in Rome, Ephesus, and Corinth

Aquila and Priscilla, introduced by Luke (see Acts 18:2–3), appears three times in Paul's letters initially as Prisca and Aquila Romans (16:3) and includes the gratefulness of Paul, and all of the churches suggesting Prisca and Aquila are indeed coworkers in Christ Jesus (Walker, 2008). From the beginning, Prisca and Aquila are willing to be used by God. Through the hardship of making their home as movable as the tents, they made, accepting the task of leading a home church, and risking harm of life by preaching and teaching that Jesus is the Messiah of God (Keller, 2010), Prisca and Aquila exhibit followership through all aspects of life. Paul welcomes and asks for a greeting from the Church (1 Cor. 16:19), making them discipleship, the best-known married couple in the New Testament (Keller, 2010).

By way of the first mention of Priscilla from Luke's Acts (18:26), it is inferred that she instructs Apollos in a whole way of God (Den Dulk, 2020). Luke's mention of Priscilla first coupled with his inclusion of Pontus as Aquila's and Alexandria as Apollos' heritages may be to subvert the undermining of ethical stereotypes. Aquila, Priscilla (Prisca), and Apollos answering a call of what Paul suggests as not wise, not robust, and not noble, then proclaim, "But God chose what is foolish in the world to shame the strong" (1 Cor. 1: 27, Den Dulk, 2020). Anyone familiar with the common negative view of Pontus realizes the absurdity of a person from this region influencing a person of Alexandria—the epicenter of learning. Luke's mention of this gentilic point adds a twist in Apollos' eloquent speaking Alexandria, intellectual's instruction, which Apollos humbly receives. Apollos, an ardent, enthusiastic, spiritual believer, and Aquila and Priscilla, the experienced, skilled, spiritual, faithful believers, sharing knowledge of the way of the faithful in the Messiahship of Jesus.

Interestingly, Apollos and Aquila from differing backgrounds and though Apollos, a teacher (Barton, 1924) and Aquila and Priscilla, missionaries (Keller, 2010), through the shared vision of faith in the saving grace of Christ resurrection, which transcends culture, move each toward engaging in exemplary followership in Paul's mission of spiritual salvation. Kelley (1992) supposes organizations aplenty with visionary roles "like Moses descending from the mountaintop, the leader unveils the new order..." (p. 207), and all the dependent followers stop their wandering and applaud. Exemplary followers expect to put themselves on the line, thus the motivation to develop a strategy with leaders.

Acts 18:18–28 as a Hermeneutical Model of Followership

Cultural habits of the early Church perpetuate a need to determine the extent of Jewish acculturation within the biblical text (Osborne, 2006). Investigating the extent of supracultural indicators reveals if a text is normative (supracultural) or cultural, thus moving text to context and revealing authenticity. Discovering the supracultural nature of Scripture unveils the gospel and gives life in each new historical setting, which is far removed from the biblical culture and mindset. The three-step process to determine if a text is normative or cultural first involves noting the passage for supracultural indicators or the extent Scott (1979) argues the selection isolates salvation. The second step in this process is reviewing the passage for cultural practices no longer present in modern society. Third, determine the distance between the cultural statement and supracultural (Osborne, 2006).

Supracultural Indicators

Osborne (2006) suggests assessing for teaching that conforms to a cultural bias. For example, Acts 18:18 states that after reaching Cenchreae, Luke reveals that Paul "had his hair cut, for he was under a vow." Paul had followed a vow of the Old Testament Nazirites, who usually would close with a haircut among other stringent sacrifices. Paul is completing a vow in Jerusalem as was the cultural norm in that day; thus, this text is cultural. Conversely, in Acts 18:24, Luke introduces Apollos as an "…eloquent man, well-versed in the scriptures" and Acts 18:25 stating, "he spoke with burning enthusiasm and taught accurately the things concerning Jesus," clearly these passages transcend culture and bring meaning into each new historical period. The Ministry of Apollos (Acts 18:24–28) with six passages referencing the scriptures (Acts 18: 18 & 24), teaching (Acts 18:25 & 26), or the Way of Jesus (Acts 18:25), the Way of God (Acts 18:26) indicates supracultural ideologies. Osborne (2006) argues a closer review of cultural practices must be completed to reduce subjectivity and discern the supracultural nature of the text.

Cultural Practices

The second step of Osborne's (2006) supracultural process is investigating the cultural practice of the early Church no longer observed. The practice of following vows and Jewish cultural rituals occurred in the first-century Church (Acts 18:18), and paradoxically, across these lines of Scripture, Paul enters the synagogue to hold discussions with the Jew (Acts 18:19) and "…powerfully refuted the Jews in public…" (Acts 18:28). Osborne (2006) argues criticality in determining proof in cultural events and practices and linking to first-century customs. The passages of Acts 18:1–28 reflect Paul's mission to take the gospel to the Jew and Gentile alike; thus, it must be acknowledged how these Scriptures influence the twenty-first-century Church. Osborne (2006) suggests a third assessment for the distance between Greco-Roman culture and the modern world to reveal the supracultural.

Distance

To overcome cultural distance, the interpreter infers the supracultural principle within the command. Acts 18:18–28 contains cultural and supracultural ideologies. Acts 18:25 sets forth a shift in faith occurring after the baptism of John, Acts 18:25 and 18:26 point to a difference between "the Way of the Lord" (Acts 18:25) and "the Way of God" (Acts 18:26), which develop a variation of the interpretation of culture within these perspectives, and contrast revelation of Paul's adherence to an Old Testament vow (Acts 18:18). From these complex passages, we consider the uniqueness of the faith response of followers of Christ in the first and twenty-first centuries. Larkin (2011) explains baptism as the inner experience of regeneration, which suggests the baptism a new birth brought about by the Holy Spirit, the Way of God. Fruchtenbaum (2011) proposes the twenty-first-century Church as a Gentile cultured church and foreign to the Jew. Messianic Jews do not wish to lose their identity in Judaism through faith in Jesus as Messiah. Contemplating the ideas concerning regeneration through baptism and the Gentile acculturation of the modern Church brought forward by Larkin and Fruchtenbaum indicates an argument too thin to determine these passages as primarily cultural.

The supracultural concepts extracted from Acts 18:18–28 constitute teaching, knowledge sharing, identity, and vision sharing among Paul's social network of followers. Supracultural passages are normative (eternal), shrinking the distance between cultural aspects and supracultural to zero. There is little difference in Paul's mission to lift followers full of faith and with the knowledge and spirit to change society, then with the advent of Christ's saving grace for faithful followers through the resurrection. Little difference exists in the distance between the Greco-Roman Mediterranean culture Paul establishes his mission in and the global culture in which the modern era organization likely operates.

Within this global framework, Küpers and Weibler (2008) point toward a collective leadership discourse dependent on followers and leaders' collaborative, knowledge-sharing effort to increase operations efficiency sustained business success. Similarly, Nonaka and Takeuchi (1995) purport that knowledge creation occurs through dialog and collective reflection between organizational members. Finally, Hogg et al. (2005) postulate the effectiveness of depersonalized leadership increases as leaders and followers appraise each other in terms of the group prototype. Thus, organizational behavior becomes governed by the ingroup prototype, more so than by a leader. These imperatives point toward the value of followership typology and implicit followership behavior.

Followership Typology

Like a coin with an obverse and reverse, such is leadership and followership within an organization, unlike the game of chance in a coin toss, followership should not be a game of luck. Scant literature in understanding followership development exists with a predominance of leadership research approaching follower behavior as a result of leader influence. Three authors prevail as idea generators of followership, including Ira Chaleff, Barbara Kellerman, and Robert Kelley. Chaleff (1998) postulates a change in culture with followers focus on the mission and the courage to influence the organizational position leader. The success in sustained change appears challenging in a model that depends mainly on the follower's skill to affect change through organizational leadership. Kellerman (2007) likewise brings forward a supposition with followership on a metric of engagement. While favorable toward identifying likely response or effort a knowledge worker is expected to apply to an organizational task, Kellerman's model is insufficient in encouraging follower development. Kelley (1988) postulates the key to followership lies in the followers' ability to think critically and act independently. Kelley suggests influential followers and care over themselves carry concern and are committed to a cause, idea, or mission. One might call this organizational health. Next, this chapter takes a closer look at Kelley's (1992) followership development process.

Becoming a Follower

Recent research (Gao & Wu, 2019; Oc & Bashshur, 2013; Sy, 2010) focuses on prototypical follower behavior. Others (Carsten et al., 2010; Yang et al., 2020) disseminate knowledge regarding cognitive construction and social constructionism theories concerning follower behavior. While this is interesting, academia has scarcely contributed toward what much of its leadership scholarship identifies as the most critical commodity within an organization—followership.

Kelley (1992) stresses organizations should design environments to accommodate and retain followers. Followers often look within organizations for ways to fulfill a personal vision—what they have been called to do. Followers are primarily driven by interpersonal relationships, which Kelley describes as:

- Apprentice (learners focused on leadership from the follower perspective)
- Disciple (conduits through education for a culture of knowledge)
- Mentee (entrusts others in development, which may include emotional as well as professional skill)
- Comrade (involves a team or group relations and work)
- Loyalist (to leader, vision, mission); dreamer (following a personal dream is driving force)
- Lifeway (a path to service) as a path to followership.

According to Kelley, the paths toward followership develop "some sense of enoughness" (p. 86) in defining work/life balance. The paradox of followership asks people can both think for themselves and perform a followership role. Through a qualitative questioning process of organizational members, Kelley identified two dimensions or types of followers, those who think for themselves, are innovative and active or engaged, and those on the opposite spectrum, those who give no thought and are passive or worse disengaged.

Along the follower dimension spectrum, five followership types (see Fig. 5.1) exist, which include (Kelley, 1992):

- Alienated Followers: Think freely and critically; non-participatory
- Conformist Followers: Content taking orders and deferring to their leaders
- Passive Followers: Non-thinkers; require supervision
- Exemplary Followers: Perform well in every aspect; exercise independence, critical thinking, separate from the leaders or the group, are actively engaged
- Pragmatist Followers: Straddle the fence; question decisions, but not too critically.

Kelley (1992) introduces readers to the fictional character Leo from the Hermann Hess novel Journey to the East. Leo's fictional character is a good spirit and manages to keep things organized, helping or leading the team's movement forward. All is well until Leo vanishes. Then, the team unravels and meets failure.

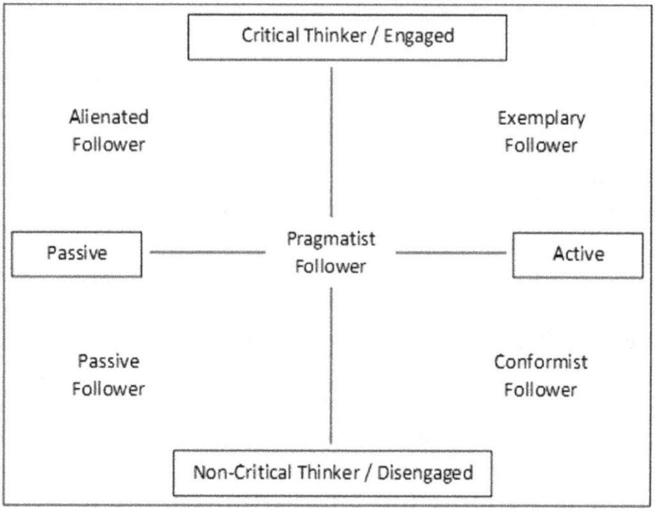

Fig. 5.1 Followership styles along two dimensions (*Note* Robert Kelley's typology of followers along two dimensions: Independent critical thinker and disengaged non-critical thinker. Adapted from "The power of followership: How to create leaders people want to follow, and followers who lead themselves" by R. E. Kelley (1992). Copyright 1992 by Robert E. Kelley)

Kelly (1992) suggests Leo as "the quintessential exemplary follower" (p. 25). Interestingly, Greenleaf (2002) postulates Leo exists with a "natural feeling …to serve first" (p. 27), thus, a servant leader. Can Leo be both? Suda (2013) suggests followership roles as closely intertwined with leadership roles people shift between on a condition-dependent basis. If this is so, Kelley and Greenleaf are conditionally correct. Kellerman (2007) questions in an era of cross-cutting teams of knowledge workers, who exactly is leading and who is following, Kelley (1988) mentions followership may be situation-dependent, and Chaleff (1998) suggests many positional followers are simultaneously positional leaders. Followership may be the dominator of our lives.

Recent research (e.g., Bjugstad et al., 2006; Ekundayo, 2010; Epitropaki & Martin, 2004) suggest followership remains understudied and contested as a viable study variable, with implicit leadership theory (ILT) research limited to the underlying conception of their behavior a topic in need of deeper discussion. Sy (2010) argues that while thirty years of research exists concerning ILT, scant literature exists concerning the notion of follower implicit theory. Steffens et al. (2015) postulate that shared group membership between the leader and followers may influence prototypical identity as in or out of the group. Interestingly, these authors bring forward correctly so that being of a group does not correlate as being for the group.

The work of Steffens et al. (2015), along with that of Oc and Bashshur (2013), argues that because leaders exist within the same group as followers, several variables exist (e.g., member decisions, behavior, attitudes) which are open to the future study of others-focus leadership theory. There exists a need to understand better how followers socially constructed view of leaders is influenced as the role of leader diminishes. This is important in the twenty-first-century organization summarized by the pivotal work of Drucker (1999) as the knowledge economy era. Drucker's work advances the importance of implicit theories concerning followers in an age in which worker knowledge is a primary organizational commodity. Through two decades of implicit theory research followership in which is approached by extending the understanding of influence through others-focused leadership, such as servant leadership and leader behavior influencing follower happiness. Drucker (1999) introduced the knowledge worker era juxtaposes the breath of member knowledge spread with organization skill in the global market. Further research is called for concerning the Implicit Follower Theory whereby a better understanding of follower expectation of leader behavior is gained.

Chapter Takeaways

The New Testament text of Acts makes known that Paul, through the hospitality of Aquila and Priscilla, finds shelter and coworkers in the trade of tent-making and faith sharing. As proclaimers and followers of Messiah Jesus, Aquila and Priscilla lift and strengthened other like-minded followers of Christ such as Apollos. Through their shared vision and mission, the trio, Aquila, Priscilla, and Apollos, were intuitive in raising believers as exemplary followers able to transition in their role as follower–leader. In a global environment, these first-century citizens within a diverse Greco-Roman culture showed success through normative practices that transcend historical periods. Within twenty-first-century knowledge economy organizations, there is no less calling for collaborative followership behavior. Emerging others-center leadership, however, slow to emerge, reflects a basis toward role reversing leader–follower behavior. Despite a strong emergence two decades ago, followership development has experienced shifting interest. To make a significant and sustained move forward, we must intentionally develop strategic organizational paths that link decision-making and point of action at the follower. Followership in the knowledge economic era is a presence that strengthens organizational outcomes. Informed dialog of a fresh perspective concerning leadership inclusive of a leader–follower is needed to enhance twenty-first-century organization development.

Reflective Questions

- What can we learn from the ideological analysis of biblical text?
- How do supracultural indicators influence our understanding of biblical scripture?
- Thinking about the teaching interaction between Priscilla (Prisca) and Apollos, what cultural barriers may have existed in this exchange? Thinking critically, how were the obstacles overcome?
- In our generation, how can organizations overcome knowledge-creating barriers?
- Thinking about Apollos, what actions can followers take to become exemplary followers?
- What influence does a pragmatist follower have in an organization?

References

Alexander, L., & Green, J. B. (1995). The relevance of Greco-Roman literature and culture to New Testament study. In J. B. Green (Ed.), *Hearing the new testament: Strategies for interpretation* (2nd ed., pp. 109–126). William B. Eerdmans Publishing Co.

Barton, G. A. (1924). Some influences of Apollos in the new testament, I. *Journal of Biblical Literature*, 207–223.

Bjugstad, K., Thach, E. C., Thompson, K. J., & Morris, A. (2006). A fresh look at followership: A model for matching followership and leadership styles. *Journal of Behavioral and Applied Management, 7*(3), 304.

Carsten, M. K., Uhl-Bien, M., West, B. J., Patera, J. L., & McGregor, R. (2010). Exploring social constructions of followership: A qualitative study. *The Leadership Quarterly, 21*(3), 543–562.

Castelli, E. A. (2004). Interpretations of power in 1 Corinthians. *Michael Foucault and Theology: The Politics of Religious Experience*, 19–38.

Chaleff, I. (1998). Full participation requires courageous followership. *The Journal for Quality and Participation.*

Den Dulk, M. (2020). Aquila and Apollos: Acts 18 in light of ancient ethnic stereotypes. *Journal of Biblical Literature, 139*(1), 177–189.

DeSilva, D. A. (2004). *An introduction to the New Testament: Contexts. methods, and ministry formation*. Intervarsity Press.

Drucker, P. F. (1999). *Management challenges for the 21st century*. Harper Business.

Dvorak, J. D. (2007). John H. Elliott's social-scientific criticism. *Trinity Journal, 28*(2), 251.

Ekundayo, J. (2010). Time to focus on Followers: Looking at the other side of the Leadership 'coin.' *Academic Leadership: The Online Journal, 8*(4), 78.

Epitropaki, O., & Martin, R. (2004). Implicit leadership theories in applied settings: Factor structure, generalizability, and stability over time. *Journal of Applied Psychology, 89*(2), 293.

Fruchtenbaum, A. G. (2011). *The Remnant of Israel: The history, theology, and philosophy of the Messianic Jewish Community*. Ariel Ministries.

Frye, J., Kisselburgh, L. G., & Butts, D. (2007). Embracing spiritual followership. *Communication Studies, 58*(3), 243–260.

Gao, P., & Wu, W. (2019). Effect of leaders' implicit followership theory on subordinates' career success. *Social Behavior and Personality: An International Journal, 47*(5), 1–14.

Greenleaf, R. K. (2002). *Servant leadership: A journey into the nature of legitimate power and greatness*. Paulist Press.

Hart, J. H. A. (1905). Apollos. *The Journal of Theological Studies, 7*(25), 16–28.

Henry, M. (1991). *Mathew Henry's Commentary on the Whole Bible New Modern Edition* (Vol. 6). Hendrickson Publishers Marketing LLC.

Hogg, M. A. (2001). A social identity theory of leadership. *Personality and Social Psychology Review, 5*(3), 184–200.

Hogg, M. A., Martin, R., Epitropaki, O., Mankad, A., Svensson, A., & Weeden, K. (2005). Effective leadership in salient groups: Revisiting leader-member exchange theory from the perspective of the social identity theory of leadership. *Personality and Social Psychology Bulletin, 31*(7), 991–1004.

Horrell, D. G. (2016). *Ethnicisation, marriage, and early Christian identity: Critical reflections on 1 Corinthians 7, 1 Peter 3, and modern New Testament scholarship.*

Keller, M. N. (2010). *Priscilla and Aquila: Paul's Coworkers in Christ Jesus.* Liturgical Press.

Kellerman, B. (2007). What every leader needs to know about followers. *Harvard Business Review, 85*(12), 84.

Kelley, R. E. (1988). *In praise of followers* (pp. 142–148). Harvard Business Review Case Services.

Kelley, R. E. (1992). *The power of followership: How to create leaders people want to follow, and followers who lead themselves*. Broadway Business.

Küpers, W., & Weibler, J. (2008). Inter-leadership: Why and how should we think of leadership and followership integrally? *Leadership, 4*(4), 443–475.

Larkin, C. (2011). *Rightly dividing the Word*. Martino Publishing.

Leon, H. J. (1995). *The Jews of Ancient Rome*. Hendrickson.

Maier, P. L. (Ed.). (1999). *Eusebius—The church history: A new translation with commentary*. Kregel Academic.

Meeks, W. A. (2003). *The first urban Christians: The social world of the apostle Paul*. Yale University Press.

Moessner, D. P. (1986). 'The Christ Must Suffer': New Light on the Jesus-Peter, Stephen Paul Parallels in Luke-Acts. *Novum Testamentum, 28*(3), 220–256.

Mott, S. (1982). *Biblical ethics and social change*. Oxford University Press.

Moxnes, H. (1994). The social context of Luke's community. *Interpretation, 48*(4), 379–389.

Nonaka, I., & Takeuchi, H. (1995). *The knowledge-creating company: How Japanese companies create the dynamics of innovation*. Oxford University Press.

Oc, B., & Bashshur, M. R. (2013). Followership, leadership and social influence. *The Leadership Quarterly, 24*(6), 919–934.

Osborne, G. R. (2006). *The hermeneutical spiral: A comprehensive introduction to biblical interpretation*. IVP Academic.

Robbins, V. K. (1996a). *Exploring the texture of texts*. Trinity Press International.

Robbins, V. K. (1996b). *The tapestry of early Christian discourse: Rhetoric, society, and ideology*. Routledge.

Robbins, V. K., & Neyrey, J. H. (1991). The social location of the implied author of Luke-Acts. *The Social World of Luke-Acts: Models for Interpretation*, 305–332.

Rordorf, W. (1969). Marriage in the New Testament and in the early Church. *The Journal of Ecclesiastical History, 20*(2), 193–210.

Scott, J. J. (1979). Some problems in hermeneutics for contemporary evangelicals. *Journal of the Evangelical Theological Society, 22*(1), 67–77.

Smith, B. T. D. (1915). Apollos and the twelve disciples at Ephesus. *The Journal of Theological Studies, 16*(62), 241–246.

Steffens, N. K., Schuh, S. C., Haslam, S. A., Pérez, A., & Dick, R. (2015). "Of the group" and "for the group": How followership is shaped by leaders' prototypicality and group identification? *European Journal of Social Psychology, 45*(2), 180–190.

Suda, L. (2013). *In praise of followers*. [Paper presentation] Project Management Institute Global Congress 2013, New Orleans, LA, United States.

Sy, T. (2010). What do you think of followers? Examining the content, structure, and consequences of implicit followership theories. *Organizational Behavior and Human Decision Processes, 113*(2), 73–84.

Walker, W. O. (2008). The Portrayal of Aquila and Priscilla in Acts: The question of sources. *New Testament Studies, 54*(4), 479–495.

Yang, Y., Shi, W., Zhang, B., Song, Y., & Xu, D. (2020). Implicit followership theories from the perspective of followers. *Leadership & Organization Development Journal, 41*(4), 581–596.

Young, S. L. (2015). Paul's Ethnic Discourse on "Faith": Christ's Faithfulness and Gentile Access to the Judean God in Romans 3: 21–5: 1. *Harvard Theological Review, 108*(1), 30–51.

CHAPTER 6

Transient Followership Prominence: An Act of Exemplary Followership That Changes Modern Christianity

Robert B. Huizinga

Researchers agree that leadership and followership are intertwined (Hopper, 2008; Kellerman, 2009; Maroosis, 2008; Stech, 2008). Similar to the double helix of DNA, where a pair of parallel helices are intertwined about a common axis (in this case, the axis being the act of moving the church forward in its God-directed plan to preach the gospel to all nations), leaders and followers need each other. Chaleff (2009) described the interplay of organization, leader, and follower as a triad.

> Any organization is a triad consisting of leaders and followers joined in a common purpose. The purpose is the atomic glue that binds us. It gives

R. B. Huizinga (✉)
Regent University, Virginia Beach, VA, USA
e-mail: robehui@mail.regent.edu

D. J. Dean and R. B. Huizinga (eds.), *Followership and Faith at Work*, Christian Faith Perspectives in Leadership and Business,
https://doi.org/10.1007/978-3-030-90614-6_6

> meaning to our activities. Followers and leaders both orbit around the purpose; followers do not orbit around the leader. (p. 12)

The understanding of followership is key as it impacts our understanding of the interaction of leader and follower. Some consider followers as subordinates who therefore have less power, authority, and influence than do their superiors (Kellerman, 2009), and is typically seen as the poorer cousin to leadership. A Google Scholar search for academic articles on leadership turned up 4 520,000 results, while the same search for academic articles on followership turned up 24,600 (Google, 2021). This is a leader-centric approach of followership where followers are simply recipients of the leader's will (Uhl-Bien et al., 2014). However, this view is not universal. Rost (2008) viewed followership as distinct from leadership, where the best case scenario is when followership and leadership are the twin rails of an organization which run together in the same direction but never meet. Carsten et al. (2010) noted that followership develops over time with socialization and interaction with leader and follower stimuli. This is a follower-centric approach of followership which viewed leadership as a social construction (Uhl-Bien et al., 2014). A third view is a constructionist approach where leaders and followers co-create leadership and followership (Uhl-Bien et al., 2014). This mixed approach considered followership and the relationship between follower and leader. In this interdependent relationship, followers and leaders hold things in common (Baker, 2007).

The psychology of followers is the key to understanding the leader's influence (Popper, 2011); appropriate followership is a critical element to a well-functioning organization. Kelley (1988) based the classification of followers upon two dimensions: independent critical thinking versus dependent thinking, and active engagement/positive energy versus passive involvement and negative energy. According to Kelley in the first dimension, the best followers are innovative and creative individuals with critical thought, whereas the poorest followers needed to be given constant instruction and did not possess self-motivation. Regarding the second dimension, the best followers take initiative and go above and beyond the job, whereas the poorest followers were lazy and avoided responsibility. This led to Kelley's five basic styles of followership.

"Sheep," or passive followers are passive dependent thinkers within the organization, requiring external motivation from the leaders. They see themselves as relying on the leader's judgment and thinking. Conversely,

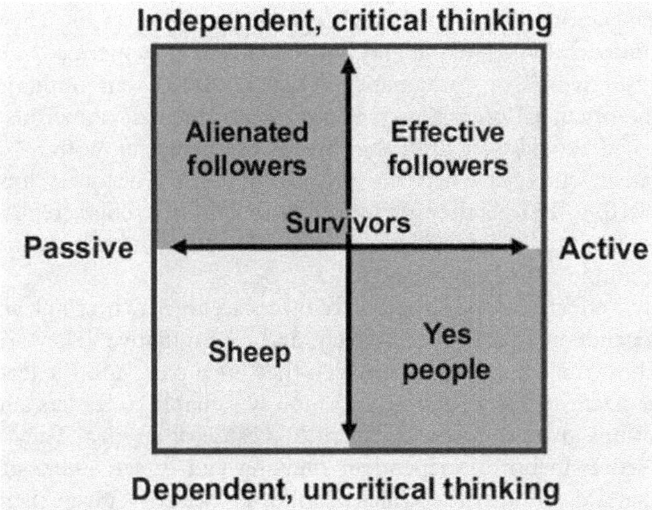

Fig. 6.1 Kelley's Followership Styles (Adapted from Kelley [1988])

other followers see them as not doing their share or needing a high level of supervision. They score low in active engagement and score low in level of engagement (Fig. 6.1).

"Yes people," or conformist followers are positive and defend the leader but require the "boss" to plan the work and simply carry out the work in a positive manner. They see themselves as gladly carrying out the instructions of the leader, while other followers experience them lacking their own ideas or unwilling to take an unpopular position (Kelley, 1992). This style of obedient follower is a role that traditional leadership literature would define as a good follower (Kellerman, 2009). Conformist followers score high in active engagement and low in independent thinking.

The "alienated followers" are the opposite of the conformist followers. They have independent thought but negative energy. Terms they may use for themselves are "the devil's advocate" or an "organizational conscience." Other followers view them as headstrong or cynical. In actions, they criticize the leader and offer cynical answers for why something will not work. They actively choose not to participate in the groups and organizations of which they choose to be members of. They score high in independent thinking and low in active engagement.

The "survivors" or "pragmatics" (Kelley, 2008) wait until they see where the organization is going. Having been through numerous leader initiatives, they will wait until the "winds of change blow over" (p. 8). "Pragmatism emerges when the organization itself becomes unstable" (Chai, 2010, p. 15). As they are unwilling to fail, they refuse to put themselves in a position of risk. They are the middle scores in both independent thinking and in active engagement.

Finally, "effective" or exemplary followers are those who think critically and independently, participate actively, and take initiative. They are valuable both to the organization of which they are a part, and the leaders of that organization. They become enormously valuable to leaders and their organizations given their commitment to a cause or an idea. They are the highest scores in both independent thinking and in active engagement. Pastors should fall into the effective follower category given their position as simultaneous leader and follower. As effective followers, they are seen to be as active and having positive energy. While not always agreeing with the leader (in this case the church board), they offer constructive alternatives to what the leader is suggesting.

With these two dimensions of followership, independent thinking and active engagement, Kelley (1992) created a 20-question Followership Questionnaire to help subjects identify their own followership style and to highlight their strengths and weaknesses relative to their followership capacities. Kelley (1992) also analyzed follower motivation which led to seven paths of followership. The paths are: comrade; loyalist; lifeway or altruist; dreamer; apprentice; disciple; and mentee. Within each followership path followers exhibit differing motivations allowing them to decide when to follow as opposed to when to lead. Some paths led to follower personal growth or move the organization forward, whereas other paths allowed follower self-expression to flourish (Kelley, 1992, pp. 49–51).

Chai (2010) investigated the relationship between congregational leadership positions and dimensions of followership styles within the context of Korean American Presbyterian congregations. Using Kelley's (1992) Followership Questionnaire to measure followership behaviors and styles, Chai asked the following questions: are the followership questionnaire scores of the pastors higher than that of elders, gwonsas, and deacons on the dimensions of followership styles; are the followership questionnaire scores of elders higher than that of gwonsas and deacons on the dimensions of followership styles; are the followership questionnaire scores of gwonsas higher than that of deacons on the dimensions of followership styles; and are the followership questionnaire scores of members who hold no leadership offices lower than that of pastors, elders, gwonsas, and deacons on the dimensions of followership styles (p. 7). Of note, "gwonsas" is a congregational title found only in a Korean church which is reserved for an elderly and godly woman who is considered above a deacon but under an elder in church position hierarchy. Overall, the analysis demonstrated that as the responsibilities of church officers increased, the followership dimension scores increased. Pastoral scoring was not significantly different from elders and gwonsas but was significantly higher than deacons or non-leaders. When compared back to Kelley's followership dimensions, pastors and elders scoring demonstrated that they were exemplary followers while deacons and gwonsas were pragmatist followers.

Kellerman (2008) offered another descriptive perspective on followership. She posits that there are five types of followers which range on a spectrum from left to right. On the left are "isolates," the followers who are detached and unwilling to make an impact on the leader's decisions or even upon the other followers. "Bystanders," while similar to isolates, have opinions on the leader's decisions, but refuse to act upon those opinions. "Participants" are engaged in the decisions of the leader to a degree, while "activists" are even further engaged and feel strongly about the leader and the leader's ideas. Finally, on the opposite spectrum from the isolates, the "diehards" are either deeply devoted to the leader and their ideas or deeply devoted to the concept of removing the leader by any means necessary.

"One responsibility of a good follower is to speak truth to power" (Bennis, 2010, p. 3). In addition to understanding the concept of followership, the impact of a follower on the leadership is therefore also worthy of discussion. Chaleff (2009) in his treatise on courageous followership noted that courageous followership can be depicted in four quadrants. On the y axis is the level of support the follower provides the leader. On the x axis is the degree of challenge that a follower gives to a leader (Fig. 6.2).

Quadrant I is the "Partner" follower. This follower gives high support to the leader's ideas while having the willingness to challenge them appropriately. This follower is exemplified as purpose-driven, risk-taking

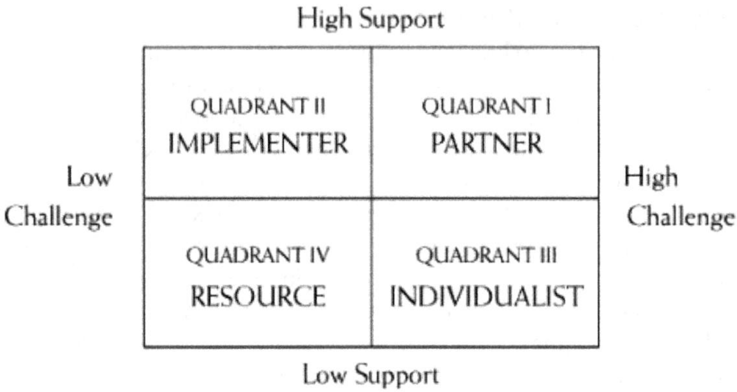

Fig. 6.2 Chaleff's Followership Styles (Adapted from Chaleff [2009])

and is on a peer relationship basis with the leader. Quadrant II is the "Implementer" follower. The implementer provides high support without excessive need for direction. While this follower is a leader's favorite, this follower is unlikely to challenge the leader when things do not appear to be going well. This follower is considered dependable, team oriented, and respectful of authority. The "Individualist" is in Quadrant III. This follower is necessary in a group dynamic as they feel free to critique the leader's ideas without providing support for carrying out the initiatives thereby potentially balancing any possibility of the Abilene paradox (Harvey, 1974). They can potentially become toxic within the group and may require leadership intervention. The individualist is confrontational, rebellious, and unintimidated by authority. Finally, the Quadrant IV follower is the "Resource" follower. This follower, while hardworking, does not go beyond the minimum expectations. They are characterized as present, uncommitted and avoids the attention of authority. It is only when they are ready to give more priority to their participation in the group or organization, that they can earn the credibility to question the leader and provide more support to the leader's thoughts.

Understanding followership overall helps in our understanding of church leaders as followers. Ricketson (2009) posited that a church is an organized group of followers with specific responsibilities. Leaders in the church should therefore embrace the concept of a *Follower First* philosophy which follows Jesus Christ, the head of the ecclesia. Under this philosophy, the modern church should empower followers such that they, not the leaders, are held responsible for the growth of the church. Finally, this Follower First stance is intended not only to pastors and lay leaders of the church, but as all members and attenders of a church are to follow Jesus Christ, it is intended to impact all Christians.

Jesus' first and last commands to the disciple Peter were to "follow me" (Mark 1:17; John 21:21). Mimesis is the ability to imitate another is speech or action. If leadership can be Christo-mimetic (Bekker, 2009), and if the Scriptures say a great deal more about followership than leadership (Chai, 2010), then followership must be Christo-mimetic as well.

The Background of the Event

As the most famous conversion story in history, Acts 9:1–9 is oft written about. An excellent review of the three reports in Acts was completed by Hedrick (1981). In this passage, Saul as a leader of Pharisees receives letters of accreditation from the Sanhedrin (the religious police force of the time) to find and persecute Christians (followers of The Way) in Damascus. Rather than simply being satisfied with his inquisition of Christians in Jerusalem, he extends his reign of terror, using the additional power of the Sanhedrin to extend his influence into a small trading city.

Saul travels the approximately 130 miles from Jerusalem to Damascus on foot, which is thought to have taken 5 or 6 days. Just in sight of Damascus, he is met by Jesus who turns the avenging religious persecutor into a blind helpless man.

However, it is the healing of Saul, specifically the role of Ananias of Damascus which is typically glossed over. It has short mention in Scripture in Acts 9:10–18 and 22:10–16 (Paul's retelling of the story), yet the followership role of Ananias and the resultant impact on modern Christianity is not well covered in the literature.

> Now there was a disciple at Damascus named Ananias. The Lord said to him in a vision, "Ananias." And he said, "Here I am, Lord." And the Lord said to him, "Rise and go to the street called Straight, and at the house of Judas look for a man of Tarsus named Saul, for behold, he is praying, and he has seen in a vision a man named Ananias come in and lay his hands on him so that he might regain his sight." But Ananias answered, "Lord, I have heard from many about this man, how much evil he has

> done to your saints at Jerusalem. And here he has authority from the chief priests to bind all who call on your name." But the Lord said to him, "Go, for he is a chosen instrument of mine to carry my name before the Gentiles and kings and the children of Israel. For I will show him how much he must suffer for the sake of my name." So Ananias departed and entered the house. And laying his hands on him he said, "Brother Saul, the Lord Jesus who appeared to you on the road by which you came has sent me so that you may regain your sight and be filled with the Holy Spirit." And immediately something like scales fell from his eyes, and he regained his sight. Then he rose and was baptized; and taking food, he was strengthened. (Acts 9:10–19, English Standard Version)

Ananias, as a follower of The Way, rises to transient prominence in Scripture as commanded by God. He lays hands on Saul, baptizes him and returns to anonymity. It is the understanding of this transient followership prominence which is worthy of study.

Damascus

Damascus is known as one of the most ancient cities of Syria (Smith, 1863), with varying levels of importance over time. Founded by Uz, grandson of Shem, it is originally mentioned in Genesis 14:15 as the home of one of Abraham's servants. Northeast of Jerusalem, the Damascene plain is fertile, fed by three bodies of water, including the Biblical rivers Abana and Pharpar. It was held by various Kings including David (2 Sam 8:5–6) and is subsequently razed to the ground by Assyrian soldiers (2 Kings 16:9). During the destructive period, it was dominated by Assyrians, Babylonians, Persians, Macedonians, Romans and Saracens, and finally the Turks in 1516 A.D (Smith, 1863). While it belonged to the Roman province of Syria during the time of our event, it had municipal autonomy in a federation of cities called the Decapolis (Bruce, 1988). Given the large Jewish population in the city, it had several synagogues, with the ability of each synagogue to exercise discipline over its congregants.

Damascus was an important trading center but was not an important city overall. It was not a center of intellectual pursuit like Alexandria. However, it was an important travel point on the pilgrimage road to Jerusalem (Mann, 1988). As a trading hub, it connected to northern Syria, Mesopotamia, Anatolia, Persia, and Arabia.

It is this alignment of Damascus, Jerusalem and the feasts which resulted in the alliance of the Pharisees (Saul) and the Sadducean clergy. As it was on one of the pilgrimage routes, Damascus became a checkpoint where Jewish credentials "could be checked for those going to Jerusalem for one of the great feasts" (Mann, 1988, p. 332). As both the Sadducees and Pharisees would be concerned with the integrity of the Jerusalem temple, and followers of The Way were known to be in Damascus, this temporary alliance of feuding religious leaders came together for Saul.

Ananias of Damascus

Ananias, the Damascene disciple, is not well described in the Bible. In Acts 22 he is described as a "devout man according to the law, well spoken of by all the Jews who lived there" (Acts 22:12, ESV). While not much is written of him, the fact that he is mentioned at all may suggest that he could have been the head or chief teacher of the local Christian or Nazarene synagogue, and was probably one of the original Jerusalem Christians who scattered by the first great persecution (Stokes, 1892).

> Some think he was one of the seventy disciples; some say he was a deacon; but it is certain he was not one of the first seven; others affirm he was a presbyter, and some report that he was afterwards bishop of Damascus, and died a martyr there; but these are things not to be depended on. (J. Gill, 1771).

There is a deep dimension to Ananias' faith. When told by God to seek out the "greatest enemy of Christianity," he calmly raised his objections, received God's instructions and carried them out. When seeing Saul face to face, he greeted him as a brother (v. 17). And when the healing had occurred, he baptized Saul (v. 18).

Importantly, it was not one of the apostles from Jerusalem, or Philip the evangelist (who baptized the eunuch) who were called upon for this task. Rather it was a local disciple, who was commanded to follow God's instruction. When called by God, in similar fashion to Samuel of the Old Testament, he replies: "Here I am, Lord."

Saul of Tarsus

Saul, a Pharisee and a son of a Pharisee, is introduced to us in Acts 7:58 when he was present at the stoning of Stephen. The Pharisees are understood as the more spiritual and earnest religious section of the Jewish people (Stokes, 1892). Describing himself in Acts 22, Saul is "educated at the feet of Gamaliel according to the strict manner of the law of our fathers, being zealous for God as all of you are this day" (v. 3). Known for his repression of Christians, the followers of The Way, Saul desired to root out these false believers not only from Jerusalem but even beyond the borders of Israel. Saul, now known as Paul, recounts his "zeal" to a crowd in Jerusalem in Acts 22:

> I persecuted this Way to the death, binding and delivering to prison both men and women, as the high priest and the whole council of elders can bear me witness. From them I received letters to the brothers, and I journeyed toward Damascus to take those also who were there and bring them in bonds to Jerusalem to be punished.

Saul imprisons and beats Christians (Acts 22:19) and stands by while witnessing the death of Stephen (Acts 22:20). In Acts 26:11 Paul recounts these events to King Agrippa: "And I punished them often in all the synagogues and tried to make them blaspheme, and in raging fury against them I persecuted them even to foreign cities." In short, Saul is a furious persecutor, a troubler of Christians, and a murderer (Chalk, 1966).

Saul noted in Acts 22 that he needed a letter. The Romans required that neighboring states grant privileges to a sovereign state, including extradition (Bruce, 1988). An example of this is noted where a Roman ambassador to Ptolemy VIII of Egypt writes, "If any pestilent men have fled to you from their own country [Judaea], hand them over to Simon the high priest, so that he may punish them according to their law" (1 Macc. 15:21). While Judaea is no longer sovereign, these rights were given to the Jewish nation and in particular the high priesthood by Julius Caesar in 47 B.C. (Bruce, 1988).

The Event

On his walk to Damascus, Saul understands the importance of Damascus to his quest. If followers of The Way gained a foothold there, they could spread their heresy throughout the Roman empire and potentially back to Jerusalem (Mann, 1988). As he comes in sight of the city, he is confronted by Jesus regarding his persecution of Christians. Recognizing the eminence of Jesus, Saul calls him Lord, is blinded and led by His hand into the city and into the house of Judas. The Damascene street called Straight is the setting where “the greatest enemy of Christianity becomes the greatest of all Christians” (Morton, 1959, p. 263). Saul stayed there for 3 days and did not eat or drink during this time. “Saul experienced the agony and revolution of repentance during his three long, lonely days following the Lord’s appearance” (Chalk, 1966).

Ananias, a devout man, is chosen by God directly to intervene. When the angel of the Lord first appears to Ananias and calls out his name, the disciple responds by saying, “Yes, Here I am Lord” (Park, 2009). This response, “Here I Am” (using the Greek word *kurios* denoting that God has supreme authority over Ananias), is in similar fashion to the response of Abraham (Gen 22:11), Moses (Exodus 3:4), and Samuel (1 Samuel 3:4–8) to God’s call. He has two limited tasks given by God: heal and baptize Saul (Acts 22:12–16) (Lundgren, 1971). He is not called to lead Saul, nor to let the Damascene synagogue emerge as the center of Christianity.

Understandably, Ananias is very concerned about meeting Saul. He is going to see the chief of persecutors, whose rage is well understood: “Lord, I have heard from many about this man, how much evil he has done to your saints at Jerusalem. And here he has authority from the chief priests to bind all who call on your name” (9:3b, 14). God’s instruction is clear: Saul is to be God’s instrument that will allow the church to grow. Ananias travels to the Straight street, sees Saul and speaks to him as a brother:

> The God of our fathers appointed you to know his will, to see the Righteous One and to hear a voice from his mouth; for you will be a witness for him to everyone of what you have seen and heard. And now why do you wait? Rise and be baptized and wash away your sins, calling on his name. (22:14–16)

Ananias lays hands upon him, Saul is healed and then baptized by Ananias. Importantly, Ananias’ response and actions allow Saul to move from prosecutor to Paul the fellow Christian (D. Gill, 1974). Upon his conversion, Paul immediately begins to preach at the Damascene synagogues. And with his conversion, Paul becomes a fellow sufferer for the faith: “I will show him how much he must suffer for my name" (9:16). After the baptism, Ananias is presumed to depart. Other than the above mention by Paul, he is not mentioned in the Bible again.

Transient Followership Prominence in Scripture

Leadership and followership are intertwined, and for every form of leadership there is a corresponding form of followership. The most desired followers (exemplary) were described by Kelley as those who think critically and independently, contribute with eagerness and independence while working toward the objectives of the organization. They are the highest scores in both independent thinking and in active engagement. Chai's (2010) study noted that when using Kelley's followership dimensions, pastors and elders scoring demonstrated that they were exemplary followers. They listened to the spiritual calling by God and acted in a humble manner. Beyond Kelley's work, Willson (2012) states that exemplary followers prioritize group purposes ahead of personal purpose, show trust and trustworthiness and understand the needs of others. In our pericope, Ananias is called by God to *follow* His command: heal and baptize Saul. He is not called to lead Saul in any way, he is not called to leadership prominence within his synagogue, he is not called to lead a revolt against the Sadducees or Sanhedrin. He puts God's purposes ahead of his own (his very life), he understands the needs of Saul (calling him brother and creating a psychological collective relationship) and shows trust by healing Saul turning him from a helpless blind man.

An aspect of exemplary followership is restorative followership. Zoogah (2014) notes that "A follower's role therefore is to alter, improve, or enhance the relationship by providing solutions that enable the relationship to excel" (p. 91). Here, we see Ananias improving the relationship between Saul and the church/Christ by performing a miracle and then baptizing Saul. He takes these actions despite the grievous threat that Saul is to the followers of The Way. Ananias simply follows God's command ignoring the threat to his own life and in doing so changes the course of the modern church.

Interestingly, Woods (2009) examined the impact of active engagement of the follower on the leader. He hypothesized that active followership led to high levels of leader-member exchange (LMX), whereas passivity led to low LMX. In our case, the LMX relationship is between God and Ananias. In his study, he found that as one moves from a least desirable followership type (sheep) to most desirable (exemplary), the LMX quality scores increase. This is telling for us as Christians as we seek to follow God's call on our lives, despite the personal cost, our relationship with Him improves.

Just as leadership may be transitory (see the book of Esther), we must acknowledge that followers who are called to a higher form of followership may be transitory. Ananias' role as a lead follower is "for a time such as this," and after his active engagement in the healing and baptizing of Saul he returns to his prior role within society. He is no longer mentioned in Scripture, which is telling given the critical nature he played in Saul's life. One might have thought that Saul, suffering some of agony and revolution of repentance, might have mentioned him and elevated his role in Saul's life beyond that in Acts 22. However, God ordained that Ananias should play a prominent but transient role as a follower of The Way.

Conclusion

Followership, like leadership, is neither static nor unidimensional. Rather, it changes in response to the leadership/organizational structure, and like a dance interacts with the external environment. Kelley (1992) notes that organizations should desire exemplary followers who are independent, enthusiastic, and use their intellect to support organizational objectives. Ricketson (2009) notes that the *Follower First* philosophy empowers followers such that they are responsible for the growth of the church which is Christo-mimetic in form.

Three key elements are seen in the life of Ananias: a *transient* calling to *exemplary followership* of *prominence* within a seminal event in the life of the church. The healing of Saul and his subsequent transition to Paul, who defined the role and goals of the early Christian church, required Ananias to hear God's call (like Samuel), to act upon it for a defined time (like Esther), and then to return to his regular role as a follower of The Way. After his key actions, this Damascene disciple is no longer mentioned in Scripture. This is follower Christo-mimesis in action. "Wherever the word is proclaimed and people turn to God, there the Holy Spirit falls on the new disciples through the agency of the apostles" (DeSilva, 2004,

p. 330). Through Ananias' agency, Saul is changed, and the church was positively altered.

Chapter Takeaways

Jesus' first and last commands to the disciple Peter were to "follow me" (Mark 1:17; John 21:21). Mimesis is the ability to imitate another is speech or action. If leadership can be Christo-mimetic (Bekker, 2009), and if the Scriptures say a great deal more about followership than leadership (Chai, 2010), then followership must be Christo-mimetic as well.

Paul's conversion event has been covered extensively in many texts, however what is not well covered is the role of Ananias. Three key elements are seen in the life of Ananias: a transient calling to exemplary followership of prominence within a seminal event in the life of the church. *After his key actions, this Damascene disciple is no longer mentioned in Scripture.* This is follower Christo-mimesis in action. "Wherever the word is proclaimed and people turn to God, there the Holy Spirit falls on the new disciples through the agency of the apostles" (DeSilva, 2004, p. 330). Through Ananias' agency, Saul is changed, and the church was positively altered.

Reflective Questions

1. How can Christ followers *be* better followers, without assuming a form of leadership?
2. Would you agree that God can call people to a more prominent form of followership which is not the same as a form of leadership?
3. If you could imagine Ananias and his life, how do you think he felt being called to meet with Saul?
4. In the same light, how do you think he felt not being called to a continual form of leadership or even a higher form of followership, according to what we know from Scripture.

References

Baker, S. D. (2007). Followership: The theoretical foundation of a contemporary construct. *Journal of Leadership & Organizational Studies, 14*(1), 50–61.

Bekker, C. J. (2009). Towards a theoretical model of Christian leadership. *Journal of Biblical Perspectives in Leadership, 2*(2), 142–152.

Bennis, W. G. (2010). Art of Followership. *Leadership Excellence, 27*(1), 3–5.

Bruce, F. F. (1988). *The Book of Acts*. In G. D. Fee (Ed.), *The New International Commentary on the New Testament*. William B. Eerdmans Publishing Company.

Carsten, M. K., Uhl-bien, M., West, B. J., Patera, J. L., & McGregor, R. (2010). Exploring social constructions of followership: A qualitative study. *The Leadership Quarterly, 21*(3), 543–562. https://doi.org/10.1016/j.leaqua.2010.03.015

Chai, D. H. (2010). *Leading as followers: A followership study of the Korean congregational leadership of the Presbyterian Church (U.S.A.)*. Spalding University.

Chaleff, I. (2009). *The courageous follower: Standing up to and for our leaders* (3rd ed.). Berrett-Koehler Publishers.

Chalk, J. A. (1966). From Blasphemy to Belief. *Herald of Truth Documents. 5*. Highland Church of Christ. https://digitalcommons.acu.edu/hot_docs/5

DeSilva, D. A. (2004). *An introduction to the New Testament: Context, methods & ministry formation*. Inter-Varsity Press.

Gill, D. (1974). The Structure of Acts 9. *Biblica, 55*(4), 546–548.

Gill, J. (1771). *John Gill's Exposition of the Entire Bible* (R. Meyers, Ed.) (10.4.0). e-Sword.

Google. (2021). Google Scholar Search. Retrieved February 16, 2021, from www.google.com

Harvey, J. B. (1974). The Abilene paradox: The management of agreement. *Organizational Dynamics, 3*(1), 63–80.

Hedrick, C. W. (1981). Paul's conversion/call: A comparative analysis of the three reports in acts. *Journal of Biblical Literature, 100*(3), 415–432. http://www.jstor.org/stable/3265962

Hopper, L. (2008). Courageous followers, servant-leaders, and organizational transformations. In R. Riggio, I. Chaleff, & J. Lipman-Blumen (Eds.), *The Art of Followership*. Jossey-Bass.

Kellerman, B. (2008). *Followership: How followers are creating change and changing leaders*. Harvard Business School Publishing.

Kellerman, B. (2009). *Followership*. https://www.youtube.com/watch?v=kgLcAF5Lgq4

Kelley, R. E. (1988). In praise of followers. *Harvard Business Review, 66*(6), 142–148.

Kelley, R. E. (1992). *The power of followership: How to create leaders people want to follow, and followers who lead themselves*. Doubleday/Currency.

Kelley, R. E. (2008). Rethinking followership. In R. E. Riggio, I. Chaleff, & J. Lipman-Blumen (Eds.), *The Art of Followership*. Jossey-Bass.

Lundgren, S. (1971). Ananias and the calling of Paul in Acts. *Studia Theologica—Nordic Journal of Theology, 25*(1), 117–122. https://doi.org/10.1080/00393387108599922

Mann, C. (1988). Saul and Damascus. *The Expository Times, 99*(11), 331–334. https://doi.org/10.1177/001452468809901104

Maroosis, J. (2008). Leadership: A partnership in reciprocal following. In R. E. Riggio, I. Chaleff, & J. Lipman-Blumen (Eds.), *The Art of Followership*. Jossey-Bass.

Morton, H. (1959). *In the steps of the master* (23rd ed.). Methuen & Co., Ltd.

Park, J. H. (2009). Overcoming internal barriers: The "Conversion" of Ananias and Peter in Acts 9–10. *Journal of Asia Adventist Seminary, 12*(1), 19–35.

Popper, M. (2011). Toward a theory of followership. *Review of General Psychology, 15*(1), 29–36. https://doi.org/10.1037/a0021989

Ricketson, R. (2009). *Follower first: Rethinking leading in the church*. Heartworks Publications.

Rost, J. (2008). Followership: An outmoded concept. In R. E. Riggio, I. Chaleff, & J. Lipman-Blumen (Eds.), *The Art of Followership*. Jossey-Bass.

Smith, W. (1863). *Smith's Bible Dictionary*. Thomas Nelson; SuperSaver Edition.

Stech, E. L. (2008). A new leadership-followership paradigm. In R. E. Riggio, I. Chaleff, & J. Lipman-Blumen (Eds.), *The Art of Followership*. Jossey-Bass.

Stokes, D. D. (1892). The Acts of the Apostles. In W. Robertson Nicoll (Ed.), *Expositor's Bible Commentary*. A. C. Armstrong and Son.

Uhl-Bien, M., Riggio, R. E., Lowe, K. B., & Carsten, M. K. (2014). Followership theory: A review and research agenda. *The Leadership Quarterly, 25*(1), 83–104. https://doi.org/10.1016/j.leaqua.2013.11.007

Willson, A. (2012). Attaining peak performance. *1000 Lives Plus* (6), 1–20.

Woods, C. R. (2009). *Followership as a complement to leadership: An analysis of the relationship between leader member exchange and followership types*. Capella University.

Zoogah, D. B. (2014). *Strategic followership: How followers impact organizational effectiveness*. Palgrave Macmillan.

CHAPTER 7

Stephen: Deacon, Martyr, and Agent of Change

R. Lewis Steinhoff

Introduction

With a study of Stephen, we are immediately drawn to specifics of his character, his boldness, his knowledge of the scripture, and his willingness to die for the cause of Christ. These observations are based solely on what we read in Acts 6–8. One striking quality about Stephen that made him ideal for the deacon position was that he was ready. He was qualified and passionate about who he was and why he was here on Earth. Stephen is the model of devoted followership and servant leadership; qualities every Christian should strive to emulate.

Literature on Stephen can support the overall study by pinpointing details that we might otherwise miss. An example of this is his name. Stephen is a Greek name not a Hebrew name. In fact, we find he was a Hellenistic Jew and Hellenists embraced the Greek culture and spoke the Greek language. Likewise, facts about the name Stephen can draw

R. Lewis Steinhoff (✉)
San Diego Christian College, Santee, CA, USA

D. J. Dean and R. B. Huizinga (eds.), *Followership and Faith at Work*, Christian Faith Perspectives in Leadership and Business,
https://doi.org/10.1007/978-3-030-90614-6_7

readers away by the questions that arise. For example, how did a Greek speaking Jewish man learn so much scripture? Why would he have been in Jerusalem if he were from outside Jerusalem?

In this chapter, we will discuss the qualifications of Stephen to be one of the first deacons and compare those qualifications to the present-day church office of Deacon as defined in 1 Timothy 3: 8–13. We will then take a comprehensive look at the accusation against him and his famous defense as captured in the sermon of Acts 7. We will then look at his subsequent martyrdom. Most importantly, we will analyze Stephen as a follower and transformational leader. Last, we will look at how Stephen was the catalyst for the spread of Christianity. The chapter will end with reflection on how Stephen's follower and leader characteristics can shape followers and leaders in the twenty-first century. This reflective analysis will be built around the research of Robert Kelley, Robert Greenleaf, and James MacGregor Burns.

Qualifications

The story of Stephen begins with a statement of need. We see in Acts 6 the following:

> In those days when the number of disciples was increasing, the Hellenistic Jews among them complained against the Hebraic Jews because their widows were being overlooked in the daily distribution of food. So the Twelve gathered all the disciples together and said, "It would not be right for us to neglect the ministry of the word of God in order to wait on tables. Brothers and sisters, choose seven men from among you who are known to be full of the Spirit and wisdom. We will turn this responsibility over to them and will give our attention to prayer and the ministry of the word.
>
> This proposal pleased the whole group. They chose Stephen, a man full of faith and of the Holy Spirit; also Philip, Procorus, Nicanor, Timon, Parmenas, and Nicolas from Antioch, a convert to Judaism. They presented these men to the apostles, who prayed and laid their hands on them. (Acts 6:1–6, NIV)

The Hellenistic Jews were primarily Jewish Christians who had adopted the Greek language and culture. The Hebraic Jews were Aramaic speaking Jewish Christians. The Hellenists are complaining that their widows are not being taken care of. A couple of observations here before we continue. The Twelve gather "all the disciples"—this includes both Jewish Christian groups and maybe others—and they direct the disciples to choose seven men to "wait on tables." Charles Ryrie (1978) notes, "the Greek word for 'serve' is the one from which we derive 'deacon,' but these were 'deacons only in the sense of being servants'" (p. 1548). Ryrie (1978) also notes that every deacon selected has a Greek name. This implies the disciples—"all the disciples"—chose men who could culturally relate to and communicate with this forgotten group, the widows. This passage also identifies what the important characteristics are; "full of the Spirit and wisdom."

However, we cannot ignore that this event perhaps paved the way for what would become the requirements for the church office of Deacon as later defined in 1 Timothy 3.

> In the same way, deacons are to be worthy of respect, sincere, not indulging in much wine, and not pursuing dishonest gain. They must keep hold of the deep truths of the faith with a clear conscience. They must first be tested; and then if there is nothing against them, let them serve as deacons.
>
> A deacon must be faithful to his wife and must manage his children and his household well. Those who have served well gain an excellent standing and great assurance in their faith in Christ Jesus. (1 Tim 3:8–10, 12 &13, NIV)

The list of deacons starts with Stephen and the words "a man full of faith and of the Holy Spirit" are attributed only to him. Given Luke is writing on this account, he could have had a special fondness for Stephen, or these attributes could have stood out in Stephen over the others. Either way, when you compare these attributes with those listed in 1 Tim 3:8–10, 12 & 13 we see similarities. One other similarity is that the Twelve, or the Apostles, "prayed and laid their hands on them." This was an incredible site to the other disciples because it showed they were worthy of respect and that they were being entrusted with an important function. Rushbrooke (1940) makes this observation about Stephen and the filling of the Holy Spirit:

> He is not endowed with the Spirit because he is a martyr; he becomes a martyr because of the presence that fills his life. He is not "a man full of the Holy Spirit" because he is a church officer; he was chosen -for office because his fellow members found him already Spirit-filled. The tone and temper of his life marked him as one in vital touch with the Lord Christ. (p. 5)

Rushbrooke (1940) adds the Holy Spirit works independently from other things about Christianity. It is not dependent on the laying on of hands, or holy oil or baptism, but rather those things known as the fruit of the Spirit identified in Galatians 5:22 *"love, joy, peace, forbearance, kindness, goodness, faithfulness, gentleness and self-control."* Though the Book of Acts was written about 60 A.D., most Biblical timelines put Stephen about three years after the death, burial, and resurrection of Christ and of course sometime after the Day of Pentecost when the Holy Spirit arrives on the scene. It is quite possible Stephen was raised in a Christian home.

I am often taken by the sheer knowledge and wisdom some of the followers of Christ had back then. Peter's sermon on the Day of Pentecost in Acts 2 is one example as is Stephen's Defense which we will examine next. Did these men excel with scripture memorization and history? Did they each have committed family members that diligently taught them the scriptures? Or perhaps were the words they spoke God-breathed into them at the time. Remember these thoughts and questions as you walk through the next section.

The accusation against Stephen and his defense will be examined next. As we examine these things, we should ask why did these things happen to such a good man? Seems like an easy enough question, but could just the clear presence of God in a man bring others to anger? We will see how this is indeed what happened.

Stephen's Accusation and Defense

Stephen is next seen proclaiming Jesus and getting in trouble for doing it. But notice the first verse of this passage; "*Now Stephen, a man full of God's grace and power, performed great wonders and signs among the people*" (Acts 6:8, NIV). So, in addition to "spirit, "wisdom," and "faith," we see "grace" and "power" associated with Stephen.

The Accusation

The result was rising opposition. We see how the opposition begins with arguing but then quickly escalates to outright lies and false testimony against Stephen.

> Opposition arose, however, from members of the Synagogue of the Freedmen (as it was called)—Jews of Cyrene and Alexandria as well as

> the provinces of Cilicia and Asia—who began to argue with Stephen. But they could not stand up against the wisdom the Spirit gave him as he spoke. (Acts 6:9,10, NIV)

Stephen spoke so passionately the opposition could not stand up to him and as the verses that follow show, false accusations were brought up against him and they stirred up others and even coerced some to testify against him. I pause here to ask, who else endured this kind of opposition at the end of his life? Jesus, of course.

I would like to interject an important point here before moving on to Stephen's defense, Hamon (1977) posits Stephen may have been under stress during this time period based on "observances" and that we can observe three things about his personhood.

> Stephen was an inventor. In presenting claims of Jesus and His disciples, Stephen spoke from a point unique to any frame of reference, Greek or Semitic. Yet something beckoned him outside the safety of conventionality, and he answered the call.
>
> Stephen remained an integrated person under the stress of argumentation and accusation. Stephen's adversaries…'could not withstand the wisdom and the Spirit with which he spoke (Acts 6:10)'…and Stephen had …become infused with the Holy Spirit such that he was 'full' of the Spirit. (Hamon, 1977)

Just before Stephen begins his defense, verse 15 states, "*All who were sitting in the Sanhedrin looked intently at Stephen, and they saw that his face was like the face of an angel*" (Acts 6:15, NIV). It should be obvious to the reader that God was present, and that God was on his side. Though the Sanhedrin did not want to admit this, they most likely knew it to be true. It is a safe assumption that Stephen knew his time was short and that now was the time to take a stand for Christ. The other thing this verse suggests is two more godly characteristics possessed by Stephen, peace and joy.

The Defense

"*Then the high priest asked Stephen, 'Are these charges true?'*" (Acts 7:1, NIV). And, with this question, Stephen begins his long defense. It is also known as Stephen's Sermon. The sermon is 51 verses in length. Ryrie (1978) describes the text of the sermon "as your fathers did, so do ye"

(v. 51) and notes, "Stephen recited the privileges of the nation Israel and their rejection of God's messengers; then he laid blame for the slaying of Jesus squarely on his hearers" (v. 52) (Ryrie, 1978, p. 1549).

Stephen passionately and I might add, accurately, recounts the history of the children of Israel from the time of Abraham through the building of the temple by Solomon. It is what he says next that begins to stir people. The irony is that he is quoting the Old Testament (Is. 66:1,2).

> However, the Most High does not live in houses made by human hands. As the prophet says:
>
> Heaven is my throne, and the earth is my footstool. What kind of house will you build for me? says the Lord. Or where will my resting place be? Has not my hand made all these things?
>
> You stiff-necked people, with uncircumcised hearts and ears! You are just like your fathers: You always resist the Holy Spirit. (Acts 7:48–51; Is 66:1–2a, NIV)

These three verses are very important because if misinterpreted by the people listening, they can be a catalyst for extreme disagreement. Bovan (2003) notes,

> First, the story of the tension in the Jerusalem church has been particularly noted. It is clear today, for the majority of scholars, that a quarrel existed between opposing and distinct Christian groups of Jewish origin: the Twelve, who spoke Aramaic and respected the Jerusalem Temple, and the Seven, who spoke Greek and presented a liberal understanding of the Mosaic law and opposed the sacrificial function of the Temple. (p. 284)

Thus, when Stephen boldly states God does not live in the temple and that sacrifices in the temple were no longer necessary (implied in the verses Acts 7:42b & 47), this was interpreted as blasphemy by some. Some scholars have gone so far as to refer to Stephen's words regarding sacrifices in the temple as a cult (Bovon, 2003).

When we look at the final three verses in full context, we see the possible trigger that spurred the high priest to do what he did next.

> You stiff-necked people! Your hearts and ears are still uncircumcised. You are just like your ancestors: You always resist the Holy Spirit! Was there ever a prophet your ancestors did not persecute? They even killed those who predicted the coming of the Righteous One. And now you have

> betrayed and murdered him— you who have received the law that was given through angels but have not obeyed it. (Acts 7:51–53, NIV)

Even though he is defending himself, he boldly accuses the Sanhedrin of having hearts and ears that are uncircumcised. This is the equivalent of telling them that they are not set apart as the physical circumcision sets apart and have been resisting letting the Holy Spirit come into their hearts. To add a little more context, according to Harbour and others (1988) note Israel (the traditional Jews) told their history from the position of "God's salvation for an elect people" but add, "Stephen told it as a history rejecting God's leaders and leadership, a history of resisting the Holy Spirit, a history of climaxing in the violent rejection of the righteous Messiah" (p. 1374). He was figuratively pointing his finger at them.

He shows the boldness to speak to the hierarchy of the day, a trait of courageous followership. Stephen's list of godly characteristics continues to grow: Spirit, Wisdom, Faith, Grace, Power, Peace, Joy, and now Boldness. Next, we will examine his martyrdom and how that led to the spread of Christianity.

The Martyrdom

To believe in God so passionately that you are willing to die for him is a testament to the boldness and courage of Stephen. As stated earlier, at this point in the story, he knows he is going to die. He has thoroughly upset the Sanhedrin and says some things that seal his fate.

> When the members of the Sanhedrin heard this, they were furious and gnashed their teeth at him. But Stephen, full of the Holy Spirit, looked up to heaven and saw the glory of God, and Jesus standing at the right hand of God. 'Look,' he said, 'I see heaven open and the Son of Man standing at the right hand of God. (Acts 7:54–56, NIV)

Rushbrooke (1940) notes Stephen was the only person in Acts to call Jesus the Son of Man a name Jesus called himself. Jesus referred to himself as the Son of Man throughout the Gospels and is identified that way in Acts and Revelation. Rushbrooke (1940) posits, "The reason is that he is the first to realize that the Christ is no mere Jew, but the Saviour of the human race" (1940, p. 9). The Apostles, though saved and filled with the Holy Spirit, were still living as Jews. They had not grasped the full meaning of their faith whereas Stephen had. Therefore, it makes sense that Stephen would be the first martyr. One could conclude here that the follower (Stephen) had become the leader in this moment in time which is another quality of courageous followership.

The "Son of Man" title is more relatable to human beings. It really is the more appropriate title for Jesus while on Earth. Some have noted the fact that Jesus is standing instead of sitting at the right hand of God illustrates a welcoming posture to Stephen as he is about to die. We will never understand the euphoria Stephen must have felt—though in tremendous pain from the stoning—seeing his blessed savior ready to welcome him.

> At this they covered their ears and, yelling at the top of their voices, they all rushed at him, dragged him out of the city and began to stone him. Meanwhile, the witnesses laid their coats at the feet of a young man named Saul. (Acts 7:57–58, NIV)

The result of conviction, they (the Sanhedrin and others perhaps) chose not to accept the gift of God's salvation and instead began the process of killing Stephen. There are numerous definitions of what stoning entailed. Some would have taken time to execute such as burying an individual up to their chest or neck or tying them to a post. Others would have tortured first by throwing smaller rocks. Based on what we read in the Stephen account, it seems to depict a very quick event; medium and large stones immediately onto a kneeling Stephen.

Verse 58 seems almost out of place or irrelevant to the story unless it points to something later. People standing around laying their coats at the feet of Saul. Why? We will explore this in the next section. But first we see the ultimate act of a courageous follower of Christ. Love.

> While they were stoning him, Stephen prayed, 'Lord Jesus, receive my spirit.' Then he fell on his knees and cried out, 'Lord, do not hold this sin against them.' When he had said this, he fell asleep. (Acts 7:59–60, NIV)

To the very end, Stephen cared for and loved his fellow man. He knew they needed Christ. Before we examine the resulting spread of Christianity, it is necessary to understand why or how the resulting actions came about. We see in Stephen a committed follower, yet we also see a leader. Therefore, next we will review the literature of followership—namely that of Robert E. Kelley—and applicable leadership concepts of James MacGregor Burns.

Followership

In this section we will briefly review the research of Robert E. Kelley. There are a growing number of researchers investigating followership. I am focusing on Robert Kelley's work because he was a pioneer in the field and has continued to refine his thoughts on followership. Others such as Kellerman (2007) and Chaleff (2009) have added to the research by introducing engagement and courageous followership into the discussion. What is fascinating about this literature review is the way Kelley builds off servant leadership concepts and introduces elements of followership that have proved foundational to more contemporary experts in the field. Ultimately this section connects traits identified as those of Stephen and what kind of follower he truly was.

Kelley (1988) originally looked at followers as being associated with critical thinking [or not] and whether they were effective [or not]. He noted that some followers are more effective than others and they could be illustrated in a box with four quadrants corresponding to Alienated Followers, Effective Followers, Yes People, and Sheep. The Alienated and Effective followers showed Independent, Critical Thinking behaviors. The Yes People and Sheep were Dependent, and Uncritical in their thinking. Likewise, Effective and Yes People were Active participants and Alienated and Sheep were Passive. In the very middle of the box Kelley identified Survivors.

Twenty years later, Kelley (2010) revised his quadrants to Alienated, Star or Exemplary, Yes Person or Conformist, and Sheep or Passive Followers. Survivors—the middle box—was replaced with Pragmatic Followers. The other big change was that Effectiveness was now identified in terms of energy; there is now Negative Energy and Passive Engagement and Positive Energy and Active Engagement. We'll come back this later.

Another very important thing came out of this later work. Kelly's (2010) Seven Paths of Followership illustrated in a circular fashion, where the polar labels were Followers Seek Self-expression and Followers Seek to Transform Themselves. The equatorial labels were Relationships have primary Importance and Personal Goals have Primary Importance. The seven paths then form a circle—think pieces of pie—working clockwise around the circle:

- The Apprentice's Path—"They understand the need to learn the ropes and pay their dues...hope to win the confidence of peers and supervisors" (p. 186);
- The Disciple's Path—"To bond with and emulate the leader...one who believes" (p. 187);
- The Mentee's Path—"Involves an intensive one-on-one relationship between mentor and follower...mentees entrust themselves" (p. 187);
- The Comrade's Path—"Intimacy from belonging. Once you feel part of something, you transcend feelings of isolation and even feelings of self" (p. 188);
- The Path of Loyalty—"Requires emotional commitment to another...willingly given and unshakeable from the outside" (p. 188);
- The Dreamer's Path—"Committed to their personal dream rather than to a particular leader...They are so focused on achieving their dream that it does not matter whether they are in the leader or follower role" (p. 188); and,
- The Lifeway Path—Follow out of conviction...followership is compatible with their personal makeup...may be inherently altruistic or naturally skilled at following" (p. 188).

When I think of Stephen, the Disciple's Path and Lifeway Path seem most descriptive. The Disciple's Path was illustrated by Kelley (2010) as follows:

> For example, having read Plato's dialogues, the seventeen-year-old Aristotle left his hometown for Athens to study in Plato's Academy. For the next twenty formative years, Aristotle worked and studied with a brilliant group of disciples under Plato's leadership. (Kelley, 2010, p. 186)

Disciples give up everything to follow another and they feel enlarged as a result. Though Stephen most likely was not going for the feeling, he knew he was enlarged if he was aligned with Jesus. The boldness he showed all the way to his death was beyond anything the Twelve had shown up to that point. His scriptural wisdom exhibited a desire to learn and a skill of persuasiveness. In a Crosswalk.com article, White (2017) suggests, "instead of saying, 'Everything rises and falls on leadership,' perhaps the deeper truth is, 'Everything rises and falls on followership.'" He concludes you cannot be a leader without first being a follower. I tend to agree with this except in extraordinary cases such as when a charismatic leader rises during a point in history where a leader is needed. So, the question to ask is, was Stephen a leader or follower?

Likewise, the Lifeway Path of followership describe those that "may be inherently altruistic or naturally skilled at following…following is a way of serving…they make helping others their goal" (Kelley, 2010, p. 187). So, what is altruism? Psychology Today defines altruism as, "acting to help someone else at some cost to oneself." Stephen arrives on the scene as the first appointed Deacon. He is selected to serve! He paid the ultimate price. This kind of followership is very similar to servant leadership. Greenleaf (1977, 2002), the pioneer of Servant Leadership, noted…

> Servant and leader-can these two roles be fused in one real person, in all of status and calling? If so, can that person live and be productive in the real world of the present? My sense of the present leads me to say yes to both questions. (Greenleaf, 1977)

Greenleaf and his contemporaries generally identify several component constructs for servant leadership which included Altruism, Empowerment, Humility, Agape love, Service, Trust, and Vision. It is evident from this list that Altruism and Service are common with the Lifeway path of followership.

So, was Stephen a leader or a follower? Several Biblical timelines agree that Stephen's moment was just a few years after the death, burial, and resurrection of Jesus Christ. It is quite possible Stephen could have been a witness to much of what happened toward the end of Christ's life and after his resurrection. Most suggest that since he was a Hellenist Jew, he was foreign born. However, most also agree he lived in Jerusalem. One might also ask, why wasn't he selected to fill Judas' place among the Twelve? There were basic requirements to be an Apostle as we see in Mark 3:14–15. They had to be called by Jesus, they had to accompany/study under Jesus, and they had to be empowered by Jesus.

> Then he appointed twelve of them and called them his apostles. They were to accompany him, and he would send them out to preach, giving them authority to cast out demons. (Mark 3:14–15, NLT)

According to these three qualifications, Stephen may have been one of the 120 disciples that Peter was addressing in Acts 1:15 regarding the need to fill the vacancy left by Judas. If so, he could have studied under Jesus, but we know that he was not called to be an Apostle by Jesus. He may have been empowered by Jesus but not in the sense meant by these requirements (i.e., healing, raising the dead, casting out demons, etc.). He was clearly empowered to serve and preach. Thus, he was not a leader in an apostolic sense. However, his martyrdom changed the world.

Though there were certainly aspects of leadership seen in Stephen, and there is overwhelming evidence to support Stephen's walk down the Disciples Path and the Lifeway Path as defined by Kelley (2010), he also showed evidence of being a courageous follower.

For the sake of review, Ira Chaleff (2009) identifies seven elements of courageous followership.

1. Courage to Assume Responsibility;
2. Courage to Serve;
3. Courage to Challenge;
4. Courage to Participate;
5. Courage to Take Moral Action;
6. Courage to Speak to the Hierarchy; and
7. Courage to Listen to Followers. (Chaleff, 2009, pp. 6–8)

Chaleff starts these with the word courage. The argument is a follower with the first six elements will exhibit traits of a leader. For example, having the courage to be responsible might go beyond just being responsible for yourself as it could also include observing a need and just jumping in and taking care of the need. For the elements of Challenging and Taking Moral Action, this may include direct follower to leader engagement and obviously courage. Same with Speak to the Hierarchy. It is very clear that Stephen had a good grasp of elements one through six. However, there is a seventh one; Courage to Listen to Followers.

The seventh element is clearly for leaders. It also involves courage. Some leaders do not want to listen to followers. When Stephen sees Jesus standing [not sitting] at the right hand of God, it could have signaled to Stephen that Jesus was listening and watching. As he is dying, Stephen says to God, "forgive them for they know not what they do," and I would like to believe God (Jesus) heard him. That was a transformative moment for Stephen as he attained that desired level of self-actualization as originally defined by Maslow (1943). Maslow (1943) noted that self-actualization is…

> What a man can be, he must be. This need we may call self-actualization… It refers to the desire for self-fulfillment, namely, to the tendency for him to become actualized in what he is potentially. This tendency might be phrased as the desire to become more and more what one is, to become everything that one is capable of becoming. (p. 383)

The spiritual and physical came together in perfect union in Stephen and though being stoned to death, he was a child of God and knew he would be with Jesus in a matter of minutes.

Transformational Leadership

Earlier we discussed Greenleaf's servant leadership and noted the parts of servant leadership that describe Stephen. James Macgregor Burns was an accomplished political scientist, historian, and writer having published numerous books beginning in 1949 with the book titled, *Congress on Trial*. One of his greatest accomplishments was his book titled, *John Kennedy: A Political Profile* (1960) which was a very intimate account of a young John Kennedy before he became President. The book gained Burns much notoriety and respect. Burns later focused much of his attention on the study of leadership and in 1978 wrote the book titled, *Leadership*. In the book he introduces the concepts transactional leadership—simply put I reward you if you do something for me—and transforming leadership. It is the transforming leadership that I believe applies to Stephen the Martyr.

Burns (1978) defines a Transforming Leader as someone who, *"looks for potential motives in followers, seeks to satisfy higher needs, and engages the full person of the follower"* (p. 4). He adds, *"Such leadership occurs when one or more persons engage with others in such a way that leaders and followers raise one another to higher levels of motivation and morality"* (Burns, 1978, p. 20). If we look back at Acts 6, we see an astonishing outcome that can be missed as it falls in the middle of two significant events. Acts 6:7–8 says, *"So the word of God spread. The number of disciples in Jerusalem increased rapidly, and a large number of priests became obedient to the faith. Now Stephen, a man full of God's grace and power, performed great wonders and signs among the people*" (Acts 6:7–8, NIV). This happened just after Stephen and six others were selected to be the first deacons but before Stephen was seized by the Synagogue of the Freedmen (Jews from Cyrene, Alexandria, and other provinces) and brought to the Sanhedrin. Already the transformation had started. Stephen's ministry was more leadership than followership in that he created followers of Jesus. He was raising others to "higher levels of motivation and morality" (Burns, 1978). When this thought is juxtaposed next to Maslow's Hierarchy of Needs where the pinnacle of needs is met with Self-Actualization (Maslow, 1943), we can understand better how the events of Acts 6–8 triggered the spread of Christianity after Stephen's death.

Hamon (1977) posits four points to suggest Stephen's actions "point to an experiential process" which he suggests goes beyond self-actualization.

> Point 1—"The experiential sanctification process had begun in Stephen at his first moment of belief in Jesus…and…accelerated at the point where Stephen saw the vision of Christ" (p. 295).
> Point 2—"Stephen's prayer is one of enlightened acceptance. Stephen accepts his death as the culmination of his desired sanctification" (p. 295) which transcends Maslow.
> Point 3—"By asking God to absolve his killers of blood guilt, Stephen released them from any claim which the adversary (Satan) might have had on them concerning him" (p. 295).
> Point 4—"Transcendent actualization begins with a willful invitation of the third person of the Christian 'three-in-one' God (i.e., the Holy Spirit) into one's life through faith in Jesus Christ" (p. 296).

Connecting Burns (1978) and Hamon (1977), it is not hard to see Stephen as a Transformational Leader. Much of Transformational Leadership hinges on followers recognizing the vision of the leader, embracing it and making it theirs. When someone accepts Jesus as their personal Lord and savior—Point 1 above—they have accepted an invitation from God and have wholly embraced it. Stephen did this and shortly after he was ordained as a Deacon, he was part of the evangelism explosion that occurred and led to many coming to Jesus but also many Jews becoming very angry with him. A close cousin of Transformational Leadership is Charismatic Leadership. Point 2 above from a leader's standpoint reminds me of Jesus's command to "Take up your cross and walk," and anyone that agreed to do that as Stephen did, recognized that the ultimate outcome of sanctification could possibly lead to glorification. So, the Charismatic Leader here could be God but also Stephen. And of course, from a Follower perspective, Stephen followed so far that it ultimately led to his enlightened acceptance. Regarding Point 3 above, it takes a lot of love for "*one or more persons engage with others in such a way that leaders and followers raise one another to higher levels of motivation and morality*" (Burns, 1978, p. 20). Stephen's prayer to God to absolve those killing him of any blood guiltiness, i.e., sin, was agape love through and through and it resulted higher levels of motivation and morality. That single act alone may have demonstrated love like never have been seen before; except for Jesus Christ himself. Point 4 is about achieving self-actualization and beyond and hones in on the Holy Spirit. Burns (1978) beautifully describes something like this using teachers and leaders as the catalysts. He notes...

> The problem for them as educators, as leaders, is not to promote narrow, egocentric self-actualization but to extend awareness of human needs and the means of gratifying them, to improve the larger social situation for which educators or leaders have responsibility and over which they have power...and...They seek to help students rise to higher stages of moral reasoning and hence to higher levels of principled judgement. (p. 449)

Hamon (1977), when explaining Point 4, posits this about one's awareness of one's position in Christ and one's uniqueness as a person. He posits...

> As this awareness increases, so does the awareness of the limitations sinful human conditions place on one which frustrate realization of the potential for hallowed 'Christ-like' personhood. As one attempts to resolve the imbalance between the completed position and the limited condition in daily Christian life the Holy Spirit teaches that such resolution is only done by the One who created the potential and Who makes possible the actualization of that potential, God. (p. 296)

Up to this point, we have been identifying distinguishing traits, or godly characteristics, about Stephen. We have also examined followership and leadership traits Stephen had. The last section highlights the result of Stephen's moment in time. We investigate how Stephen, through his courageous followership and transformational leadership, was the catalyst that sparked the spread of Christianity.

The Spread of Christianity

Several things contributed to the beginning of the spread of Christianity, but one event appears to stand out from the rest and that is the martyrdom of Stephen. We see in Chapter 8, with emphasis added, the following:

> And Saul approved of their killing him. On that day a great persecution broke out against the church in Jerusalem, and all except the apostles were scattered throughout Judea and Samaria. Godly men buried Stephen and mourned deeply for him. But Saul began to destroy the church. Going from house to house, he dragged off both men and women and put them in prison. Those who had been scattered preached the word wherever they went. (Acts 8:1–4, NIV)

We see here the witness' coats were thrown at the feet of the one who approved of (consented to) the stoning of Stephen. The scripture then immediately states, "On that day…" the persecution started and the subsequent spread of all "except the apostles" to Judea and Samaria. Stephen was the catalyst for change. Why not the Apostles? It is unclear why they stayed back or were spared being forced out of Jerusalem. They represented the Church at Jerusalem and of course would play a role in policy and missionary work later. We also know that all the apostles became martyrs except for John who was used by God later to write the Revelation of God. The point of Acts 8:1–4 is that a movement started. God used hostility and persecution toward Christians to move Christians beyond Jerusalem. This is defined even better in Acts 11 where we see the result of the scattering.

> Now those who had been scattered by the persecution that broke out when Stephen was killed traveled as far as Phoenicia, Cyprus, and Antioch, spreading the word only among Jews. Some of them, however, men from Cyprus and Cyrene, went to Antioch and began to speak to Greeks also, telling them the good news about the Lord Jesus. The Lord's hand was

Table 7.1 Summary of Stephen's traits, followership behaviors, and leadership behaviors

Holy Bible Text (Acts 6–8 & 11)	*Followership (Kelley)*	*Courageous Followership (Chaleff)*	*Servant Leadership (Greenleaf + Contemporaries)*	*Transformational Leadership (Burns)*
Holy Spirit	The Apprentice's Path	Courage to Assume Responsibility	Altruism	Looks for potential motives of the follower
Wisdom	The Disciple's Path	Courage to Serve	Empowerment	Seeks to satisfy higher needs of the follower
Faith	The Mentee's Path	Courage to Challenge	Humility	Engages the full person of the follower
Grace	The Comrade's Path	Courage to Participate	Agape love	Raise one another to higher levels of motivation/ morality
Power	The Path of Loyalty	Courage to Take Moral Action	Service	Transcendent actualization (Hamon)
Peace	The Dreamer's Path	Courage to Speak to the Hierarchy	Trust	
Joy	The Lifeway Path	Courage to Listen to Followers	Vision	
Boldness				

with them, and a great number of people believed and turned to the Lord. (Acts 11:19–22, NIV)

Salvation was being preached to both Jews and Greeks and both were becoming believers! Stephen was the catalyst that ignited the spread and the results of many Jews and Greeks being saved! He was an agent of change, a courageous follower, and transformational leader.

Chapter Takeaways

Table 7.1 shows the results of the examination of the story of Stephen in Acts 6–8 and in the review of the literature. The underlined characteristics represent my assessment of Stephen's traits and his character.

Reflective Questions

1. Was Stephen a follower or a leader? Why?
2. If Stephen was an agent of change, what was Paul (formerly Saul)?
3. Was Saul convicted by what he saw done to Stephen?
4. We discussed Transcendent Actualization in Stephen when he sees Jesus standing at the right hand of God. Was this a perfect coming together of wills; Stephen's and God's?
5. What is the take-away from this study of Stephen and how might we apply it to our own lives?

References

Bovon, F. (2003). The dossier on Stephen, the first martyr. *Harvard Theological Review, 96*(3), 279–315.

Burns, J. (1978). *Leadership*. Harper & Row.

Chaleff, I. (2009). *The courageous follower: Standing up to & for our leaders* (3rd ed.). Berrett-Koehler Publishers.

Greenleaf, R. K. (1977/2002). *Servant-leadership: A journey into the nature of legitimate power and greatness*. Paulist Press.

Hamon, S. A. (1977). Beyond self-actualization: Comments on the life and death of Stephen the martyr. *Journal of Psychology and Theology, 5*(4), 292–299.

Harbour, B. & many others. (1988). *Disciple's study Bible*. Holman Bible Publishers.

Kellerman, B. (2007). What every leader needs to know about followers. *Harvard Business Review, 85*(12), 84.

Kelley, R. (2008). In praise of followers. *Harvard Business Review*, November–December, 142–148.

Kelley, R. (2010). Followership. In G. R. Hickman (Ed.), *Leading organizations: Perspectives for a new era* (2nd ed.). Sage.

Kelley, R. E. (1988). In praise of followers. *Harvard Business Review Case Services*, 142–148.

Maslow, A. (1943). A theory of human motivation. *Psychological Review, 50*, 370–396.

Ryrie, C. (1978). *The Ryrie study Bible*. Moody Press.

Rushbrooke, J. H. (1940). A man full of the holy spirit. *The Review and Expositor, XXXVII*(1), 3–13.

White. (2017). https://www.crosswalk.com/blogs/dr-james-emery-white/followership.html

CHAPTER 8

Reading Your Leader: Essence of Followership

Boniface Toulassi

Introduction

Nobody can be a leader without first being a follower, could there be leadership without followership? Is followership the consequence or the source of effective leadership? Why should followers stay on the sidelines of the leadership pyramid whereas they contribute 80% to the organizational success and growth? Does ranking make greatness? Andrew did prove that to become a leader one has to be a follower, and a smart and initiative taking one. Crucially, times have changed and leaders to really see the urgency to change and take up the intentionality to respect, develop, and empower followers.

In part, cultural values and norms guide people's behaviors in a society. As a result, it influences the social construction of both leadership and followership roles and behaviors as well (Rokeach, 1973). Culturally

B. Toulassi (✉)
Regent University, Virginia Beach, VA, USA
e-mail: bonitou@mail.regent.edu

D. J. Dean and R. B. Huizinga (eds.), *Followership and Faith at Work*, Christian Faith Perspectives in Leadership and Business,
https://doi.org/10.1007/978-3-030-90614-6_8

and traditionally, paternalistic and hero-type leadership views and treats followers as people of lower status, a marginalized group, for whom "the leader is the principal driver of innovation and change" (Blair & Bligh, 2018, p. 129). Surprisingly, Jesus's goal was to educate His disciples not to lead like nations do (Mark 10:41–44) and to refine their faith. To that end, Jesus created this miracle of feeding the five thousand people in John 6:1–15 to teach servant leadership through lateral and participative leadership through problem-solving skill development. Apostle Andrew evidenced this new deal by developing and using his self-awareness, personal conviction, courage, creativity, curiosity, ability to inspire, ability to listen, ability to innovate, eager to experience, and willingness to reflect (Bisoux, 2005).

Clearly, proactive followers become active problem-solvers and co-contributors dynamically demonstrating both followership and leadership on their own behalf and of the team (Chaleff, 1995; Kellerman, 2008; Shamir, 2007; Uhl-Bien et al., 2014). Humanly speaking, feeding five thousand people is not a joke nor a dream. This road to practical followership was set on a huge scale, even the setting for the story. It all pointed to immensity contrasted with scarcity, abundance with nothingness. This abundance does not come from careful calculation nor planning especially that this gigantic need, its time and geographical location, Bethsaida (1:44) proved human powerlessness. However, Andrew tapped from his personal knowledge of Jesus Christ, used his self-leadership and personal power to usher collaborative leadership which ended up solving the problem.

In the pages to come, discover who apostle Andrew was, Andrew's contribution to problem-solving through connectivity to and with people. At the end, some takeaways and reflective questions help reminiscent the key aspects and thoughts developed in this work.

Who Was Apostle Andrew?

Andrew was not in the first class of apostles. According to the Bible usage Andrew is mentioned 13 times in the New Testament. The first reference in Matthew 4:18 and the last in Acts 1:13. In consequence, Barclay (1975) was right to say, "there is no great deal of information about him" (p. 105). As such, in light of the norms of decision, priority, and subordination were determined by status or power gap. The interaction of power distance with tightness and looseness explains differences in followership orientation and the tolerance of divergent ideas (Blair & Bligh, 2018). However, with the feeding of five thousand people in John 6:1–15, Andrew became an indispensable intermediary (Bovon, 1994).

Semantically, Andrew means *Manliness* in Greek while *The Hitchcock's Names Dictionary* translated the name as "a strong man." For Barclay, the name Andrew has two meanings in the Greek Manuscripts: *Prōton* means "*first*" and *Prōi* means "*early in the morning*" (p. 105). For Robertson (1960), "*Proton* is an adverb supported by Aleph AB fam. 13, indicating that Andrew sought "his own brother Simon" (*ton adelphon ton idom Simona*)" (p. 27). But Aleph L W reads *protos* (nominative adjective) meaning that Andrew was the first who went after his brother. Putting the exclamation and explanation together, even "the little that we know about Andrew perfectly brightened his character: the most attractive men in the apostolic band with two outstanding characteristics. He is the man with missionary heart" (p. 27). With the miracle of the multiplication of the bread (John 6:1–15), from his less visible status, Andrew's actions became his best archives and spoke louder than words as Laurie (1952) rightly affirmed:

> How we need more Andrews today! Every time we read of him in Scripture, he is bringing someone to Jesus...If we had more Andrews, we would have more Simon Peters - one person bringing another to Jesus. So simple. So effective. So, neglected. (p. 261)

The above quote echoes Woodruff and woodruff (2009) explanation according to which the name Andrew means "manly" or "of valor." Leaving his first Rabbi, John the Baptist, for Jesus Christ the apostle made the latter the most important thing in his life.

At this level one may argue that the unseen is not necessarily hidden (Vickers, 2001). By helping with the resource provision to feed thousands of people, Andrew changed the old perspectives that leaders have of followers, "The Yes-People" (Hickman, 2010). As a matter of fact, as first called (*Protoclete* for the Greeks), Andrew, the icon in the Byzantine Church, preached the gospel in Greece (St Andrew Parish, 2020). He was crucified in Patras in about the year 60 on an X-shaped cross known as the cross of St. Andrew (the Crux Decussate). Known to be the Patron Saint of Russia and Scotland, the flag of the latter displays the Cross of St. Andrew. His self-leadership was very instrumental in the miracle of "feeding to repletion of 5000 people," a "sacramental meal" "that nourished hearts and souls" (Barclay, 1975, p. 238).

Tight or loose, cultures are subjected to change and innovation, and Jesus was ushering the way. In clear, Jesus was teaching the undeniable lesson than position does not determine nor mean effectiveness. Andrew's self-interest or altruism was definite, positive, and inclusive (Zhao et al., 2020). Only self-efficacy, the power of connection, and problem-solving skills explain Andrew's success.

Andrew: The Iconic Connector and Problem-Solver

The miracle of the feeding of the 5,000 is the only sign recorded in the four Gospels (besides Jesus's resurrection. This fact alone points to its importance (Walvoord & Zuck, 1985, p. 293). In the Gospel of John, Andrew symbolized connectivity with people and to people: his brother, the inquiring Greeks, and the boy with the barley loaves and fish. This echoes a high note of interpersonal relationships skills. The apostle connects to and with people. Behaviorally, Andrew inspires confidence and trust in leading individuals to their goals (establishing their roles). He embodied a blending of the various skills, a collaboration. Amazingly mirrored through Lipman-Blumen (2010) Nine-factor L-BL achieving styles behavioral model, Andrew comes out relational, direct, and instrumental. This model is divided into three sets, the relational consisted of (collaborative who join forces, contributory who helps, and vicarious who mentors), the direct set made up of (intrinsic who excels, the competitive who outperforms, and the power who takes charge), Andrew exemplified the instrumental set to vitalize his relational direct sets. With the instrumental set consisted of personal (who persuades), social (who networks), and entrusting (who empowers), Andrew proved how he persuades people to build networks that empower others and solve problem. the apostle clicks and connects to other's tasks (relational), masters his own task (direct), and maximizes interactions (instrumental).

Rightly, by asking His disciples to feed the impossible number of people (John 6:5–6), Jesus enacted the task of enabling and collective empowerment. Guided by an internal standard of excellence, Andrew judged their current result by comparing to none. He had previous results like connecting Perter to Jesus and the inquiring Greeks to Jesus but never had he the best past result which fits best the current equation to solve. However, Andrew relished "pitting themselves against a significant challenge" (Lipman-Blumen, 2010, p. 171). This "politics of commonality" was a direct contribution to the equitable development of all participants in the project. This takes self-regulation on Andrew's part and the skill of understanding other people's minds (Riggs et al., 2006; Zimmerman, 2000). Like Jesus, successful leaders adopt subordinate-oriented communication and obtain subordinates' commitment to change (Luo et al., 2016). Andrew's self-balance and ability to understand others made him successful in helping solve the socio-organizational equation with two unknowns set by Jesus: where to find the resource and the amount needed to acquire or buy the resource. Andrew, by bringing this boy might have de-escalated organizational stress, anger, and conflicts (Strayer & Robert, 2004, 136–137). No wonder the community wanted Jesus their king, a feeding pipeline (John 6:15, NIV). This highlights Andrew as a problem-solver.

Andrew as a Problem-Solver

Andrew was a problem-solver. In other words, and to be accurate with the pericope understudy, Andrew does not solve this problem, but rather points to the solution. Whatever we say, problem-solving is one of the important skills in an individual's life. It requires three elements: the person must recognize the existence of the problem while possessing the motivation to solve it, and there must be some obstacle to directly solving the problem, and a behavior that brings about the solution (Donahoe & Palmer, 1994). It starts with a crisis and takes initiatives, and functional relationships. Then leads to focus which influences a variety of affective, cognitive, and behavioral employee outcomes (Lanaj et al., 2012; Johnson et al., 2017). Here, Andrew exhibited greater satisfaction and effort when his regulatory focus is aligned with the focus of an external target (Brockner & Higgins, 2001). Because this alignment existed, I mean the focus [feeding people] with the boy with loaves and fish [external target], the apostle felt right about what he was doing. This intensified his motivation to engage in their work and relationships with others. Such sensation of 'feeling right' also stemmed from the approval of his means reinforced by the environment and his leader. His confidence led to a stronger engagement in work-related behaviors. Moreover, problem-solving has steps or problem-solving process the first of which is problem identification.

Problem identification. To solve a problem takes determining the causes, the scope, and ways to solve it. Knowing that "God test people to refine their faith, never to tempt them to do evil" (Walvoord & Zuck, 1985, p. 293), Jesus' question to Philipp (6:5–6) about where to buy bread for these people was not for information but was part of His program of educating the disciples. Philip was from Bethsaida (1:44) which was the closest town, and he would know the local resources (Walvoord & Zuck, 1985, p. 293). The answer to Jesus' question was that it was impossible, humanly speaking, for thousands of people to get bread late in the day from the little neighboring villages.

> The amount needed was a large sum of money: literally, "200 denarii." One denarius was the wage for a day's work; this would have been eight months' wages. Even if the bread had been available, the disciples did not have nearly that much money. The disciples were supported by people who responded to Jesus' ministry. (Walvoord & Zuck, 1985, p. 293)

In contrast with Philip, Andrew had gone into the crowd to determine its resources. All he could come up with was a little boy's lunch. Man's inability sets the stage for a manifestation of Jesus' compassion and power (Walvoord & Zuck, 1985, p. 293). Technically, Andrew might have applied the model known to be plan, do, check, act. This interactive four-stage approach involves systematically testing possible solutions, assessing results, and implementing the ones that are shown to work as follow:

Plan: Identify and analyze the problem or opportunity, develop hypotheses about what the issues may be, and decide which one to test.
Do: Test the potential solution, ideally on a small scale, and measure the results. [Andrew decided to talk to the boy and take him to Jesus in case the boy accepts]
Check/Study: study the result, measure effectiveness, and decide whether the hypothesis is supported or not. [Would the boy accept?]
Act: If the solution was successful, implement it. [Upon agreeing, Andrew took the boy to Jesus] (*My Brackets*).

Having accepted follower classification as a disciple, all that mattered to Andrew was to be with Jesus and serve Him as well as he could.

Since crisis is a change triggered uncertain event, organizational innovation practices are required to handle its consequences (Bessant et al., 2015). Andrew might have used his past data and knowledge to that end instead of organizational competitiveness or position (Anderson et al., 2014; Yang et al., 2016). Problem-solving also takes pragmatism and initiatives.

Problem-solving takes pragmatism and initiatives. Acting summarizes pragmatism and initiative taking in a context. Andrew found a boy with the hope of solution (The barley loaves Jn 6:). How did Andrew get the courage and the knowledge to go through the crowd? Here, the principle of contextuality might apply: All things are interconnected and the meaning of anything depends on its context. For the apostle, Jesus is the whole reason why not only did he see a boy but brought him to Jesus. Between the person and the object of attention and the salience of an object, Andrew thought exactly like Jesus might have expected: just do something and I would complete it all well. People question what Andrew told the small boy, and we know that: Andrew knows how to talk to people and convince them to action. This was enriched by his personal behavior and relationship with Jesus which he to understand other's situation and interpretation (MacDougall, 1992).

In clear, contrary to the general assumption that followers "are alienated, sheep, or passive followers, Yes-People, or Conformist" (Hickman, 2010, p. 183), only eager to take orders, to defer to the leader's authority, and to yield to the leader's views or judgment, and lacking initiatives or influences (Oyetunji, 2013), Andrew emerged as pragmatist and smart star follower. This took functional relationships.

Functional relationships. Functional relationships in problem-solving take four elements: "people, meaning (values), society, and environment" (MacDougall, 1992, p. 93). Expounded, in addition to the functional values that are the meaning that people have and give to their needs and solutions, the society stands for the institutions whereas the resources may be both natural and cultural. Generally, people seek meaning through society using or affecting their environment. But Andrew influenced the environment to give meaning to people and society (Kendrick & Drew, 2016, p. 23). Further, using Lipman-Blumen social behavioral category, Andrew accomplished his tasks by assembling networks of associates. He selected individuals with relevant abilities, experience, or contacts for specific [can we use your loaves!]. As a unique component and a direct reflection of dyadic communication (Williams & Spiro, 1985), Andrew's communication style plays a pivotal role in explaining different work outcomes and in determining the quality of leader–member exchange (LMX) relationships.

The above paints Andrew as a self-sacrificial leader, a total or partial abandonment, either permanently or temporarily of his personal interests, privileges, or welfare in the division of labor, distribution of rewards, and exercising of power (Choi & Mai-Dalton, 1998, 1999). Zhou et al. (2016) supported that Self-sacrificial leadership generates positive affect in followers and is strongly influenced by environmental uncertainty (Choi & Mai-Dalton, 1998). Andrew was a leader who abandoned or postponed his individual interests and privileges to expend personal costs in order to benefit their collective, strongly motivate their followers (Hoogervorst et al., 2012). With collective empowerment, people found their place, their role, their identity, and their voice in the system. This was the goal Jesus wanted. Everyone is somebody precious and can contribute something precious. One may also argue that there was an interconnection of individuals in all parts of the system [Andrew, the boy, and his mother, the other apostles, and the crowd]. Though the parts did not have a clear conception of their roles, they contributed to the goal of feeding the crowds. This represents a clear picture of a fruitful development of relationships with others, clarity about purpose, meaning, and value in their work (Kirk & Shutte, 2004, p. 243).

Apostle Andrew's fruitful development of others by others justifies why Lipman-Blumen argued that the command-and-control model of leadership is faltering seriously. In fact, the two overarching realities in leadership and organizations today are the changing nature of our times and gender differences: and here, the worth of each individual. In this miracle of feeding the thousands, the connective leadership derives its label from its character of connecting individuals, not only to their own tasks and ego drives, but also to those of the group and community that depend upon the accomplishment of mutual goals. The event connected individuals to others and other's goals, using a broad spectrum of behavioral strategies. It revealed or forced or created the recognition of networks of relationships that bind society in a web of mutual responsibilities. The outcome reaches out beyond its own traditional constituencies to presumed adversaries, using mutual goals, rather than mutual enemies to create group cohesion and community membership (Gardner, 1990).

Connectivity and activity shed light onto the reality that Jesus was teaching His disciples where they are (current reality) and where He wants them to be (vision). Moreover, with authenticity and assistance, Andrew lent a helping hand to somebody in need. Andrew saw Kotter's (1996) urgency of change, created the guiding coalition, developed a vision and strategy, communicated the change vision, empowered broad-based action, generated short-term wins, consolidated gains, and produced more change. Better, Andrew anchored new approaches in the culture using the awareness of the need to change, the desire to participate and support the change, having the knowledge on how to change, and the ability to implement required change using dialogue and problem-solving skills but to reinforce and sustain the change. Jeff Hiatt developed this ADKAR approach which works best with individuals m rather than organizations. It is most effective when managing individuals or staff in helping them see and accept the value of change—and his or her role within the organization in helping to make the change happen.[1] In the text understudy, comparing or reading Andrew in the microscope of the ADKAR Approach presents the following tableau:

- Awareness of the need for change: [Finding material to feed 5000 people: Here Andrew saw the risk of not changing and the nature of the change]
- Desire to participate and support the change: [Looking for someone who has a little]: Andrew exemplified the personal motivation to support the change and converted himself into an organizational driver to support the change
- Knowledge on how to change: [Instead of waiting always on Jesus, let us try our best]: Andrew understood how to implement change using dialogue and problem-solving skills
- Ability to implement required skills and behaviors: [Having the courage to convince the boy to yield his lunch package]. Andrew demonstrated ability to implement the change and overcame the barriers that may inhibit implementing the change (crowd, shame)

[1] https://www.ellucian.com/insights/change-leadership-models-and-methods.

- Reinforcement to sustain the change: [Gather the rest into 12 baskets]. The result kept the change in place through the recognitions, rewards, incentives, and successes (*My brackets*).

One item that stood out in this change process is Andrew ability to use dialogue for change.

Dialogue for Change

A dialogue is based on a principle of give and take, and is not a one-way communication (Kirk, 2004). By Asking His disciples to feed the thousands, the disciples were under obligation to engage with one another and help other participants to be active through dialogue. Other than the apostles, somebody had to tell Andrew that there was a boy with lunch. Also, the boy who brought his lunch must agree to let go of his meal and be brought before Jesus. All this was helping the members to collectively explore the possibilities and potential of connecting with a common goal (effective team-working) and create and sustain a creative space where collective leadership flourishes. This fosters collaboration and enables different voices to be heard. Jesus proved how a leader cares and puts himself into the shoes of his followers, adding social responsibilities to his spiritual ones, building souls and communities. Indeed, leadership does not come from one direction and tales critical thinking and capacity building which positioned Andrew as an inestimable gift and liaison between people and people and people and solutions.

Critical Thinker and Capacity Building

Neil and Sue Thompson discussed the CIA model in their 2009 book, *The Critically Reflective Practitioner*. It is a versatile problem-solving and time and stress management tool that identifies three ways to respond to challenges:

Control: identify the issues or elements of the situation that you control [Only Jesus can feed people, not me].

Influence: identify the elements that you cannot control, but that you can influence [Andrew knew he could not feed nor have means to but could talk to a boy].

Accept: identify the things that you can neither control nor influence and adapt accordingly [finding the loaves and fish is what I can do. Multiplying them is beyond my ability] (*My Brackets*)

As Kelley's (1992, 1988) independent follower with active engagement, Andrew built capacity. The apostle embraced critical thinking as the correct way of assessing statements and a reasonable reflective thinking which focused on deciding what to believe or do (Ennis, 1991). Critical thinking helps a person develop the ability to control individual decisions and actions (Blindu, 2020). Thus, though some argue that critical thinking has six aspects or four (Facione, 2011; Torrance et al., 1992), Andrew thought necessary to find, synthesize, analyze, and solve problems. Fluency is the ability to generate a number or many ideas whereas flexibility is the ability to produce diverse ideas. Like his brother Peter, Andrew had originality and elaboration (ibid.). Originality to generate responses to ideas that are not common among most or rare/unique and elaboration to develop and issue ideas. By so doing, the apostle turned the power of little to more than many.

Andrew's ability to see things differently holds the prospect of beneficial social change. It is like Argyris and Schön's (1996) double loop of learning, especially that a change goes beyond adaptation to reframe attitudes, beliefs, and cultural values (Chapman, 2002). Together, the three mousquetaires (Jesus, Andrew, and the boy) made a direct contribution to the equitable development of all participants in this project. Working together this congruence with capacity building principles solidified team efforts and teamwork, making collaborative inquiry and practice robust enough to provide the work with its focus and direction.

Andrew, an Inestimable and Gifted Liaison

To be a successful connector means that one is a qualitative liaison. Actually, in this connective era, everyone is inextricably linked, yet the same applies at the time of this miracle. Someone needs to stand. Here, nobody can read Andrew's heart, but if cognition leads to conation, Andrew fits Lipman-Blumen contributory agency: satisfaction by helping the other person(s) succeed. Fortunately, Jesus the leader contributed to individual innovative behavior (Anderson et al., 2014) and how to manage change in times of crisis (Boin et al., 2013). Also, the above requires experience and attachment, but essentially a follower who reads his leader's mind. This takes a gift, not a natural one, on the contrary a spiritual gift: the gift of perceiving. The Greek word translated as "perceiving" is *propheteia*. It means "revealing, manifesting, showing forth, making known, and divulging vital information" (Winston, 2002, p. 168). The functional gift of prophecy in Romans 12 is the extraordinary ability to discern and proclaim truth. Did Andrew perceive a boy has five loaves of barley bread and fish? While thinking, Fortune and Fortune (1987) proved that everyone has a functional gift:

> each person's gift was built into them when God formed them; that this gift can be observed from childhood; that this gift is to not be neglected, for to neglect it is to neglect God's purpose and plan for that person's life; that this gift affects how the person views the world and circumstances around them; and (5) that this gift gives only one perspective of the whole. "God purposely limited and focused our giftedness so that we would work together and to remain dependent on each other in order to grasp the whole truth". (p. 25)

In light of the above, reading Andrew through the lenses of *The five-factor model*, the apostle is extravert (surgency or positive affectivity), agreeable and opened to experiences (intellect or unconventionality) (John & Srivastava, 1999). With this personality functioning, Andrew brought high functioning ability to the group of apostles. The apostle had personal selection, development, in which inclusion is critical, and connection is inevitable (Lipman-Blumen, 2000). Descriptively, the apostle exercised personal self-esteem, organizational based self-esteem, and self-categorization which made him a successful connector and problem-solver. In addition, Andrew knew how to maintain his self-esteem for group effectiveness. One underlining factor might be how Andrew's secure attachment with Jesus grew into a solid familiarity. If this is proven right, with this communication style, the work performance is not determined by leadership style only such agreement or fit in this communication style guides the group regulation process and promotes interaction quality. These nurture a sense of belonging among the work-group members (Abu-Bakar & McCann, 2014).

This raises the question pertaining to what may explain Andrew's high energy level and motivation to connect? The answer may reside in attachment theory which helps predict the actions of the leader and of the follower in their relationship (Shorley & Chaffin, 2018, p. 518). Andrew's actions indicated how securely attached he was to Jesus. In brief, he knew his leader for exactly who He is. This form of attachment favors dyadic communication (Abu-Bakar & McCann, 2014; Yrle et al., 2002) which links to various aspects of coworker relationship quality, such as degree of intimacy self-disclosure relational closeness relational expectations and interactional richness (Berscheid, Snyder, & Omoto, 1989; Kelley & Burgoon, 1991; Prager, 1989; Tesch & Whitbourne, 1982). Secure in himself and in his attachment with Jesus, Andrew focused on personal effectiveness and efficacy. These might have from his personal competency associated with effective management behavior (Murdock & Scutt, 1997).

With Jesus, the apostle maximized his potentials and exercised situational followership with openness, self-disclosure. With such attachment, the apostle trusts in the style of leadership and includes a pro-social orientation to followers and greater effectiveness (Mayseless, 2006). Logically, "openness in combination with perceptiveness and communication made a person much more effective" (Sharma & Writer, 2015, p. 38). As such, great leaders train leaders, not lifetime followers. The secure attachment Andrew has developed with Jesus or benefitted from Jesus led to the apostle internal security.

Internal security: Internal security is the socio-psychological profile of a person, the selfhood (Khalymon et al., 2020). Andrew's lived out his organization-based self-esteem, a personal worthiness within the work and organizational context to the point of a chronic self-esteem (Pierce et al., 1989). Korman (1976) underlined three major elements that determine an employee's "chronic" self-esteem within the work and organizational context: they are signals from work environment structures, messages from significant others in the workplace, and direct experiences of success (or failure) accompanied by internal attributions to the self as the cause of that success (or failure). With this internal security comes a healthy self-esteem which has a highly positive effect on that of the group. In other words, a positive self-esteem influences group esteem. Andrew's actions also meant a self-categorization, which is a specific form of cognitive categorization which relates to people's sense of self. The apostle chose the social identity approach and "derived his sense of self from, categorizing himself at various levels of abstraction, including at a personal and at collective level" (Steffens et al., 2018, p. 25).

In sum, apostle Andrew left a legacy, not that of position but action. To bring this home, both leaders and followers do think too much of power instead of service. Andrew rightly deconstructed this pre-conceived notion of leadership and followership and epitomized self-efficacy and community building through the adequate and appropriate assessment of problems and delicately solving them, linking, and networking people with and through people and to solutions. Is serving and building community the better side of leadership and/or followership? Why then cling onto position?

Chapter Takeaways

Apostle Andrew deconstructed implicit theories of followership by maximizing his personal effectiveness to generate new ideas and produce change through functional relationships and dialogue. The apostle also possessed informational power (a boy with five loaves of bread) and used them to full effect, avoiding the negative power base that followers might instinctively rely on. With his ability to manage stress and team through strong decision-making skills and communication skills, Andrew adopted the right solution approach, while working with the control influence, and acted to the fulfillment of the needs of the people. Andrew's position and structural power find their validity and strength in embracing the opportunity to perform, the willingness to perform, and the ability to perform (Ivancevich et al., 2009).

Andrew's commitment to build unity and achieve goals went beyond emotional pains and societal norms. Andrew's categorical imperative has some clues to learn from: secure attachment, internal security, know your leader and your calling. This prepares the follower to a genuine definition and for facing hardships with joy and organizational expectations.

Reflective Questions

- Is serving the greatest missing factor in the leader–follower relationship?
- As a leader, do I have a personal respect for who a follower is or in his performances only? Why or why not?
- What are the consequences of not being recognized as unique? How to overcome the lack of visibility through goal achievement and orientation?
- How do self-knowledge and divine calling heal employees from organizational setbacks, frustrations, and unfairness?
- When and how does little mean more?

References

Abu-Bakar, H. A., & McCann, R. M. (2014). Matters of demographic similarity and dissimilarity in supervisor–subordinate relationships and workplace attitudes. *International Journal of Intercultural Relations, 41*, 1–16. https://doi.org/ccj4

Anderson, N., Potočnik, K., & Zhou, J. (2014). Innovation and creativity in organizations: A state-of-the science review, prospective commentary, and guiding framework. *Journal of Management, 40*, 1297–1333. https://doi.org/32w

Argyris, C., & Schön, D. A. (1996). *Organizational learning II: Theory, method, and practice* (p. XXIX). Addison-Wesley. ISBN 0-201-62983-6.

Barclay, W. (1975). *The gospel of John: The new daily study Bible* (Vol. 2). John Know Press.

Berscheid, E., Snyder, M., & Omoto, A. M. (1989). The relationship closeness inventory: Assessing the closeness of interpersonal relationships. *Journal of Personality and Social Psychology, 57*, 792–807. https://doi.org/bz7g6d

Bessant, J., Rush, H., & Trifilova, A. (2015). Crisis-driven innovation: The case of humanitarian innovation. *International Journal of Innovation Management, 19*, 1540014. https://doi.org/gdqfdf

Bisoux, T. (2005). *What makes leaders great*. Aacsb.Edu/Careerconnection. https://bized.aacsb.edu/articles/2005/september/what-makes-leaders-great

Blair, B. A., & Bligh, M. C. (2018). Looking for leadership in all the wrong places: The impact of culture on proactive followership and follower dissent. *Journal of Social Issues, 74*(1), 129–143. https://doi.org/10.1111/josi.12260

Blindu, A. C. (2020). *The role of formal education in developing critical thinking skills of engineering students* (p. 2). Annals of the University Dunarea de Jos of Galati.

Boin, A., Kuipers, S., & Overdijk, W. (2013). Leadership in times of crisis: A framework for assessment. *International Review of Public Administration, 18*, 79–91. https://doi.org/csx3.

Bovon, F. (1994). The words of life in the Acts if the Apostle Andrew. *Harvard Theological Review, 87*(2), 139–154.

Brockner, J., & Higgins, E. T. (2001). Regulatory focus theory: Implications for the study of emotions in the workplace. *Organizational Behavior and Human Decision Processes, 86*, 35–66. https://doi.org/10.1006/obhd.2001.2972

Chaleff, I. (1995). *The courageous follower: Standing up to and for our leaders*. Barrett-Koehler Publishers Inc.

Chapman, E. (2002). The social and ethical implications of changing medical technologies: The views of people living with genetic conditions. *Journal of Health Psychology, 7*, 195–206.

Choi, Y., & Mai-Dalton, R. R. (1998). On the leadership function of self-sacrifice. *The Leadership Quarterly, 9*, 475–501. http://doi.org/c68cbj

Choi, Y., & Mai-Dalton, R. R. (1999). The model of followers' responses to self-sacrificial leadership: An empirical test. *The Leadership Quarterly, 10*, 397–421. http://doi.org/d2vcdc

Donahoe, J. W., & Palmer, D. C. (1994). *Learning and complex behavior*. Allyn & Bacon.

Ennis, R. (1991). Critical thinking: A streamlined conception. *Teaching Philosophy, 14*(1), 5–24.

Facione, P. (2011). Critical thinking: What it is and why it counts. 1998. *Insight Assessment, Pearson Education, 9*, 1–28.

Fortune, D., & Fortune, K. (1987). *Discover your God-given gifts* (Working Paper). Virginia Beach, VA: School of Leadership Studies, Regent University.

Gardner, W. J. (1990). *On leadership*. Free Press.

Hickman, R. G. (2010). *Leading organizations: Perspectives for a new era* (2nd ed.). Sage.

Hoogervorst, N., De Cremer, D., van Dijke, M., & Mayer, D. M. (2012). When do leaders sacrifice? The effects of sense of power and belongingness on leader self-sacrifice. *The Leadership Quarterly, 23*, 883–896. http://doi.org/mmr

Ivancevich, J., Konopaske, R., & Matteson, T. M. (2009). *Organizational behavior and management* (9th ed.). McGraw-Hill Irvin.

John, O. P., & Srivastava, S. (1999). The Big Five trait taxonomy: History, measurement, and theoretical perspectives. In L. A. Pervin & O. P. John (Eds.), *Handbook of personality: Theory and research* (2nd ed., pp. 102–103). Guilford Press.

Johnson, E. R., Lin, S., Kark, R., Djik, V., & King, D. D. (2017). Consequences of regulatory fit for leader-follower relationship quality and commitment. *Journal of Occupational and Organizational Psychology, 90*(3), 379–406.

Kellerman, B. (2008). *Followership: How followers are creating change and changing leaders*. Harvard Business Press.

Kelley, D. L., & Burgoon, J. K. (1991). Understanding marital satisfaction and couple type as functions of relational expectations. *Human Communication Research, 18*, 40–69. https://doi.org/bdgtpw

Kelley, R. (1992). *The power of followership*. Doubleday.

Kelley, R. E. (1988). In praise of followers. *Harvard Business Review, 66*, 142–148.

Kendrick, K. H., & Drew, P. (2016). Imperative directives: Orientations to accountability. *Research on Language and Social Interaction, 49*(1), 1–19.

Khalymon, S., Polovnikov, V., & Volynets, P. (2020). Socio-psychological profile of a person who confidentially provides assistance to the operational unit. *Anuario de Psicología Jurídica, 30*, 13–20. https://doi.org/10.5093/apj2019a10.

Kirk, P., & Shutte, A. M. (2004). Community leadership development. *Community Development Journal, 39*(3), 234–251.

Korman, A. K. (1976). Hypothesis of work behavior revisited and an extension. *Academy of Management Review, 1*, 50–63. https://doi.org/10.5465/AMR.1976.4408762

Kotter's. (1996). *Leading change*. Harvard Business School Press.

Lanaj, K., Chang, C.-H. "D.", & Johnson, R. E. (2012). Regulatory focus and work-related outcomes: A review and meta-analysis. *Psychological Bulletin, 138*(5), 998–1034. https://doi.org/10.1037/a0027723

Laurie, G. (1952). *Breakfast with Jesus*. Tyndale House Pub. ISBN-13: 9780842353281

Lipman-Blumen, J. (1996). *The connective edge: Leading in an interdependent world*. Jossey-Bass.

Lipman-Blumen, J. (2000). *Connective leadership: Managing in a changing world*. Oxford University Press.

Lipman-Blumen, J. (2010). Connective leadership: What business needs to learn from academe. *Change: The Magazine of Higher Learning, 30*(1), 49–53.

Luo, W., Song, L. J., Gebert, D. R., Zhang, K., & Feng, Y. (2016). How does leader communication styles promote employees' commitment at times of change? *Journal of Organizational Change Management, 29*, 242–262. https://doi.org/ccj7.

MacDougall, D. (1992). Films of memory. *Visual Anthropology Review, 8*(1), 29.

Mayseless, O. (2006). Studying parenting representations as a window to parents' internal working model of caregiving. In O. Mayseless (Ed.), *Parenting representations: Theory, research, and clinical implications* (pp. 3–40). Cambridge University Press.

Murdock, A., & Scutt, C. N. (1997). *Personal effectiveness* (3rd ed.). Routledge.

Oyetunji, C. O. (2013). The relationship between followership style and job performance in Botswana private universities. *International Education Studies, 6*(2), 179–187.

Pierce, J. L., Gardner, D. G., Cummings, L. L., & Dunham, R. B. (1989). Organization-based self-esteem: Construct definition, operationalization, and validation. *Academy of Management Journal, 32*, 622–648. https://doi.org/10.2307/256437

Prager, K. J. (1989). Intimacy status and couple communication. *Journal of Social and Personal Relationships, 6*, 435–449. https://doi.org/bmfmmp

Riggs, N. R., Jahromi, L. B., Razza, R. P., Dillworth-Bart, J. E., & Mueller, U. (2006). Executive function and the promotion of social-emotional competence. *Journal of Applied Developmental Psychology, 27*, 300–309.

Robertson, A. T. (1960). *Word pictures in the new testament* (Vol. v). Baker Book House.

Rokeach, M. (1973). *The nature of human values*. The Free Press.

Shamir, B. (2007). From passive recipients to active co-producers: Followers' roles in the leadership process. In B. Shamir, R. Pillai, M. Bligh, & M. Uhl-Bien (Eds.), *Follower-centered perspectives on leadership: A tribute to the memory of James R. Meindl* (pp. ix–xxxix). Information Age Publishers

Sharma, R., & Writer, S. (2015). Cognitive-behavioral approach in mentoring college students for personal effectiveness: An empirical study. *Scholedge International Journal of multidisciplinary & Allied Studies, 2*(5), 36–42. ISSN-2394–336x.

Shorley, S. H., & Chaffin, S. J. (2018). Leader-follower attachment: Implications assessment in organizational contexts. *Journal of Personality Assessment, 100*(5), 518–528. https://doi.org/10.1080/00223891.2018.1472100

Steffens, N. K., Haslam, S. A., Jetten, J., & Mols, F. (2018). Our followers, our lions, theirs are sheep: How social identity shapes theories about followership and social influence. *Political Psychology, 39*(1), 23–42.

St Andrew Parish. (2020). *About St. Andrew, Our Patron Saint*. Retrieved this September 8, 2020 from http://www.standrewparish.cc/about-us/about-st-andrew-our-patron-saint/

Tesch, S. A., & Whitbourne, S. K. (1982). Intimacy and identity status in young adults. *Journal of Personality and Social Psychology, 43*(5), 1041–1051.

Torrance, E. P., Ball, O., & Safter, H. T. (1992). *Torrance test of creative thinking streamlined scoring guide figural and B. Bensenville*. Scholastic Testing Service Inc.

Uhl-Bien, M., Riggio, R. E., Lowe, K. B., & Carsten, M. K. (2014). Followership theory: A review and research agenda. *The Leadership Quarterly, 25*, 83–104. https://doi.org/10.1016/j.leaqua.2013.11.007

Vickers, M. H. (2001). *Work and unseen chronic illness: Silent voices*. Routledge. ISBN: 0415243475

Walvoord, F. J., & Zuck, B. Y. (1985). *The Bible knowledge commentary: An exposition of the scriptures by Dallas Seminary Faculty- New testament*. Victor Books.

Williams, K. C., & Spiro, L. R. (1985). Communication style in the salesperson-customer dyad. *Journal of Marketing Research, 22*(4), 434–442.

Winston, B. (2002). *Be god leader for god's sake. From values to behaviors*. A revision of the 1997 edition of Be a Manager for God's Sake. Regent University.

Yang, F., Qian, J., Tang, L., & Zhang, L. (2016). No long take a tree for the forest: A cross-level learning related perspective on individual innovative behavior. *Journal of Management & Organization, 22*, 291–310. https://doi.org/cszf.

Yrle, A. C., Hartman, S., & Galle, W. P. (2002). An investigation of relationships between communication style and leader–member exchange. *Journal of Communication Management, 6*, 257–268. https://doi.org/dgr4f7

Zhao, W., Ye, C., & Ding, X. (2020). *Preferred service investment in the dual-channel supply chain: Leader-follower relationships and product characteristics*. Mathematical Problems in Engineering. Retrieved June 8, 2020 from http://web.a.ebscohost.com.ezproxy.regent.edu:2048/ehost/pdfviewer/pdfviewer?vid=3&sid=802ac092-0e85-4ab8-af1c-a936c92fbcde%40sessionmgr4006

Zimmerman, B. J. (2000). Attaining self-regulation: A social cognitive perspective. In M. Boekaerts, P. R., Pintrich, & M. Zeidner (Eds.), *Handbook of self-regulation*. Academic Press.

CHAPTER 9

Open Vessels and Flowing Waters: The Followership Legacy of Apostle John

Nancy Nkirote Muriuki and Percy Opio

Who Is John the Apostle?

John, who is the subject of this chapter, was among the 12 disciples whom Jesus personally called to follow Him. A review of the New Testament in the Bible reveals that he is believed to be the author of the Gospel according to St. John (deSilva, 2004). John is introduced to the world in Mathew 4:21–22 (ESV) as one of two fishermen and "sons of Zebedee" that immediately abandoned their father and fishing business to follow Jesus who later christened them Boanerges, or "Sons of Thunder" (Mark 3:17) because of their zeal in following Him. The fact that John was willing to stop what he was doing to follow Jesus shows his zeal. John

N. N. Muriuki (✉) · P. Opio
Regent University, Virginia Beach, VA, USA
e-mail: Nancy.Muriuki@pacuniversity.ac.ke

P. Opio
e-mail: percy.opio@pacuniversity.ac.ke

D. J. Dean and R. B. Huizinga (eds.), *Followership and Faith at Work*, Christian Faith Perspectives in Leadership and Business,
https://doi.org/10.1007/978-3-030-90614-6_9

was also referred to by Paul, another apostle, as one of the pillars of the Church (Galatians 2:7–9, ESV). Schaff (2002) summarizes John's character as "He is at once the apostle, the evangelist, and the seer, of the new covenant" (p. 253). He goes further to state that John was the "…bosom-friend of Jesus who had become his most perfect reflection so far as any human being can reflect the ideal of divine-human purity and holiness (p. 253)." It is revealed that John even referred to himself as "the one whom Jesus loved" (John 13:23, John 19:26, John 20:2, John 21:7, John 21:20, ESV). Instances where Jesus wanted to reveal events to a select few from among His disciples disclose that John was always among them—when Jesus raised Jairus' daughter from the dead (Mark 5:37, ESV); during the transfiguration (Matthew 17:1–11, Mark 9:2–8, Luke 9:28–36, ESV); and when Jesus prayed at the Garden of Gethsemane on the night of the betrayal (Matthew 26:36–46, ESV). John's zeal as a follower of Jesus is also reflected in his uncompromising character when he asked if Jesus would allow him to "call fire from heaven" to consume those who differed in their beliefs (Luke 9:54, ESV). John's importance as a follower is further brought to the fore during Jesus' crucifixion (John 19:26–27, ESV) when Jesus asked John to take care of his (Jesus') mother. After resurrection, the zealous John outrun his fellow disciple (Simon Peter) when they heard that Jesus' body was taken out of the tomb (John 20:1–10, ESV)—the fact that John was among the first to be informed demonstrates his closeness to Jesus. So fundamental to the New Testament is John as he went on to contribute five books (The Gospel of John, 1 John, 2 John, 3 John and Revelation)—more than any other disciples, and became one of the strongest pillars of the Early Church.

Research Statement

Leaders-centric research has dominated the scholarly world since the twentieth century while followership received little or no attention until the late 1980's when Robert Kelly wrote his seminal article "In Praise of Followers" (Martin, 2015). Kelly argued that despite the neglect, followers contributed to organizational outcomes just as leaders do. Since Kelly's inaugural work, the concept of followership has continued to grow exploring the subject in a twofold approach; (a) from a role based perspective considering followership within a hierarchical structure and (b) from a relational construct based on how followers relate to leaders in driving organizational results (Sarver, 2020). One area where the application of both approaches is seen to have harvested tremendous results is in the spread of the Christian gospel through the work of Jesus Christ and his first twelve followers (disciples).

Whereas Jesus' leadership model has been applied in many organizational settings, there is scanty citation of the impact of his follower-centric approaches whose influence surpassed his physical presence. This chapter will explore the follower–leader relationship between the apostle John and Jesus to unfold the follower development of John and its transcending impact on the mission of his leader. The chapter will focus on the following two research questions:

1. What can we learn from the follower-leader experience of John and Jesus' relationship?
2. How can we apply the learnings of apostle John's follower-leader experience in the modern-day workplace?

Introduction

The book of John in the Bible gives us a first-hand encounter of John's followership of Jesus when Jesus was physically present with him. John's subsequent writings—1 John, 2 John, 3 John, and Revelation, reveal a scenario where John's followership of Jesus continues to develop and is unaffected by Jesus' physical absence. However, in between Jesus' crucifixion, death, and burial (John 19:17–42, ESV) and His resurrection and appearance to the disciples (John 20–21, ESV), we experience a scenario where the disciples appear to be "absent" and dejected (John 20:9–10, ESV). They did not participate in preparing Jesus' body for the tomb (John 19:38–42, ESV). They seemed to have gone back to their old ways—fishing (John 21:1–3, ESV) ... until Jesus appears again (John 21:4–9, ESV) and the scene comes back to life. The follower-leader relationship seems to be "restored"—if it ever was disrupted. This chapter explores lessons on followership from Jesus and His disciple—John (also known as one of the son of Zebedee). It begins with a historical review of John's context to understand what followership meant during the Early Church era.

The chapter will also reveal how these insights can be applied in organizations today. A critical analysis of John's followership will show similarities with selected scholarly perspectives. The concept of "open vessels and flowing waters" implies a follower-leader relationship that is open, genuine, transparent, transformational and transcends the leader's physical presence. It reveals a follower–leader relationship that influences the follower beyond the formal relationship with the organization or the leader.

Contextualizing Followership in the Early Church

An academic and cultural analysis of followership will be used to get a glimpse into how people in the Early Church era perceived followership. DeSilva (2004) states that while there is no clear indication of the place and time, a papyrus fragment of part of John's Gospel discovered in Egypt places the writing in the early second or late first century. According to Fergusson (2013), the Roman, Greek, and Jews' integrated perspectives influenced the early Christian's worldview. The Romans provided political and administrative leadership, which influenced the development of the church's hierarchy, while the Greek's influence was mainly in language, education, literature, and philosophy. The Jewish influence was religious.

The early Christians shared values that guided their social interaction, relationships, and ordering of the world—concepts like purity and pollution, honor and shame, patronage and reciprocity, and family were common themes that defined their worldview (DeSilva, 2004). These themes played a crucial role in ordering their world, attaining social status, recognizing leadership, and maintaining reputation. It can be argued, therefore, that recurring themes and the impact of the three worldviews—Roman, Greek, and Jewish, influenced followership. Robbins (1996) states that an analysis of a text's social and cultural texture can reveal the social and cultural person living in a world of particular text. A brief analysis of selected social and cultural texture will help show how following Jesus can be perceived against the respective recurring themes of purity and pollution, honor and shame, patronage and reciprocity, and family.

The discourse in John 1:29–51 reveals how Jesus called the first disciples and the basis upon which they voluntarily decided to follow Him. Through the use of Robbin's (1996) social and cultural texture analysis, the world of the disciples and Jesus will be revealed. John 1:29–34, ESV shows a conversionist view of the world as sinful (vs. 29), and that salvation can be attained through a supernatural transformation of oneself through a process of baptism (vs. 33) and because of the presence of a new "subjective orientation" (vs. 29, 34, 36, 38, 41, 45). The use of purity codes like "Lamb of God," "Spirit," "Holy Spirit," "Son of God," "Rabbi," "Messiah," "King of Israel" and "law" (vs. 29, 32, 33) classify Jesus' status and validates Him as one worthy of being followed. By following Jesus, therefore, it was possible to attain honor and purity in a shameful and polluted world.

In verses 31–51, the action moves to the calling of followers, and the reader is introduced to dyadic contracts based on the concept of patronage and reciprocity as a result of following Jesus (vs. 42, 49–51). With the Hebrews perceiving God as their patron (DeSilva, 2004) and the purity codes validating Jesus' status in proximity to God, it was possible to achieve this relationship of patronage and reciprocity together with honor by following Jesus. Toward the end of the discourse (vs. 43–51), we encounter the riposte between Philip and Nathaniel, where the former tells the latter "We have found him of whom Moses wrote about in the Law and also the prophets wrote, Jesus of Nazareth" (vs. 45). Nathaniel's response is "Can anything good from Nazareth?" (vs. 46). Philip then challenges Nathaniel to "Come and see" (vs. 46). The result of this riposte is the conversion of Nathaniel into a follower of Jesus (vs. 49–51), re-validation of Jesus' status as one who would genuinely bring honor, purity, and is worthy patronage.

Over the past several years, followership has been gaining interest from several scholars as the growing importance of the follower to the leader's success continues to be highlighted. The following section juxtaposes scholarly and African cultural perspectives of followership with a Biblical context.

Perspectives of Followership

Scholars have analyzed the leader-follower relationship to arrive at different follower traits and behavior linked to a leader's success. While there may be different perspectives, one area of agreement is that the follower-leader relationship determines the leader's success (Chaleff, 2009; Kelley, 2008; Kellerman, 2008). These perspectives reveal that although the focus has always been the leader in delivering positive organizational performance, followers play a crucial role.

In Acts 1:8, before His ascension into heaven, Jesus' expectation of His followers (disciples) was to go out and be His witnesses across the world after the Holy Spirit came upon them. Challef (2009) perceives followership as a courageous process of standing up to and for leaders and states that "Whether we lead or follow, we are responsible for our actions, and we share responsibility for the actions of those whom we can influence" (p. 13). This statement implies that followers too have responsibilities and have the power of influence over others—one of the duties bestowed upon the disciples as followers was to influence the world. Chaleff (2009) defines effective followership from seven dimensions of courageous behavior—taking responsibility, serving, challenging, transformative action, taking moral action, speaking to hierarchy, and listening to followers. He further defines followership and leadership roles as inevitable and interchangeable within the social context. He states that followers should not revolve around the leader but the core values and purpose of the organization—the leader's alignment to the purpose and core values to which the follower subscribes determines the follower-leader relationship. Winston (2002) states that employees and followers prefer leaders who are honest, open, and who positively steer the organization within a context of love—what he refers to as "agapao" leadership. The Beatitudes (Mathew 5:1–12, ESV) define the values that Jesus' followers should revolve around.

Kellerman (2008) perceives followers as influencers and states that while leaders (good or bad) are entirely dependent on followers to fulfill their vision, the word "follower" has been disliked and has connotations that suggest passivity and dependency. However, unlike Chaleff (2009) and Kellerman (2007) perceives follower effectiveness from a typology of engagement levels. These levels include; *isolates*—detached and uninvolved; *bystanders*—observers who go unnoticed; *participants*—engaged and driven by their passion; *activist*—driven by strong feelings about the leader or organization; and *diehards*—driven by their cause. Kellerman further states that while the leader needs to know whether participants, activists, and diehard followers support them or not, this support (or lack of it) is inconsequential concerning the isolates or bystanders' effectiveness. In Mathew 10:5–42 (ESV), Jesus sends out His Twelve Apostles with clear instructions of where to go and what to do (vs. 5–15), what to expect (vs. 16–25), and how to respond (vs. 26–33). He also makes them aware of the level of dedication to Him that He expects from them (vs. 34–39). There is no room for isolates and bystanders but an inclination toward activists and diehards.

Kelley (2008) arrived at five styles of followership that he uses to differentiate followers; *passive* followers—dependent on the leader for motivation; *yes-people* or conformists—depend on the leader for direction; *alienated* followers—independent thinkers but exude negative energy; the *pragmatics*—watch the direction the wind is blowing and follow in order to survive; and the *star* followers—independent thinkers who engage and have positive energy. Jesus' expectations of His disciples would not accommodate what Kelley classified as passive, alienated, or pragmatic followers. While the conformist is desirable for values-alignment and the initial call to follow and acknowledge Jesus as Son of God (Mathew 10; Mark 1:16–20; Luke 5:11), star followership was expected of each follower to achieve the purpose for which Jesus came to earth (Mathew:10; Luke 9:1–6).

From an African perspective, Ubuntu is a worldview encompassing a value system of communalism and interdependence of humanity that should be the basis of living in harmony, and for societal governance (Idoniboye-Obu & Whetho, 2013). Ubuntu means the belief that a person is a person through other people—I am because we are (ibid). A study by Thomas (2014) reveals that Africans tend to identify more with groups because of high in-group collectivism instead of individuality. The research further shows that high collectivism causes followers to avoid challenging leadership and encourages them to become less critical thinkers. These perspectives (Ubuntu and in-group collectivism) imply that communal values and the desire for societal harmony influence followership in an African context. Followership can also be a means for self-preservation—I am because we are, and it is, therefore, more comfortable to follow a leader based on shared ethnic or cultural background. In John 14:6, ESV Jesus says, "I am the way, the truth, and the life. No one comes to the Father except through me." In verses 11–13 of the same chapter, He says, "Truly, truly, I say to you, whoever believes in me will also do the works that I do; and greater works than these will he do because I am going to the Father. Whatever you ask in my name, this I will do, that the Father may be glorified in the Son." While followership from this perspective leads to self-preservation (of the human soul), it is not meant to glorify the community but the Father because, in this case, "I am because He is."

In a global environment characterized as volatile, uncertain, and ambiguous (VUCA), not only influential leaders are needed to navigate through this terrain, but also courageous, exemplary, and diehard followers. Can any lessons be applied from John's follower relation with

Jesus? The next sections seek to answer this question by first exploring John's follower relation with Jesus and his followership characteristics.

Followership According to Jesus

The words "follow me" appear to be the keywords Jesus used to recruit his followers Peter, Andrew, John, James, and Paul (Mathew 4:18–22, 3:16–20; Luke 5:1–11; Mark 1:16–20; John 1:35–51, ESV). The word "*follow*" occurs at least 90 times in the four gospels, and so it may be argued that, to a large extent, Jesus defined the philosophy followership. John and other disciples were fishermen before they met Jesus, who would make them fishers of men; thus, the request to "follow me" had a clear purpose; the followership vision, mission, and process were apparent right from the point of initial calling. According to Jesus, followers are not called to remain followers forever but rather to learn from the leader and take over the responsibilities to fulfill the mission, which in His case is making more and more followers who would, in turn, become leaders as they made more followers. The cycle would continue forever to include every generation.

Jesus' followership perspective was about total commitment. On calling John and his brother James, He asked them to "come and follow me," and immediately they left their father and fishing business to follow Him. The calling required quick decision-making with complete focus and no turning back (loyalty). The Bible is silent about what happened to Zebedee after his sons and Jesus left him, so it would appear that Jesus considered the mission that he had come to fulfill more important than anything else. He expected his followers to act with haste and leave everything else behind—a perspective expressed repeatedly in the gospels; "… If you would be perfect, go, sell what you possess and give to the poor, and you will have treasure in heaven; and come, follow me" (Mathew 19:21, ESV), "So therefore, any one of you who does not renounce all that he has cannot be my disciple" (Luke 14:33, ESV), "…. If anyone would come after me, let him deny himself and take up his cross and follow me" (Mathew 16:24, ESV).

For Christ, followership did not require prior training or preparation though He never recruited any idler. He transformed his followers into disciples portraying a strategic leadership/followership approach. He took them to his first mission in Galilee and nearby towns, leading by example and later on assembled them to explain His expectation (Mathew 4, 5, 6,

7). Things flowed from one step to another within an open transformative environment. As a result, John's followership characteristics are highly reflective of his close walk with Jesus.

John and Jesus' Relationship

The depth of John's followership is best described by the words in Acts 4:13, ESV "Now when they saw the boldness of Peter and John, and perceived that they were uneducated, common men, they were astonished. And they recognized that they had been with Jesus." Peter and John had met and healed a lame man as they entered the temple for prayers and were arrested preaching the resurrection message. They were, however, freed and the people testified that indeed, they had been with Jesus.

Zebedee's sons became followers of Jesus without prior notice or preparation. Like the other first disciples, they were picked from their natural situations performing what their regular duties then were—fishing (Mathew 4:18–22, ESV). Notably, Zebedee's sons made an instant response to the call as "immediately they left the boat and their father, and followed Him" (Mathew 4:22, ESV). This propitious action is manifested in John's passionate followership of Jesus that transcended their physical presence with each other. The Bible testifies of the apostle's zealous followership marked with his expressions of unsurpassed spiritual depth calling people to believe; "For God so loved the world that he gave his only begotten Son that whoever believes in him should not perish but have eternal life" (John 3:16, ESV); "If we say that we have no sin, we deceive ourselves, and the truth is not in us" (1 John 1:8, ESV); "In the beginning was the Word and the Word was with God, and the Word was God" (1 John 1:1, ESV).

The depth of their relationship is further demonstrated by the closing words in John's gospel when he states that "Now there are also many other things that Jesus did. Were every one of them to be written, I suppose that the world itself could not contain the books that would be written" (John 21:25, ESV). John is also referred to as "the disciple whom Jesus loved," "son of thunder," "Evangelist," "John the Elder," "John the Apostle," and the "Pillar" due to his supportive role in the early church. These titles reveal John's transformation from a fisherman to an influential public speaker and author.

The relationship can be described as an undisrupted encounter of profound love and understanding (John 13:23; 19:26; 21:17; 20:2, ESV) as John walked with Jesus all through even to the cross when the others could not. John was also part of Jesus' inner circle (Mark 5:37; Mathew 1:7–12. 26:37, ESV). On three occasions, Peter, James, and John witnessed special events that the other disciples did not; (i) raising of Jairus' daughter from the dead (Mark 5:37); (ii) the glory of His transfiguration (Mathew 17:1–11, Mark 9:2–8, Luke 9:28–36, ESV), and (iii) betrayal night experience—in the Garden of Gethsemane where they prayed and kept watch at His instruction (Mathew 26:36–46, ESV).

But of all John's accounts, the book of Revelation is the most fascinating. First, it is believed that John was exiled by the anti-Christ authorities of the time when the revelation of Jesus came upon him. The prologue of the book records, " I, John, your brother and partner in the tribulation and the kingdom and the patient endurance that are in Jesus, was on the island called Patmos on account of the word of God and the testimony of Jesus" (1:9, ESV). According to Collins quoted by Achtemeier (1985):

> Early tradition says that John was banished to Patmos by the Roman authorities. This tradition is credible because banishment was a common punishment used during the Imperial period for several offenses. Among such violations were the practices of magic and astrology. The Romans viewed a prophecy as belonging to the same category, whether Pagan, Jewish, or Christian. Prophecy with political implications, like that expressed by John in the Book of Revelation, would have been perceived as a threat to Roman political power and order. Three of the islands in the Sporades were places where political offenders were banished. (p. 755)

Secondly, the book reveals that the spirit which was in John during Jesus' physical presence on earth remained intact even during Jesus's physical absence, hence the vision of the apostle—Jesus made it known by sending his angel to His servant John, who testifies to everything he saw (1:1–2, ESV). Other accounts of the relationship include John's gospel, first, second, and third Letters. While residing at Ephesus, a request was made by some elders in Asia to write the gospel to thwart and disprove unorthodox messages about the nature and deity of Jesus' (Zondervan, 2003; Fredriksen, 1991). The theme of the gospel is Jesus, Son of God. According to John (20:31, ESV), the purpose of the gospel is "so that you may believe that Jesus is the Christ, the Son of God, and that by believing you may have life in his name." John declares—"we have seen 'his glory'" (1:14, ESV) and ends with a confession "My Lord and my God" (20:28, ESV). The word "believe" is used multiple times referring to the call for salvation—an eternal commitment to Christ; to John, followership was a total commitment to the leader.

John emphasizes that Jesus is the truth, the holy spirit is the spirit of truth and God's word is truth, and the truth sets people free (8:32, ESV) and makes them clean (15:3, ESV). His choice of words symbolizes a complete mental transformation; "light" "love" "flesh" "witness" "know" "darkness," "world." Jesus is light and shines in the darkness (1:4–5, ESV). His aggressiveness in his leader's defense is revealed when he states that the temple must not be turned into a marketplace—it's a house of prayer (John 2:14–15, ESV).

In the Epistles, John's theme is truth and righteousness, exhorting his spiritual children (followers) to lead a life of holiness, cautioning the church against those who opposed the apostolic truth (1st 2nd and 3rd John). For the apostle, Christian love must discern between false and truth and not provide an "open door" to false teachings. John allows no compromise between light and darkness, truth and lies, righteousness and sin, or even love and hate. The weight of these messages demonstrate the depth of John's followership. Thus, the mission of his leader is emphasized with complete clarity and certainty.

On the other hand, Jesus approached the recruitment, training, and deployment of John strategically as revealed by the following:

1. Initiation of the disciples into ministry.
   Immediately after Zebedee's sons left their fishing business and followed Jesus, He toured Galilee and beyond on a mission of healing and preaching in which they accompanied him (Mathew 4:23-25 ESV).

   > And Jesus went about all Galilee, teaching in their synagogues, preaching the gospel of the Kingdom, and healing all kinds of sickness and all kinds of disease among the people. Then His fame went throughout all Syria; and they brought to Him all sick people who were afflicted with various diseases and torments, and those who were demon-possessed, epileptics, and paralytics; and

> He healed them. Great multitudes followed Him—from Galilee, and *from* Decapolis, Jerusalem, Judea, and beyond the Jordan.

This strategy of exposure to the workings of Jesus inducted John to what Jesus had invited them to do "to make you fishers of Men" (Mathew 4:19, ESV). Interestingly, Jesus does not appear to have talked much after asking them to "come and follow me" but instead rolled into action. The growing success and fame of Jesus initiated and inspired John into the ministry as great multitudes followed Jesus from all the four cities he first preached.

2. Introduction to kingdom values and principles.
   Jesus introduced his disciples to Kingdom values and principles as a fundamental step toward their transformation. After the healing and preaching mission in Galilee, Jesus retreated to a mountain and the disciples followed him there. Again, without wasting any time, He began to enlist the expected behavioral values in kingdom business; humility, patience, kindness, peace-making, righteousness, empathy, integrity, mercifulness, and perseverance all expressed as the Beatitudes (Mathew 5:1–12, ESV).
   His induction continued as He explained to them who they were as His followers and what their responsibilities would be which included being "light and salt of the earth" and "going an extra mile." He urged them to lay up their treasures in heaven and to keep seeking, asking and knocking at their heavenly father, and to build on the rock that was Him so that they could bear the good fruit of bringing many to the Kingdom- not only through preaching but also by living as good examples (Mathew 5,6,7, ESV).
3. Commissioning and continuous training
   Jesus formalized his team by naming the twelve of whom the apostle John was part. The Scriptures record that:

> Jesus went up on a mountainside and called to him those he wanted, and they came to him. He appointed twelve that they might be with him and that he might send them out to preach and to have authority to drive out demons. These are the twelve he appointed: Simon (to whom he gave the name Peter), James son of Zebedee and his brother John (to them he gave the name Boanerges, which means "sons of thunder") Andrew, and Philip, and Bartholomew, and Matthew, and Thomas, and James the son of Alphaeus, and

> Thaddaeus, and Simon the Zealot, and Judas Iscariot, who betrayed him (Mark 3:13–19, ESV).

> These pronouncements take the relationship of John and Jesus to another level where the apostle among his colleagues are now appointed to act on His behalf "...that they might be with him and that he might send them to preach and have authority to drive out demons" (Mark 3:14–15, ESV). According to (Kelley, 1992), it is not Jesus but his disciples who changed the world.

Jesus nicknamed John and his brother James Boanerges. The scripture is silent about any explanation for this reference. However, it may be due to their passionate defense of Jesus' mission (Mark 3:17, ESV) and Jesus getting a divine insight into their inner commitment. According to the scriptures, some Samaritans did not welcome Jesus into their village, so James and John were furious and wanted to call fire from heaven. Nevertheless, Jesus declined their request, and instead, reprimanded them. The brothers also seem to have deciphered what the Kingdom would be like and wanted to be there soon. After Jesus told them about his suffering, their request was to... "Grant us to sit, one at your right hand and one at your left, in your glory..." (Mark 10:35–44, ESV). But again, Jesus challenged them. While the other disciples found this request inappropriate, it would signal the zeal of their followership of Jesus.

Finally, on the cross, Jesus delegated the responsibility of caring for his mother to John (John 19:26–27, ESV). John remained in Jerusalem, caring for her and preaching the gospel while the other disciples went back to fishing. After resurrection, John outran Peter and was the first to witness the empty tomb on getting information that Jesus' body was no longer inside (John 20:1–10, ESV). After being with Jesus, John later became a church elder in Asia (current-day Turkey).

The above description of John and Jesus' relationship provides an understanding of John's followership characteristics, further analyzed below.

Followership Characteristics of John

As part of the classification of John's followership characteristics, his strengths and weaknesses are summarized and mapped with the selected scholarly typologies.

John's Strengths

1. Instantaneous-his swift response to leave his father and fishing business to follow Jesus was remarkable. This strength is also demonstrated when he ran to the tomb upon learning that Jesus's body was not there.
2. Commitment-John followed Jesus faithfully with total loyalty without wavering even in the face of danger.
3. Aggressive-Jesus nicknamed John and his brother "sons of thunder." The apostle's expressions in the scriptures are revealed in strong non-compromising words, for instance, "you must be born again." He challenged situations, especially when he threatened to call fire from heaven when a village refused to entertain Jesus.
4. Open and Transparent-John concealed neither his thoughts nor his feelings. On two occasions, he advised Jesus even at the risk of a reprimand. He wanted to call fire from heaven and stop a man who was not a disciple from preaching the gospel.
5. Transformational-John transformed from a fisherman to an apostle.
6. The apostle of love-Though not mentioned directly, John is described as the "apostle of love."
7. Servant Follower-Like servant leaders, the apostle valued his leader. He was humble as he avoided naming himself as the "apostle of love" in the gospel.
8. High Emotional Intelligence-The apostle John empathized with Jesus so that when Jesus rebuked him, John understood and changed his attitude. When Jesus asked him to take care of his mother, he did not question him.
9. Transcending Followership-John continued to relate with Jesus long after their physical presence with each other, as evidenced by the books of the Bible he authored.

John's Weaknesses

1. Temperamental-John and his brother were nicknamed "sons of thunder," probably because of their quick temper. The fact that John wanted to call fire from heaven further shows this nature.
2. Task Orientation-Though John speaks loudly and meticulously about love, he appears to have been focused on the task as we see Peter speaking most of the time when they were together.

Classification of John's Followership

The above summary depicts John as an engaged diehard in the words of Kellerman (1992), while a star follower according to Kelley (2008), and possesses all the characteristics of a courageous follower in Challef's analysis. He is a Partner (high support and high challenge) with Christ, his leader. The Table 9.1 summarizes John's followership typologies. In the African context, the Ubuntu concept is demonstrated in Jesus and John dependability.

Chaleff (2009) defines follower as "…the condition that permits leadership to exist and gives it strength" and that "Dynamic followers recognize their own aspirations in the leader's vision …follow their own light, which the leader intensifies... give 110 percent... because they are inspired... are interdependent with the leader... add value to both themselves and the leader through this relationship" (pg. 19). Apostle John's follower-leader relationship with Jesus exemplifies Challef's (2009) perspective of followership . While John's characteristics exhibit aspects of Kellerman's , Kelley's, and the Ubuntu model of followership, a greater inclination can be seen toward Challef's five dimensions of courageous followership—the courage... to serve, ... to challenge, ... to participate in transformation, ... to take moral action, ... to speak to hierarchy.

Table 9.1 John's followership typology

Characteristic	*Typology*			
	Ira Chaleff	*Barbara Kellerman*	*Robert Kelley*	*Ubuntu traits*
Instantaneous	Taking action	Participant	Conformist	Yes
Commitment	Responsibility	Activist	Star	Yes
Aggressive	Challenging	Diehard	Star	Yes
Open & Transparent	Responsibility	Diehard	Star	Yes
Love	Moral action	Activist	Star	Yes
Servant Follower	Serving	Diehards	Star	Yes
Emotional Intelligence	Moral action	Activist	Star	Yes
Transcending	Transformative Action	Activist	Star	Yes
Temperamental	Challenging	Diehard	Star	No
Task-Oriented	Responsibility	Activist	Star	Yes

The reemergence of epidemics (SAR-CoV-1, SAR-CoV-2, Ebola) and pandemics (COVID-19) have had adverse social and economic effects on regional and global populations respectively. It is at a time like now that courageous followers like apostle John are needed. The millions of health workers who put themselves at risk because of their passion to serve humanity; the workers who have accepted pay-cuts or no pay but continue to work diligently to keep their organizations running; the workers who will challenge their leaders to apply a humane approach to declaring employees redundant; and those working diligently to develop treatment or vaccines; and most of all the people reaching out to help the needy—these are the courageous followers who are ensuring that the world recovers from these crises. It is important for leaders to recognize these followers as the true heroes that navigated us through the storms just as Jesus recognized John.

Open Vessels and Flowing Waters Model of Followership

John's relationship with Jesus presents a fascinating transformational journey whose impact is infinite. The world continues to learn from the teachings of Jesus Christ and his example of a visionary servant leader who mentored his disciples and left the most amazing succession plan on earth. The twelve disciples have multiplied into millions across the world, including those of us writing this book over 2000 years after the events occurred. Since Jesus met his disciples, who experienced a physical follower-leader relationship, his leadership influence flowed into willing hearts, hereby described as "open vessels" into whom he deposited the word of his mission. But even Jesus, as God's messenger, can be described as an open vessel for he described himself as being sent (follower); this channel of God—Jesus-Disciples has remained open since Jesus came. Again, we see John demonstrating an atmosphere of ease when giving his leader a suggestion in one of their encounters.

The development of John from fisherman to the disciple of love and a sage who authored several books in the New Testament would not have been possible if Jesus, his leader, did not open himself to him fully and keep the relationship flowing so much so that the Holy Spirit was able to reveal to John what to write in the Book of Revelation. Without this "open vessel and flowing waters" system, the leader's influence on the follower is short-lived and will not lead to the transformation of the person or the organization. In the words of Chaleff (2009), "The leader's openness to diversity, empowering others, breakthrough thinking, and being challenged and learning from followers will drop precipitously. Followers will abandon their unique perspectives and healthy dissension, which are at the heart of the creative process and innovation" (p. 5).

A vital aspect of the relationship between Jesus and John is that John's followership of Jesus transcended their physical interaction on earth and was intact even after Jesus' ascension to heaven, and when John played the role of the leader in different situations. As Jesus was ending his earthly mission, he delegated the responsibility for taking care of his mother to John.

John preserved his relationship with Jesus in writing five books of the Bible. This act of receiving from Jesus and sharing from his mind and heart his experiences with Jesus and things yet to come seen in a vision in itself represents an open vessel (John) receiving living water flowing (message of the Kingdom) from Jesus. Jesus also was an open vessel, freely pouring living water to whosever believed. In turn, the apostle John becomes the open vessel from which flows living water (God's word in the scriptures) that is read by whosever wills. The Book of Revelation marks a continued spiritual flow of divine mysteries symbolizing a continual reflection of and meditations on John's experiences with Jesus. These revelations imply that follower experiences/influences from the leader continue to produce impact long after their physical presence is over. According to Jesus, followership is not a short-term relationship but one that lasts forever with great rewards here on earth and in the life to come (Mathew 19:27–29, ESV). Thus, *Open Vessels and Flowing Waters Followership Model* depicts a followership system which is;

1. Transparent-There are no barriers to creative thinking by the follower and the leader freely empowers.
2. Transformational-Continuous, open learning and unlearning transcends the physical presence of the leader (fisherman to "fisher of men").
3. Genuine-There are no unnecessary disruptions to followership (even though the working environment is open and free of thinking/speaking barriers—flowing waters—followers do not just leave anyhow—retention is high not through coercion but free will).
4. Open-The relationship is open all the time—during extraordinary and challenging times e.g., crucifixion, one continues to think about

the other all the time. Jesus prayed for himself, his disciples, and those who would become their followers (flowing waters). Thus, the mission of Christ would continue long after Him and also after the disciples

5. Transcending-There is progressive growth—the relationship is continuous (progressive development) for the leader, follower, and the organization—a follower is identified, recruited, and prepared to take over from the leader. It ends up creating leaders out of followers, leaders transforming followers for lasting growth and impact that not even the physical presence can stop. The employment relationship should not lead to deterioration or death (stress, ill-health etc.) but instead endeavor to be a river of life (Revelation 22: 1–3). Families of the follower, their social circles and society at large are positively influenced by how the leader has impacted the follower as illustrated in Fig. 9.1.

Application of John's Followership Characteristics to the Contemporary Workplace

The nature of organizations dictates that followership and leadership coexist as complementary. While leaders set the vision and direction, followers implement tasks that drive the vision to accomplishment. Therefore, leadership and followership do not exist as dichotomous roles; while the size of an organization may determine the proportion of its top leadership to other staff, every worker regardless of rank, reports to someone higher in authority. So practically, a number of them play dual roles of leader and follower at different times, depending on the assignment at hand. Many lessons can be learned from John's followership relationship with Jesus:

1. Followership vision.
   Leaders need to be well-prepared before they invite new members to their teams. Jesus was clear on the purpose and mission of calling his disciples, the process of training and who the follower would become. Employers should not think of the here and now only but of the future of those they engage including how their interactions with the organization impacts their families and society.

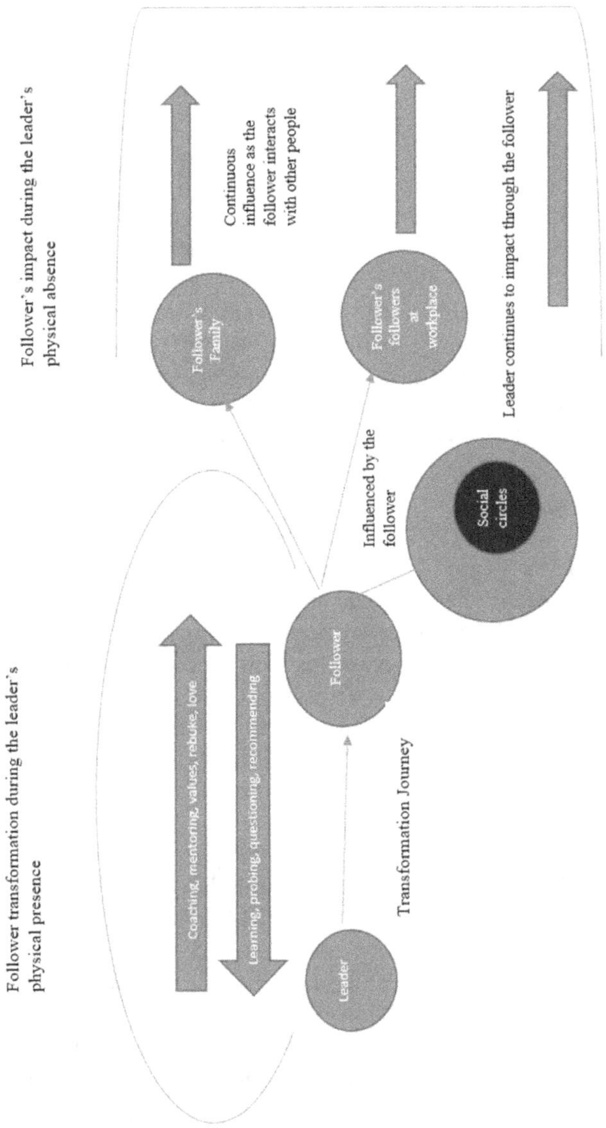

Fig. 9.1 Open vessels and flowing waters model

2. Availability of the leader.
   Jesus personally recruited, inducted, trained, equipped, and deployed John. Unlike in many organizations where leaders are too busy to have their followers accompany them to assignments in their initial days, Jesus was available until he handed over hands-on-experience to John.
3. Leaders are made.
   Jesus called unschooled, untrained fishermen and transformed them into great influencers of all ages, and there is none (except Judas due to divine will) that He lost on the way. Therefore, an employee's potential/talent should be identified correctly, developed and directed to the rightful purpose for maximum productivity, Rolle (2017). Leaders should be patient and willing to coach/mentor their followers with a positive attitude to develop them into great followers/leaders who would ultimately pass-on the baton, not just of organizational knowledge but positive values that impact society over many generations.
4. Succession planning.
   According to Kelley (1992), it was the followers and not Jesus who changed the world. Organizations can benefit significantly if empowerment of employees is the aim from the start. Jesus taught by example and only spoke when he needed to instruct or rebuke and left the most amazing successions plan ever known. The secret is that no one will live forever; Jesus was aware of the timeline of his assignment and wasted no time. His three years of ministry on earth could represent one's entire life and speak to the need for knowledge and skill transfers as soon as yesterday. This way, many beautiful ideas and visions will no longer rest in graves.
5. Transcending followership.
   The impact of the leader-follower relationship has a lifelong effect on society for many generations Leonard (2014). What we learn from John and Jesus reveals the truth that has lived with us for a long time; that our experiences at the workplace shape who we become in several ways; depending on followership characteristics, one carries the influence of the leaders they relate with by shaping behaviors at the family level and in society. Thus the leader-follower relationship experiences are ultimately transferred wherever one goes for the rest of their lives. These relationships represent open vessels and flowing waters that flow continuously.

6. Open vessels and flowing waters.
   Organizations can benefit immensely if they adopt the system suggested by the "open vessels and flowing waters" concept. It leads to a long-lasting transformational impact of the organization and society beyond the immediate generation of followers/leaders and geographical boundaries.

Chapter Takeaways

Followership is a recent subject in the scholarly field. Scholars have recognized that followers are as important as leaders and that the study of followership will improve workplace experiences for both leaders and followers and ultimately, organizational performance. This chapter has reviewed the followership version modeled by Jesus through apostle John and the lens of Kellerman (2008), Challef (1995, 2009, 2017), Kelley (1991, 1988), and Ubuntu, and how the findings can be applied to present-day organizations. The analysis reveals similarity between all the four perspectives and John's follower characteristics in most aspects and further a transcending relationship in which John's follower interactions with Jesus influence his life long after the leader's physical presence. We propose a model of open vessels and flowing waters whereby organizations recognize the leader-follower relationship's long-lasting impact long after the employment contract's lifespan.

Reflective Questions

- What can we learn from the follower-leader experience of John and Jesus' relationship?
- How does John's follower characteristics compare with the current scholarly literature on followership?
- How can we apply the learnings of apostle John's follower experience in the modern-day workplace?
- How can organizations structure their environments such that everyone's potential is allowed to unleash positively?
- Is there scholarly literature on how the leader-followership relationships impact followers (plus their families and society) after the employment relationship is over? Should it be a concern?

References

Achtemeir, P. J. (1985). *Harper's Bible dictionary*. Haper & Row.

Chaleff, I. (1995). *The courageous follower: Standing up to and for our leaders*. Berrett-Koehler Publishers, Inc.

Chaleff, I. (2009). *The courageous follower: Standing up to and for our leaders* (3rd ed.). Berret-Koehler Publishers, Inc.

Chaleff, I. (2017). In praise of leadership styles assessments. *Journal of Leadership Studies, 10*(3), 45–48.

DeSilva, D. A. (2004). *An introduction to the new testament contexts, methods and ministry formation*. Inter-Varsity Press.

English Standard Version Bible. (2001). *ESV online*. https://esv.literalworld.com/.

Fergusson, E. (2013). *Church history (Vol 1): From Christ to the pre-reformation*. Zondervan Academic. Kindle Edition

Fredriksen, P. (1991). Apocalypse and redemption in early Christianity from John of Patmos to Augustine of Hippol. *Vigiliae Christianae, 45*(2), 151–183.

Idoniboye-Obu, S., & Whetho, A. (2013). Ubuntu: 'You are because I am' or 'I am because you are'? *Alternation, 20*(1), 229–247.

Kelley, R. E. (1988). In praise of followers. *Havard Business Review, 66*, 142–148.

Kelley, R. E. (1991). Combining followership and leadership into partnership. In R. H. Kilmann, I. Kilmann, & Associates (Eds.), *Making organizations competitive: Enhancing networks and relationships across traditional boundaries* (pp. 195–220). Jossey-Bass.

Kelley, R. E. (1992). *The power of followership: How to create leaders people want to follow and followers who lead themselves*. Doubleday

Kelley, R. E. (2008). Rethinking followership. In R. E. Riggio, I. Chaleff, & J. Lipman-Blumen (Eds.), *The Warren Bennis signature series: The art of followership: How great followers create great leaders and organizations* (pp. 5–15). Jossey-Bass/Wiley.

Kellerman, B. (2007). What every leader needs to know about followers. *Harvard Business Review, 85*(12), 84.

Kellerman, B. (2008). Followership: How followers are creating change and changing leaders. *Harvard Business School*.

Leonard, R. A. (2014). *The role of followership during periods of absent leadership*.

Martin, R. (2015). A review of the literature of the followership since 2008: The importance of relationships and emotional intelligence. *SAGE Open, 5*(4), 2158244015608421.

Robbins, V. K. (1996). *Exploring the texture of texts: A guide to socio-rhetorical interpretation*. Trinity Press International

Rolle, S. (2017). A genre analysis of the parable of the pounds as it relates to Kelley's followership types. *Journal of Biblical Perspectives in Leadership, 7*(1), 179–194.
Sarver, C. A. (2020). *Be the example: Christ-centered followership in the Pastoral Epistles*. A Thesis Presented to the Faculty of The Southern Baptist Theological Seminary.
Schaff, P. (2002). *History of the Christian Church, volume I: Apostolic Christianity. A.D. 1–100* (Revised ed.). CCEL
Thomas, B. (2014). Comparison of Rwandan and American followership styles. *Faculty Publications—School of Business, 84*, 124–135. http://digitalcommons.georgefox.edu/gfsb/84
Winston, B. (2002). *Be a leader for God's sake*. Regent University.
Zondervan. (2003). *NIV Life in the Spirit Study Bible*. Zondervan.

CHAPTER 10

Nicodemus: An Example of Courageous Followership Conquering Groupthink

R. Mark Bell

In this chapter, Chaleff's (2009) courageous followership model is considered as a viable method for overcoming groupthink when applied by an individual group member. Nicodemus' role as a member of the Sanhedrin is analyzed in this vein using a social intertexture approach. Nicodemus is only presented in the Gospel of John, and he only enters the narrative at three points. Scholars and commentators have long pondered, from various viewpoints, the significance of John's inclusion of Nicodemus. This chapter does not attempt to address these questions in great detail but, instead, is focused on developing a clearer understanding of Nicodemus' role as a courageous follower and how that courageous followership role may have been useful in his overcoming the groupthink experienced within the Sanhedrin. To lay the appropriate foundation, certain relevant points of background information concerning groupthink, the

R. Mark Bell (✉)
Wayland Baptist University, Plainview, TX, USA
e-mail: bellm@wbu.edu

D. J. Dean and R. B. Huizinga (eds.), *Followership and Faith at Work*, Christian Faith Perspectives in Leadership and Business, https://doi.org/10.1007/978-3-030-90614-6_10

Sanhedrin, and Nicodemus in John's gospel are provided. As the major theoretical construct utilized in the study, a review of the followership literature is provided including historical aspects of followership, bad followership, and a special focus on courageous followership. The social intertexture analysis method is described and then applied to John's narratives involving Nicodemus in order to clarify understanding regarding several critical aspects of those passages. Ultimately, a discussion of the conclusions derived from the study is provided with special focus on recommendations for followers, leaders, and groups. This chapter adds value to the overall understanding of Nicodemus because, if he is and ought to be viewed as a courageous follower, many questions concerning him are either answered or are rendered unnecessary. This chapter's ultimate value may be found in the final analysis where it is determined that the practice of courageous followership is a useful method for individual group members in overcoming the groupthink phenomenon.

Background Information

The primary focus of this chapter is determining the extent to which Nicodemus was exhibiting courageous follower attributes and, if so, how those courageous follower actions drove his ability to overcome the strong mainstream position within his group—the Sanhedrin. In order to reach that point, it is necessary to first explore some background information concerning elements of groupthink that can at least partially inform the actions of the Sanhedrin group related to Jesus and what is understood relative to John's inclusion of Nicodemus in his gospel. Groupthink theory and the Sanhedrin group are only briefly discussed here as Bell (2016) provided a full review of the groupthink theory and established evidence indicating the Sanhedrin were immersed in a state of groupthink. John's gospel presents three different accounts of Nicodemus that are reviewed along with some of the commentaries which attempt to explain Nicodemus and his role in the Sanhedrin group.

Groupthink

The groupthink theory is likely best understood as a flawed decision-making process. Janis' (1982) work is considered the seminal work on the topic and details the antecedents, symptoms, and potential outcomes of the groupthink theory. According to Janis, three antecedents precede the existence of groupthink including highly cohesive groups, flawed structures within organizations, and certain situational realities. Janis categorized the eight symptoms of groupthink into three types including the group overestimating their own power and moral standing, the group's close-mindedness relative to challenges and opposition, and the varying steps the group would take to apply pressure on its members to conform. Janis noted only the highly cohesive group antecedent was always present in a groupthink scenario and any number or combination of the symptoms might be present. All of the potential outcomes associated with groupthink, according to Janis, are manifested in bad decision practices including failures in planning, failures to consider options or risks, biases in research or information processing, and the like.

Groupthink has generally been studied using historical case studies in order to test the theory and chronicle the existence and accuracy of the aforementioned antecedents and symptoms. Most of these historical case studies blame groupthink for some serious disasters such as: (a) the Bay of Pigs invasion and the Watergate scandal ('t Hart, 1991), (b) the Iraq war (Badie, 2010), (c) the 1986 Space Shuttle Challenger accident (Hughes & White, 2010), (d) the 1996 Mount Everest climbing team disaster (Burnette et al., 2011), and others. Based on the work of Bell (2016), one could ultimately blame groupthink for contributing to the first-century trial, conviction, and execution of Jesus Christ by the Jewish Sanhedrin. The majority of these studies adequately chronicle the antecedents, symptoms, and flawed decisions occurring in each case but fail to offer much in terms of how to avoid groupthink. The majority of writers fall back on one of Janis' (1982) original suggestions of assigning someone in the group the role of an official objector. That suggestion has merit for organizational leaders and group leaders who start from an objective viewpoint and can assign such an individual, but the suggestion fails to provide organizational followers and/or group members with any tools for overcoming groupthink at the individual level. The purpose of this chapter is to determine whether Nicodemus exhibited courageous followership and if that exhibition helped him as an individual to overcome the groupthink occurring in his group.

The Sanhedrin

In most respects, the group known as the Sanhedrin dominated the political, legal, social, and cultural aspects of first-century Jewish life. The sect of Pharisees dominated the Sanhedrin (deSilva, 2004) and focused heavily on a legalistic application of Torah law (Perrin et al., 2013). The Sanhedrin elevated themselves and their positioning within the Jewish community as a group set apart being adherents to the ultimate standards of ritual purity (Malina, 2001). As a result, the Sanhedrin retained fellowship with a select few—primarily themselves, and they disassociated themselves from most foreigners, common Jews, and the like. The Sanhedrin worked to consolidate power and authority, exhibit controlling influence, eliminate dissension, and institutionalize their distinct separation from the general Jewish population (deSilva, 2004). Bell (2016) has asserted that groupthink symptoms were demonstrated by the Sanhedrin in relation to their treatment of Christ. Additionally, Bell found five distinct groupthink symptoms demonstrated by the Sanhedrin including: (1) unquestioned belief in inherent group morality, (2) rationalizations of warnings, (3) self-censorship, (4) illusions of unanimity, and (5) direct pressure on dissenters to conform. These findings suggest that elements of the groupthink dynamic may have been present in the Sanhedrin group, at least in its engagement with Jesus. Part of Bell's study briefly touched on Nicodemus' role in the group and how some of his actions indicated his intention to "completely disassociate with the Sanhedrin group" (p. 35). Whether or not full groupthink was at play within the Sanhedrin in connection with its engagement with Christ, it is clear that strong opinions about Jesus made it dangerous for in-group Sanhedrin members to challenge the group's conclusion about who and what Jesus was. Based on Bell's research, there is room in research to determine how Nicodemus may have been able to overcome the strong voice of the mainstream perspective among the Sanhedrin as an in-group member. The present chapter serves to answer that call.

Three Views of Nicodemus in John's Gospel

Nicodemus is present in three separate "scenes" within John's gospel. First, Nicodemus is introduced in John 3:1–21 where he is identified as a Pharisee and a ruler of the Jews. In these verses, Nicodemus approaches Jesus under the cover of darkness. He conducts an interview of Jesus posing questions and being further confused by the answers. Second, Nicodemus is present in John 7:45–52 during an internal Jewish leadership discussion concerning the validity of Jesus' claims and how Jesus' followers were opposing Jewish law. Nicodemus questions the logic of the Jewish leadership in this instance and apparently does so alone. Third, Nicodemus assists Joseph of Arimathea in preparing Jesus' body for burial after the crucifixion in John 19:38–42. On this occasion, Nicodemus provided a significant amount of the necessary spices to prepare the body according to Jewish burial customs and participated in the burial.

Scholars have long struggled to unravel the mystery of Nicodemus. Bassler (1989) describes this struggle as a "fascination for scholars" (p. 635) desiring to capture the essence of John's Nicodemus. Farelly (2013) notes unraveling this mystery is challenging because Nicodemus is elusive and ambiguous at best. Indeed, the effort to understand Nicodemus extends back in time to at least the second century (Bassler, 1989). Although a variety of scholarly opinions exist, writings concerning Nicodemus can be loosely organized in three categories. These categories include Nicodemus as timidly seeking, Nicodemus as a secret convert, and Nicodemus as progressively distancing himself from the Jewish leadership. Each of these three views of Nicodemus is briefly explored for contextual and conceptual understanding.

The Timid Seeker

Those who view Nicodemus as timidly seeking, Jesus as Savior will note indications of this timidity in each of the three narratives where he appears. This view holds that fear of retribution from the Sanhedrin drove Nicodemus to timidly seek out Jesus at night, under the cover of darkness, where the possibility of being seen was minimized. While disagreeing with their position, Whitenton (2016) notes many scholars have held this view suggesting Nicodemus's initial meeting with Jesus was conducted at night for the purpose of avoiding the potential malevolence of other members of the Sanhedrin. In this view, it is also the fear of his colleagues that dictates the defense of Jesus provided by Nicodemus when he appears in John's gospel the second time. Bassler (1989) claims Nicodemus did certainly offer a defense of Jesus in this instance, but it was offered "rather tentatively" (p. 635). It is fear that again dominates the circumstances surrounding Nicodemus' effort to assist Joseph of Arimathea in preparing and burying Jesus' body. Bassler states when John mentioned Joseph's secret discipleship as being attributed to "fear of the Jews" (p. 641), it is this fear which dominates the overall context of the burial scene. Hence, this "fear of the Jews" also applies to Nicodemus by what Bassler calls "clear association" (p. 641). Therefore, in this view, Nicodemus' actions are continuously and heavily influenced by fear. This fear does not arbitrarily indicate some level of weakness in Nicodemus' character. Many New Testament disciples certainly acted out of fear at times. However, fear as a primary motivating factor would certainly stand in contrast to an understanding of Nicodemus as a courageous follower.

The Secret Convert

Viewing Nicodemus as a secret convert is also a commonly held understanding of his role in the Gospel of John. In the secret convert view, clues are also evident in each scene where Nicodemus is involved. In this view, Nicodemus seeks Christ for his initial interview because he is already a believer. Deffinbaugh (2002) claims the secret conversion of Nicodemus occurred because he could not deny the evidence for Christ and was consumed by a personal conviction concerning Jesus' divinity and mission. Additionally in this view, Nicodemus' defense of Jesus would not have taken place had he not already been converted. Driscoll (1911) states it was the Sanhedrin's accusation of Nicodemus' new so-called Galilean characteristics that indicated Nicodemus had heard and embraced the truth of Jesus' message. It is relatively hard, and needless, to dispute how Nicodemus was certainly a convert by the time he assisted in Jesus' burial. Nicodemus' secret conversion is again assumed in the burial scene because of his association with Joseph—who John notes is a secret disciple (Bassler, 1989). The fact that Nicodemus' conversion seems apparent in the burial scene does not, however, automatically indicate this conversion was secretive in nature. A secret conversion at this point would contradict an understanding of Nicodemus as a courageous follower.

The Progressive Distancing

Some scholars and commentators hold the view that John is actually describing Nicodemus as progressively distancing himself from his colleagues. In this view, Nicodemus pulls further away from the Sanhedrin in each of the first two scenes and finally pulls free from them in the final scene. Ford (2013) claims Nicodemus might be best considered as one who initially was somewhat undecided whether or not to officially break with the Sanhedrin. Nicodemus appeared not satisfied with the Pharisees' legalism and may have suspected Jesus was the Messiah leading him to visit Jesus for the initial interview. If the night interview was a first step away from Jewish law for Nicodemus, then his public challenge and criticism of the Sanhedrin's application of the law to Jesus was quite a jump. Farelly (2013) describes this encounter as a public criticism of the Pharisees clearly showing Nicodemus was not "entirely 'one of them' anymore" (p. 39). In distancing himself, he essentially was simultaneously aligning himself with Jesus and other followers of the Way. After his initial step and jump away from the Pharisees, Nicodemus took one last monumental leap by assisting Joseph with the burial of Christ placing himself squarely on the side of the followers of Christ. Farelly notes this event as the "dramatic distancing" (p. 42) where Nicodemus aligns himself with Christ in the sight of both God and man. This view actually does not arbitrarily contradict the idea of Nicodemus as a courageous follower. In fact, some aspects of the third view may work in a complimentary or corroborating fashion to an understanding of Nicodemus as a courageous follower.

Table 10.1 demonstrates the three existing views of Nicodemus as found in the associated literature. None of the three existing views specifically addresses whether Nicodemus was engaged in a first-century exposition of the courageous follower model. The present study seeks to explore this potential as a more plausible explanation of Nicodemus while simultaneously determining the role of courageous followership in groupthink scenarios.

Table 10.1 Existing views of Nicodemus in John's Gospel

View	*Description*
The Timid Seeker	Fear of Sanhedrin motives Nicodemus to: (a) seek out Jesus at night, (b) tentatively offer a defense of Jesus, and (c) form a secret discipleship along with Joseph of Arimathea
The Secret Convert	Nicodemus was already a believer as: (a) he could not deny the evidence of Jesus as Christ, (b) the Sanhedrin begin to suspect his new characteristics, and (c) he helps another secret convert bury Jesus' body
The Progressive Distancing	Nicodemus pulls away from the Sanhedrin: (a) being unsatisfied with the Pharisees' legalism, (b) by a public challenge and criticism of their application of the law, and (c) forming a clear alignment with Jesus as one who assists in the burial

Followership

The concept of followership should be understood as distinct from but related to, intertwined with, or otherwise correlated to the leadership concept. Leadership might be defined as the use of influence, the casting of vision, the development of strategies, and the motivation of followers for the purpose of achieving commonly held objectives. Followership is the act of individuals who use their talents, skills, and abilities to work with leaders and other followers to accomplish the commonly held objectives. The concept of followership is reviewed in consideration of its historical aspects along with both bad followership and courageous followership.

Historical Aspects of Followership

In the related literature, the study of leadership has always dominated the study of followership, yet leadership has never occurred without followers. In their expansive review of the followership literature, Uhl-Bien et al. (2014) make the point clearly stating "it is now widely accepted that leadership cannot be fully understood without considering the role of followers in the leadership process" (p. 89). Uhl-Bien et al. traced the modern history of studying organizational followers to the scientific management literature of the early twentieth century which casts followers as intellectually inferior to leaders thus requiring the directives of management. Some of today's leaders maintain the same mindset of intellectual superiority while some of today's followers are content to allow their leader to think for them. Uhl-Bien et al. further traced the study of followers through the majority of the twentieth century noting those studies generally focused on how to improve subordinate productivity within companies. In that stream of literature, the term subordinate was a dominant way to reference non-managerial persons in organizations carrying with it many negative connotations.

Transitioning to the term follower and/or followership seems to have primarily occurred only in the last two decades of the twentieth century. Uhl-Bien et al. claimed "clearly the most cited early work on followership is that of Robert Kelley (1988)" (p. 90). Although some would claim the term follower is still indicative of lesser stature, the study of followership elevates the role of the organizational member far beyond the status of a mere subordinate. Kelley's (1988, 1992) works are now often considered classics in the study of followership. Kelley (1988) presented a different conceptualization of the role of followers in organizations claiming that much of the success of an organization can be directly attributed to followers rather than leaders. Even today many leaders and followers fail to realize the true value of the organizational follower. Kelley (1988) claimed followership, whether good or bad, could best be understood as the net effect of two dimensions of follower behavior. Those two dimensions of follower behavior are active engagement, the opposite of passive involvement, and independent critical thinking, the opposite of dependent uncritical thinking (Kelly, 1988). In this two-dimension view, the actions and outcomes of the follower's active engagement and independent critical thinking are generally assumed as positives, and the desire is for high levels of engagement coupled with high levels of critical thinking.

The behavioral dimensions of followership have remained a strong stream in the followership research. Chaleff (2009) also described two behavioral dimensions of followership including the amount of support given the leader by the follower and the willingness of the follower to challenge the leader. Chaleff claimed those two dimensions as critical in understanding courageous followership and developed four courageous follower typologies based on those behaviors. Chaleff also outlined seven aspects of courageous follower activities as part of his courageous follower model. Being a major element of this study, Chaleff's courageous follower model is reviewed more thoroughly in a subsequent section.

Similar to both Kelley and Chaleff, Kellerman (2008) viewed followership as resulting from the unique behavior patterns of followers. However, Kellerman claimed only one behavior dimension would influence the follower's followership . Kellerman stated followership results from a "single, simple metric...level of engagement" (p. 85). The level of engagement can be viewed as a spectrum ranging from zero effort/no commitment on one end to deep commitment/extreme effort on the other (Kellerman, 2008). Based on where an individual's engagement level places them on that range, Kellerman then categorizes followers into one of five classifications: "Isolate, Bystander, Participant, Activist, [and] Diehard" (p. 85). The single dimension view of followership behavior may be the easiest for leaders and other followers to comprehend as it is quickly ascertained by observation.

Kellerman and Chaleff were not the first to present followers in categories. Kelley (1988, 1992) originally presented followership typologies based on the two aforementioned behavior dimensions of active engagement and independent critical thinking. Kelley (1992) claimed followers would combine the two behaviors in various ways in response to the leader's actions and the context of the organization. The five typologies identified by Kelley (1992) are (1) the alienated (low engagement, high critical thinking), (2) the yes-people (high engagement, low critical thinking), (3) the sheep (low engagement, low critical thinking), (4) the pragmatics (lukewarm engagement, lukewarm critical thinking), and (5) the star followers (high engagement, high critical thinking). The five typologies contribute to an improved understanding of the follower role as having the potential to demonstrate strong, middle-of-the-road, or weak followership.

The contributions of Kelley, Kellerman, and Chaleff have been instrumental in advancing the overall understanding of the followership concept. Followership is now being studied in the contemporary context as part of the leadership process. Over the course of human history, people have been fascinated with leaders and leadership prompting a plethora of writings on great exemplars of leadership. Unfortunately, very little attention has been paid to great examples of followership. The present chapter serves to help fill that void.

Bad Followership

The historical development of the followership construct included allusions to followership types and/or behaviors that were less than positive in nature. Kelley's (1988) conception of the two behavioral dimensions is explained by contrasting them with their negative counterparts. For example, one understands active engagement by considering passive involvement. Kellerman's (2008) follower types, based on the one metric of active engagement, are presented as a spectrum where low engagement types are given names with negative connotations such as the Isolate or the Bystander. Kelley's (1992) typologies have a similar recognition of follower classifications that are less than desirable. In fact, four of Kelley's (1992) typologies are not positive as only the Star Follower demonstrates both strong engagement and high levels of critical thinking. All of those allusions to negative followership types are indicated by the various authors in order to present the positive followership type with the goal of helping followers improve their followership and assisting leaders in developing good followership tendencies among organizational members.

One stream of followership research moves beyond demonstrating the less than positive follower roles and points directly to the bad followership that is detrimental to leaders, followers, and organizations. Kellerman (2005) considered why some followers are willing to follow bad leaders and how bad followership is involved in bad leadership. Kellerman claims bad leaders and bad followers are either leading or following "because it is in their self-interest" (p. 42). Additionally, Kellerman claims these bad followers are pursuing and oftentimes achieving some need fulfillment in their following of the bad leader. In the book *Bad Leadership*, Kellerman developed a typology of bad leadership and included in her description how it "engaged both the leader and at least some followers" (p. 44). Additionally, Kellerman uses the same "the leader and at least some followers" phrase in six of the seven bad leadership typologies she presents. Thus, Kellerman furthered the notion that bad leadership cannot occur without some corresponding bad followership . If that is an accurate assessment of bad followership, there is certainly a great need to better understand positive followership exemplars.

Bad followership was a major focal point in Padilla et al. (2007) development of the toxic triangle model that attempts to explain the individual contributions of leaders, followers, and the situational context to a toxic organizational environment. Concerning the follower role, Padilla et al. claim their exploration was an attempt to answer the question "why are certain followers unable or unwilling to resist domineering and abusive leaders?" (p. 183). Padilla et al. categorize these bad followers as either conformers or colluders. Conformers are more passive in allowing the bad leadership as a result of their different vulnerabilities such as immaturity or unmet needs, whereas colluders are active in support of the bad leader because they see the opportunity to work with the destructive leader in a way that advances their own personal agenda (Padilla et al., 2007). If Padilla et al.'s categories are correct, both the conformers and colluders are demonstrating bad followership as neither is willing to take a bold stance against the destructive leadership environment.

The role of bad followership in toxic environments characterized by destructive leadership was the primary consideration of Thoroughgood et al.'s (2012) effort to expand the previous classification of conformers and colluders. Thoroughgood et al. developed the "taxonomy of vulnerable followers" (p. 897) that included the subtypes of conformers as lost souls, authoritarians, and bystanders and the subtypes of colluders as acolytes and opportunists. According to Thoroughgood et al., different forms of passivity characterize the lost souls, authoritarians, and bystanders such as lack of personal direction, the desire for exertion of legitimate power, or the motivation of fear. However, Thoroughgood et al. note the assertiveness of acolytes and opportunists is driven by dark personality traits, the willingness to form alliances for personal gain, or other self-interest that aligns with the destructive leader's mission. One of Thoroughgood et al.'s overall observations is "no matter how clever or devious, leaders alone cannot achieve toxic results" (p. 901). Thus, bad followership seems to serve as a complimentary force to bad leadership. Following the stream of research conducted by Padilla et al. (2007) and Thoroughgood et al., Henderson (2015) developed the Toxic Followership Types Scale based on the conformers and colluders follower types. Henderson's instrument was developed specifically to measure the two bad followership types. Although some subtle differences did exist, in the testing of the instrument, Henderson claimed to have found similar subtypes as Thoroughgood et al. had proposed. The development of a survey instrument by Henderson was an important continuance of the research stream and validation of these bad follower typologies as measurable constructs.

As has been explained by the previously mentioned research, bad followership is more than workplace apathy, poor job performance, or lack of organizational commitment. Although those followership actions are less than positive, truly bad followership corresponds with, actively supports, and/or is willingly ignorant of bad leadership. Leaders, including bad leaders, hold significant and various forms of power and influence in organizations. A good follower of a bad leader or group has a very challenging task—one where great amounts of courage are needed in order to successfully pursue the organization's mission.

Courageous Followership

Chaleff originated the courageous follower model with the 1995 publication of *The Courageous Follower*. Chaleff has updated and revised the courageous follower model in second and third editions expanding the model from its original five dimensions by adding two new aspects. In the third edition, Chaleff (2009) introduced the Followership Styles Assessment, a survey that assists individuals in determining their current courageous follower style. Chaleff claimed the third edition is the culmination of his courageous followership journey.

Chaleff's courageous followership journey appears to have been undertaken in order to answer a single but important question. Chaleff (2011) asks "should we stand up to and for our leaders?" (p. 19). Standing up for leaders has always been indicative of a personal loyalty to the leader. This type loyalty is highly valued by leaders. Standing up to leaders is indicative of loyalty to mission, to purpose, or to cause. Chaleff contends the latter loyalty supersedes the former in the hearts and minds of courageous followers. Chaleff noted the dual duties required of courageous followers as they must simultaneously support their leader while being willing to challenge the leader. It takes courage for followers to offer the brutal honesty leaders need because followers have too often been seasoned to just follow directions and not to offer much in terms of leadership assessment.

Chaleff (2016) noted the various styles that can be used to categorize the different courageous follower approaches. The use of follower typologies is helpful in making application of the concepts. Chaleff describes the two behaviors forming the basis of the typologies as "willingness to question or challenge the leader" and "support given to the leader" (p. 46). These two behaviors correspond well with the dual duties previously mentioned. The four courageous follower styles identified by Chaleff are (1) Resource (low challenge, low support), (2) Implementer (low challenge, high support), (3) Individualist (high challenge, low support), and (4) Partner (high challenge, high support). Chaleff noted how one's follower style could change depending on the leadership type presented. It is also quite likely that one's courageous follower style could change dependent on the situational context. The situational reality relative to the purpose pursued will influence both the leadership style and the followership style.

The courageous follower model is premised on the notion that both leaders and followers serve a common purpose (Chaleff, 2009). The service to common purpose is an important aspect of the model providing a foundation for its seven dimensions. The seven dimensions of the model as outlined in Chaleff's third edition include the courage to assume responsibility, to serve, to challenge, to participate in transformation, to take moral action, to speak to hierarchy, and to listen to followers. Each of the seven courageous follower dimensions is detailed in the following sections as a deeper understanding of this model is necessary before making its application with the research subject.

The Courage to Assume Responsibility

Having the courage to assume responsibility involves the follower taking an ownership stake in the common purpose shared with the leader. Chaleff (2009) states courageous followers willingly accept and seek responsibility for both "themselves and the organization" (p. 6). Chaleff further claims these courageous followers operate with a sense of authority derived from their understanding of the common purpose and do not hold a paternalistic view of the leader. Because of the high value placed on the shared purpose, these followers will take action without specific direction from the leader. They do not fear consequences, nor do they require leaders to think for them. They do not see themselves working in opposition to their leaders. These followers will seek direction when needed but will not wait for direction when deemed unnecessary. Indeed, they understand their role as working in conjunction with the leader in order to accomplish goals and objectives associated with the common purpose.

The Courage to Serve

Courageous service involves a passionate willingness to do whatever it takes to aid the leader in accomplishing the common purpose. Chaleff (2009) claims courageous followers serve by engaging the hard work of supporting the leader through challenging tasks and tough decisions. They serve by offering complementary strengths which offset leader weaknesses while willingly unburdening the leader by taking on additional duties where necessary (Chaleff, 2009). The courage to serve is best understood as a dimension where the follower places the needs of the leader ahead of his or her own.

The Courage to Challenge

The courage to challenge one's leader concerning issues of integrity, morality, ethics, effectiveness, or efficiency is demonstrated by a follower who values the common purpose more than he or she fears potential retribution. Chaleff (2009) describes this type of courage as the willingness "to stand up, to stand out, to risk rejection, [and] to initiate conflict" when the actions of the leader or the group require such examination (p. 7). These followers place high value on harmonious relationships but place a higher value on the shared purpose and personal integrity (Chaleff, 2009). An important aspect of this dimension, the value of integrity, is paramount in understanding the courage to challenge. This dimension is essentially focused on the courage needed to speak openly and honestly to those in power despite potential consequences. The courage to challenge does not necessitate conflict, but conflict often results when leaders do not value followers who challenge or have motives which contradict the shared purpose.

The Courage to Participate in Transformation

The participation in transformation involves the active participation in organizational change endeavors that so frequently characterize organizational life. Chaleff (2009) describes this as a courageous effort to "recognize the need for transformation" (p. 7) when the common purpose could be jeopardized without the change. Of course, recognition of the need for change is only the first step. According to Chaleff, these followers actively participate in the change, supporting the leader, and advocating for the change to others within the organization. The need for the courage to participate in transformation develops in today's organizations from the rapidity and frequency of change and the corresponding increase in change-resistant behaviors that tend to stifle the success of organizational change.

The Courage to Take Moral Action

In one sense, the courage to take moral action is the ultimate step a follower can take when standing in firm support of the common purpose. According to Chaleff (2009), this form of courage is embodied by a follower who not only takes a stance opposing the leader's position but does so by refusing or appealing direct orders and ultimately by resigning from the organization, if needed. This moral courage, according to Chaleff , involves significant personal risk, but true commitment and service to the shared purpose demand the risky action. Having the courage to take such action even when motivated by a sense of morality requires the conscious acknowledgment of the potential severity of the consequences. This aspect of courageous followership is primarily focused on follower reaction to leader stimuli. It is concerned with standing up for what is right, despite the extreme personal risk, as a reaction to a perceived wrong.

The Courage to Speak to the Hierarchy

Having the courage necessary to speak to the hierarchy involves some obvious challenges including the possible consequences of moving past the direct leader and the logistical challenge of being heard at a higher level where the follower is potentially not well known. Chaleff (2009) claims these challenges exist in many large organizations where actual decision-making power originates multiple layers up the chain of command. Because of the hierarchical distance between the follower and the decision-makers, followers are challenged to communicate effectively and must engage the other courageous follower principles but with contextual sensitivities and purposeful strategy (Chaleff, 2009). Persistence and relationship building would be two necessary behaviors for followers attempting to communicate at higher levels within a hierarchy. Perhaps the most important relationship would be with the follower's direct leader as he or she could more easily create the opportunity to speak with the next highest level.

The Courage to Listen to Followers

The final dimension of Chaleff's model is based on the understood premise that leaders and followers are roles which individuals fulfill depending on context. Virtually every leader is also a follower, and many followers are also leaders. Therefore, the courage to listen to followers is an activity that allows leaders to model the other courageous follower principles while reaping their benefits. Chaleff (2009) claims this courage is the responsibility of the leader in order to foster and respond productively to acts of courageous followership. Chaleff (2009) further notes this courage is more challenging than it appears but "offers powerful paybacks" (p. 8) for those involved, especially the leader. With such powerful benefits available, one would also expect the opposite is true—significant problems and organizational challenges will exist when leaders fail to listen. It is important to recognize the duality of this aspect of courageous followership because the leader's integrity will be challenged if he or she acts as a courageous follower in the follower context but, when in the leader context, does not encourage his or her followers to act likewise.

Nicodemus' Courageous Followership

As previously asserted by Bell (2016), Nicodemus was heavily involved in a group where groupthink may have been a persistent problem. The three existing views of Nicodemus' role in the group do not indicate how he as an individual was able to overcome the potential groupthink. A deeper understanding of the social aspects and dimensions of the three passages, where John presents Nicodemus, is required to address the purpose of this study. The social intertexture method was used in analyzing the texts of John's gospels involving Nicodemus. As such, the social intertexture method is briefly described followed by a detailed analysis of the three passages using the method. The analysis does ascertain whether Nicodemus was exercising courageous followership activities and whether those activities allowed him to overcome the Sanhedrin's pervasive groupthink.

Social Intertexture Method

According to Robbins (1996b), intertexture analysis involves determining how the text represents, refers to, and considers events outside of the specific text, and those events can involve social codes, roles, and institutions. According to deSilva (2004), intertexture analysis involves more than just gathering the data regarding the use of worldly phenomena from outside the text because the method requires close examination of how the worldly phenomena are used and for what purpose. Intertexture has a wide range of applicability and offers significant insight. deSilva claims virtually every New Testament passage presents itself for the opportunity to be explored through intertextuality. Social intertexture, as a subtexture of intertexture, concerns the use or representation of differing forms of social knowledge—information known by every individual in a region due to frequent interaction with others in the region (Robbins, 1996b). Social intertexture is useful as an analytical tool and as a mechanism providing a richer and deeper understanding of a text.

Three important aspects of social intertexture involve its consideration of social roles, social institutions, and social codes. These aspects each contribute to the analysis of a social phenomenon but are not simply cultural in nature because they are understood by the entire society regardless of preference or participation (Robbins, 1996b). Robbins (1996b) explains how social codes focus on the conventional practices in certain social settings. Social roles are evident when certain identities are found indicating the individual's purpose, position, or character. Robbins (1996a) cites numerous examples of social roles including chief priests, elders, scribes, murderers, king, Jews, and soldiers. Social institutions are those entities, constructs, or procedures that are set apart as authoritative, universal, and embedded. Examples of social institutions include the council, Roman soldiers, and the temple (Robbins, 1996a). For analytical purposes, the three aspects of social intertexture: social roles, social institutions, and social codes must be located within the selected texts and then systematically reviewed.

Social intertexture can be used to discover what the individuals of first-century Judaism would have understood when John writes that Nicodemus was a Pharisee and ruler of the Jews. Similarly, social intertexture can illuminate what role the law played in the Pharisee's internal discussions and the importance of Nicodemus' actions in assisting a fearful Joseph of Arimathea in conducting the burial customs. The analysis will provide clarity concerning Nicodemus' role in the groupthink-plagued Sanhedrin and whether he overcame that groupthink by using a courageous follower approach.

John 3:1–21

The first twenty-one verses of chapter three in the Gospel of John contain the narrative introducing Nicodemus in the New Testament. In these verses, Nicodemus visits Jesus for the purpose of interviewing Him. The interview leaves Nicodemus quite perplexed at times as he does not appear to completely understand Jesus' responses. Because of the interview, some of the most well-known statements of Jesus were recorded by John including the concept of being born again and, of course, John 3:16. John does not specifically address what motivated Nicodemus to make the visit and speak with Jesus. However, pure conjecture is also not necessary because Nicodemus' motives are revealed with social intertexture analysis.

As previously mentioned, one critical element of social intertexture analysis includes the study of the social roles represented in the text. There are two prominent social roles mentioned in John 3:1. First, in John 3:1 (NASB), the author writes "Now there was a man of the Pharisees…" No explicit definition is given concerning what constitutes a Pharisee, and none was needed for the original audience. However, this is an important element concerning the character of Nicodemus. Pharisees were an especially prominent sect within Judaism during the first century (deSilva, 2004). Pharisees were considerably focused on Torah law and became rather distinct from other Jews by their erection of social boundaries (deSilva, 2004). As such, they were set apart not only as teachers but also by having dominion over the populous. deSilva (2004) refers to this social separation as indicated by the Pharisees' "great authority among the people" (p. 83). Over the course of time, authority developed into the separation characteristic of a ruling class. The second social role noted in this verse involves this ruling-class characteristic as John describes Nicodemus not only as a man of the Pharisees but also as a "ruler of the Jews." As a ruler of the Jews, Nicodemus held a position as member of the Sanhedrin who governed Israel (Harrison, 1946). Therefore, Nicodemus should be understood as a member of a very elite group of religious leaders who were set apart from the average Jew having deep religious convictions and substantial authority.

Viewing Nicodemus from that social role perspective leads to a clearer understanding of his motivations as a deeply religious follower. Although his position is one of authority, Nicodemus was not the chief priest and can, therefore, be accurately considered by his role as a follower. As a follower, Nicodemus shared a common purpose with his leader and his fellow followers. It is this common purpose that provides clarity concerning Nicodemus' courageous follower attributes. Part of the shared purpose is demonstrated by, according to Harrison (1946), Nicodemus' deep interest in any person or movement that carried significant influence as did that of Jesus. Another aspect of the shared purpose was the desire for discovery of the true Messiah who had been promised by God. Nicodemus would have certainly supported the discovery of the true Deliverer and would not prejudge Jesus only to find himself opposing the true Christ (Harrison, 1946). As a Pharisee, a ruler of the Jews, and a follower among the Sanhedrin, Nicodemus' actions would have been bound by a desire to discover the true Messiah, and, as a result, he would have felt compelled to investigate influential movements within the Jewish state. Therefore, the interview with Jesus makes logical sense. Nicodemus was investigating a very influential movement for the purpose of determining whether or not this was the true Deliverer. This desire for discovery would not have separated Nicodemus from the purpose he shared with his leadership. Of course, the Sanhedrin leadership had prejudged Jesus and had done so in error. Nicodemus' interview was certainly an act of courage. Nicodemus would not let his judgment be clouded but would instead seek the truth because the truth was what the Sanhedrin was actually supposed to be seeking.

When logically extending the understanding of Nicodemus' social role, one quickly ascertains his commitment to the shared purpose. And, considering this logical extension in light of his interview with Jesus demonstrates significant courage on the part of Nicodemus. He had the courage to take upon himself the task of personally investigating this movement's leader in order to determine whether He was the Messiah that all of Israel desired. The courage to assume responsibility is the first characteristic of a courageous follower (Chaleff , 2009). Courageous followers who assume responsibility willingly accept and seek out such responsibility and base their authority to do so on their conception of the common purpose (Chaleff, 2009). Nicodemus was fulfilling this role when he courageously sought Jesus, interviewed Him, and investigated His movement. Viewing Nicodemus' actions in John 3 as those of a courageous follower contradicts many commonly held views but is logically based on a comprehensive understanding of his role in society and his organization coupled with the importance of the common purpose.

John 7:49–51

The events of John 7 involve divisions that occurred among the people and, eventually through Nicodemus, within the Sanhedrin. These divisions were a result of Jesus' teachings. John 7:45–52 presents the narrative account of the Pharisees questioning the officers concerning why they had not seized Jesus and whether these officers had also been deceived. The Pharisees clearly indicated how the many followers of Christ had been led astray from the law and were cursed. As evidence for this straying away, the Pharisees made the claim that no one from their inner circle believed in Jesus. Nicodemus took verbal exception to the Pharisees' self-serving application of the law. As a reward, Nicodemus received a stinging rebuke.

Another important element of social intertexture includes the reference of social institutions within the text. An important social institution is mentioned twice in John 7:49–51 and has conceptual relevance concerning the entire exchange among the Sanhedrin, the officers, and Nicodemus. In John 7:49, the Pharisees claim the crowd of Jesus' followers is accursed because the crowd "does not know the Law." In John 7:51, Nicodemus clearly challenges the leadership and his colleagues' application of the law by stating "Our Law does not judge a man unless it first hears from him and knows what he is doing, does it?" John's original readers needed no explanation concerning his repeated reference to the law. They would have been quite familiar with law and would have clearly understood the dynamic as a result. Social institutions such as the Jewish law were widely understood by Jews and other groups in the area. Deffinbaugh (2002) notes Pharisee law viewed itself "as the pure remnant of Judaism" (p. 105) being not only the way into the kingdom but also the source of governance for daily life as regulated by Torah law and oral traditions concerning the law. deSilva (2004) further adds to the understanding of what constituted the law by noting the Pharisees endeavored to apply the whole of Torah law through various rules and regulations that governed many aspects of Jewish life including purity, tithing, and the Sabbath. Torah law served many purposes including the avoidance of and the atonement for sin as well as the application of justice. The law was revered as it was given directly to Moses by God Himself. Therefore, when Nicodemus challenged the Sanhedrin regarding their application of the law, it was not the law itself which Nicodemus challenged. Rather, he held the socialized institution of the law in a higher regard than he did his leader or fellow followers among the Sanhedrin.

Nicodemus' act of verbally challenging the Sanhedrin was quite remarkable in consideration of the socialized institution of Jewish law—an institution where Nicodemus was certainly a participant. Nicodemus' commitment to the law must be understood by considering his deeply held religious convictions and character. At this point, Nicodemus continues to be understood as a member or follower of a larger organization and still possessing a shared or common purpose. In this instance, the common purpose involved a strong support and commitment to the law. Nicodemus' verbal challenge was a very risky action. According to Harrison (1946), Nicodemus was risking strong disapproval and scorn by challenging and contradicting the Sanhedrin. Bassler (1989) claims Nicodemus sought to challenge the hypocrisy he deemed evident rather than a mere concern "for correct legal procedure" (p. 640). Therefore, Nicodemus so revered the law and the Lawgiver that he would risk his own welfare for their sake. At this point, Nicodemus was surely aware of his leaders' and fellow followers' prejudgments of Jesus, and he was willing to take the risk to correct this injustice.

Motivated by commitment to the law, Nicodemus clearly challenged the Pharisees' hypocritical application of the law. By doing so, he again demonstrated himself as a courageous follower. At this point, Nicodemus was still a Pharisee, ruler of the Jews, and member of the Sanhedrin. He acted alone concerned with issues of integrity, ethics, hypocrisy, and morality. This incident is characteristic of Chaleff's (2009) third aspect of the courageous follower model where the follower demonstrates the courage to challenge. Chaleff describes this courageous follower aspect as the willingness to speak up, risk rejection, and initiate conflict concerning matters of integrity or matters that negatively impact the shared purpose. Nicodemus certainly fulfilled this role by speaking up independently in defense of the law's moral imperatives. He did this with an understanding of the potential consequences but did it despite those consequences as he understood the greater importance of the common purpose.

John 19:39–40

The nineteenth chapter of John is his recounting of the scourging, crucifixion, death, and burial of Jesus. In John 19:38–42, the narrative focuses on Joseph of Arimathea and Nicodemus' effort to prepare and entomb the body of Christ. John tells his readers how Joseph was already a disciple of Christ but was one in secret. Joseph requests the body from Pilate and receives permission to take it away. Nicodemus helps with the burial preparation by providing an abundance of the necessary spices, and together he and Joseph wrap the body and place it in a new garden tomb.

The important element of social intertexture present within this text involves the social codes that are alluded to by John. Jewish social code regarding burial practices is present within the text in two distinct instances. First, in John 19:39, Nicodemus enters the narrative, and we are told he came "bringing a mixture of myrrh and aloes…" Second, in John 19:40, Joseph and Nicodemus together took the body and "bound it in linen wrappings with the spices…" which John notes was "the burial custom of the Jews." These verses highlight the important social code relevant to the Jewish burial customs. These traditions could be quite complex depending on mode of death, condition of the body, and length of time since death had occurred (Lavoie et al., 1982). However, these traditions always addressed issues of body cleansing, the anointing of the body with spices, and the proper linens and methods for wrapping the deceased (Lavoie et al., 1982). Although John did not mention the washing, Lavoie et al. claim that, based on these verses in John, the body was buried according to Jewish code. Joseph and Nicodemus obviously did not accept the Pharisees' rejection of Jesus and would not accept a burial that would have shamed the Jewish Man and His family. Therefore, they took it upon themselves to ensure a Jewish burial code was adhered to in the case of Jesus.

The fact that Nicodemus wanted to ensure Jesus received a traditional Jewish burial is a clear indication that he had taken a moral stand in opposition to the Jewish leadership. The fact that John introduces Nicodemus again as the one "who had come to Him by night" should not be misunderstood as anything other than identification. Harrison (1946) mentions how this was a "circumstantial note" (pp. 51–52) and should not raise alarms concerning Nicodemus' motives but is better understood as a way of identifying that this was the same Nicodemus John had previously mentioned. As such, Nicodemus again demonstrates his courage and willingness to act despite the potential costs. We are never told of the consequences that Nicodemus suffered as a result of this action. However, his actions were a clear departure from the desires of the Jewish leadership who would not have honored Jesus by adhering to the social codes governing burial practices. It is, therefore, quite likely that Nicodemus ended his affiliation with the Pharisees and Sanhedrin either in conjunction with this action or as a direct result. However the separation may have occurred, Nicodemus had the courage to take action.

The significance of Nicodemus' efforts to uphold the Jewish social codes concerning burial customs relative to Jesus should not be minimized. It is this action that demonstrates Nicodemus' courage and his stance opposing the Jewish leadership. He had clearly left the organization because he took this moral stand. As described by Chaleff (2009), the courage to take moral action is the fifth attribute of a courageous follower. Chaleff describes this courage as involving a follower who refuses or appeals orders and will ultimately resign from the organization over issues of integrity, morality, or ethics. Further, Chaleff notes how the courage to take moral action involves significant personal risk, but courageous followers value the common purpose more than they fear the personal risk involved. Clearly, Nicodemus demonstrated the courage to take moral action and also demonstrated his commitment to the common purpose. He had found the Deliverer and could do no less than honor Him at this point by ensuring Him a traditional Jewish burial. Nicodemus had the courage to disassociate himself from the Sanhedrin and clearly aligned himself with the other followers of Christ.

Analysis Summation

Social intertexture analysis of John 3:1, 7:49–51, and 19:39–40 provides substantial information regarding the important social roles, institutions, and codes which are present in those texts. Social roles including the Pharisees and rulers of the Jews, the social institution of the Jewish law, and the important social codes surrounding Jewish burial customs are all integrally linked to Nicodemus' character, actions, and motivations concerning the common purpose shared by Nicodemus with his leaders and fellow followers. Nicodemus understood the purposes of the Sanhedrin as including seeking out the promised Deliverer, justly upholding Jewish law, and ultimately honoring the Messiah. In each of the three passages from John, it is those common purposes which drove Nicodemus' actions and words. He clearly demonstrates courageous follower attributes by having the courage to assume responsibility, challenge, and to take moral action. Understanding Nicodemus as a courageous follower is a departure from common understandings of this mysterious New Testament character. Through social intertexture analysis, however, the true Nicodemus is revealed as an exemplar of courageous followership. Chaleff (2009) is clear concerning how courageous followershipis motivated by the follower's deep commitment to the shared or common organizational purpose and mission. It is this shared or common purpose that plays an integral role in understanding Nicodemus as a courageous follower. Chaleff does not indicate that all seven dimensions of courageous followership must be present for a courageous follower to exist. As previously indicated, three aspects of the courageous follower model are applicable to the scenarios involving Nicodemus. Table 10.2 presents the three courageous follower dimensions demonstrated by Nicodemus: (1) the courage to assume responsibility, (2) the courage to challenge, and (3) the courage to take moral action along with a brief overview of Nicodemus's corresponding action.

Table 10.2 Nicodemus' courageous followership

Dimension	*Action*
Courage to *Assume Responsibility*	Nicodemus took personal responsibility for seeking out Jesus, interviewing Him, and investigating His movement
Courage to *Challenge*	Nicodemus took verbal exception to the Pharisees' self-serving application of the law
Courage to *Take Moral Action*	Nicodemus willingly contradicts the Jewish leadership's rejection of Jesus and helps to bury the body

Note Chaleff's (2009) courageous followership does not require all seven dimensions be present

Discussion

The purpose of this chapter was to determine, using a qualitative approach with a historical subject, whether courageous followership actions are useful for individuals in overcoming the groupthink present in their group. Several notable conclusions derived from the study, both directly and indirectly, are discussed. It is not enough to simply identify organizational ailments without also identifying potential antidotes. Thus, several recommendations are provided for followers, leaders, and groups in general. This endeavor has produced significant results but, as with most studies, has also produced new questions concerning the intersection of followership, leadership, and group dynamics. As such, several future research opportunities are noted.

Conclusions Derived

Several direct conclusions are derived from the study. First, Nicodemus is found as having conclusively demonstrated the attributes of a courageous follower. To be clear, Nicodemus is recognized as a courageous follower for two specific reasons—demonstrating a strong commitment to common purpose coupled with clear demonstration of at least three dimensions of courageous followership. This finding is significant as it provides a historical exemplar of courageous followership. The finding is also significant in that it presents a new view and a new way of understanding one of the New Testament's most mysterious characters. Second, courageous followership is found to be an effective method for overcoming groupthink at the individual level. Previous methods for overcoming groupthink have merit but have focused on top-down methods such as the leader recusing him/herself from contribution to group discussion until the later stages of a decision-making process or the leader's installation of a so-called devil's advocate who has the specific purpose of offering alternative viewpoints. Courageous followership, as a method for overcoming groupthink at the individual level, is certainly more of a bottom-up approach. This finding is significant because it provides a mechanism whereby followers within groups can break free from the bondage of the groupthink. It is also important to note this finding is specified as a mechanism for overcoming groupthink at the individual level and is not necessarily effective at the group level. Third, courageous followership although effective at the individual level will not necessarily prevent the group from pursuing some group-level initiated tragedy. It is a matter of historical fact that the Jewish leadership of the first century, overwhelmed with severe groupthink, was directly involved in the crucifixion of Jesus of Nazareth. Even the Roman governor of Judaea at the time, Pontius Pilate, is well known for ordering the death of Jesus not because he found Him guilty of a crime but simply to pacify the complaining Jews. Any reasonable individual would recognize the execution of an innocent person as an important tragedy. This finding is significant because the courageous follower, although breaking free from the groupthink himself or herself, may not be able to stop the tragedies that often accompany groups plagued by groupthink.

At least two indirect conclusions appear to be discernible from the present study. To be clear, these conclusions are noted as indirect, meaning they may be presumed relevant based on close proximity to the historical events and the direct findings of the study. First, courageous followership may be a lonely enterprise for the courageous follower. Nicodemus as the courageous follower exemplar is presented thrice in John's gospel and in none of those instances is he accompanied by a robust group of other courageous followers. Nicodemus came alone to the initial meeting with Jesus. He alone spoke in defense of Jesus in the Sanhedrin meeting. Only one other individual was involved in the burial of Jesus. Courageous followers should consider the reality that their courageous acts may not be initially met with vast support from other group members. Second, courageous followership may eventually be contagious and may spread to other persons associated with the organization. In reviewing the historical record, no direct links can be made between Nicodemus' courageous follower behaviors and the courageous behaviors of future Sanhedrin group members. However, the record does show examples of other Jewish leaders abandoning the groupthink of the Sanhedrin. In Acts 5:34–39, Gamaliel alone gave advice to the Council to abandon their intentions to execute the Apostles whom they had arrested. Later in Acts 15:5, information is provided indicating there was a "sect of the Pharisees who had believed" in Jesus and had converted to Christianity. It is possible that acts of courageous followership, although a lonesome endeavor initially, may serve as a form of leadership where the exemplar persuades others to follow based on his or her example. Courageous followership appears to attract followers.

Recommendations for Leaders, Followers, and Groups

Viewing Nicodemus' courageous followership activity and considering the various conclusions one can derive from the present study leads to the development of several recommendations. Inquiries such as the present study have obvious value in social science research, but such value is enhanced when ideas are gleaned for practical application in contemporary organizations. The following recommendations are suggested in that vein—practical and immediate application for organizational leaders, followers, and groups.

Recommendations for Leaders

Three significant recommendations are offered for individuals in leadership positions. First, the leader must actively engage in his or her leadership context rather than demonstrating passive involvement. Leaders in senior leadership roles who demonstrate a *laissez-faire* approach are likely to allow the existence of middle and lower-level organizational leaders who are immature or poisonous to effective followership. Passive leaders who allow juvenile leaders and toxic leaders to persist undisturbed are likely to squelch effective followership in the organization while the organization may become infected with a system-wide toxicity. Second, the leader must create and work to maintain a culture conducive to courageous followership. Leaders must promote an atmosphere where effective and courageous followership is not only permitted but pursued. The leaders should use the normal organizational culture mediums of direct communication, placement of artifacts, creation of rituals, and the like but must specifically create reward systems that promote effective followership while frequently addressing followership issues. Organizational culture is inevitably a function of what the leader pays attention to and what the leader rewards. Third, leaders must implement a recurring assessment strategy whereby levels of courageous followership are frequently evaluated. A comprehensive followership evaluation strategy would include a 360 ° evaluation process whereby followers' levels of effective followership are measured by other followers, leaders, team members, customers, other stakeholders, and the like. Effective followers are likely to value a peer-review process as much or more than the traditional top-down performance appraisal process. A followership auditing process involving an outside entity could also be implemented by organizational leaders. Much like the company's finances are subject to a periodic audit from an outside accounting firm, executive leaders could periodically bring in followership experts from outside the organization to assess the followership health of the organization from an objective viewpoint.

Recommendations for Followers

Four meaningful recommendations are provided for individuals in followership positions. First, followers should shift their paradigm to a mental state where they recognize their own value and contribution to the organization. Most organizational followers do not know how "research suggests that followers contribute an average of 80% to the success of an organization" (Koonce et al., 2016, p. xv). Followers should not become prideful and arrogant relative to their worth to the organization no more than their leadership counterparts should. However, followers too often believe they are just another number, another warm body, or another strong back. Followers must change their thinking in this regard and realize their role is important and what they do in the organization really does matter. Second, followers should commit to the organization's mission in order to fully support the common purpose. Followers cannot commit to the mission or the common purpose they share with their leader and other followers without knowing, understanding, and believing in the mission. Effective followers will demonstrate loyalty to mission above loyalty to leader or other followers. Third, followers should *follow* by example through demonstrating courageous and effective follower attributes. Obviously, to *follow* by example is to reiterate the cliché statement "lead by example" but to do so by assigning importance to the act of following while preserving the value of being an exemplar. Effective follower exemplars will demonstrate effective followership authentically—with integrity and the value of *prima facie* credibility. When following by example, courageous followers understand they are role-modeling effective followership behaviors in view of other followers and organizational leaders. Fourth, followers must develop a certain psychological armor protecting themselves mentally for the potential hazard and backlashes often experienced by courageous followers. It is a difficult suggestion to offer, but courageous followers must be mentally prepared for negative consequences. Courageous followers must be mentally prepared to be the target of unscrupulous acts, to be alone in standing for what is right, and to be strong for their family and friends who may suffer as a result of their courageous acts. A strong mental preparedness for potential undesired outcomes is the best defense a courageous follower has against those possible realities.

Recommendations for Groups

Two notable recommendations are suggested for groups involved in group-level activities. First, groups should engage in a concerted effort directed toward the internal policing of negative group behaviors. Groups should be concerned with whether the group is working in concert with the organization's mission or is working for the desires of the group. Internal policing can be problematic unless specifically assigned to certain members of the group. Once the group agrees to processes and procedures that are designed to reach objectives related to the organization's mission, the group should create a mission or purpose taskforce of members who are entrusted with frequent assessment of group activities. Second, groups should engage in courageous collaboration—a group-level application of the courageous follower model. Courageous collaboration would include group behaviors reminiscent of the courageous follower behavior. Courageous collaboration would involve group behaviors directed both internally to the group and externally to other stakeholders. Courageous collaboration would ensure attitudes of service and of a group ownership mentality, the desire for high moral and ethical standards, the willingness to challenge each other and transform as needed, and the ability to listen to parties with a vested interest. In most instances, the desire is that groups will mesh and transform into a team mindset. Courageous collaboration, in applying the courageous follower model to the group dynamic, surpasses the team mindset and would intrinsically include safety mechanisms to prevent group dysfunctions such as groupthink.

It is both important and interesting to understand how the application of courageous followership is not simply limited to followers. The execution of courageous followership is applicable to leaders and groups as well. A summary of the recommendations mentioned for leaders, followers, and groups is provided in Table 10.3. At each level, certain specific action items have been noted along with a summary description.

Table 10.3 Courageous followership application action items

Level	*Action*	*Description*
Leader	Active engagement	Executive leadership should disallow middle and lower-level organizational leaders who are juvenile or toxic
Leader	Culture creation	Leaders should promote an atmosphere where effective and courageous followership is permitted and pursued
Leader	Recurring Assessment	Leaders should implement a comprehensive followership evaluation strategy
Follower	Paradigm Shift	Followers should recognize their own value and contribution to the organization
Follower	Mission Commitment	Followers should fully support the common purpose as expressed by the organization's mission
Follower	Follow by Example	Followers should role-model effective followership behaviors for other followers and organizational leaders
Follower	Psychological Armor	Followers should protect themselves mentally from the potential hazards of courageous followership
Group	Internal Policing	Groups should engage in a concerted effort to eliminate negative group behaviors
Group	Courageous Collaboration	Groups should pursue a group-level application of the courageous follower model

Future Research Opportunities

Various future research opportunities exist based on the results and limits of the present study. These future research streams include additional investigation related to groupthink and continued examination of the courageous followership model. As related to groupthink, the present work indicates how courageous followership may help individuals within groups overcome groupthink. Thus, the present work presents a possible individual level solution to groupthink used by an in-group member. At least two areas of focus should stem from this finding. First, some replication of this study should be conducted to further validate these findings. Additional research could indicate whether other historical cases of groups immersed in groupthink and individual members who overcame the groupthink are available for study. The groupthink phenomenon lends itself to study from a historical view, but additional research with the courageous follower model and groupthink should be conducted with contemporary human subjects. Second, because the present chapter focuses on an in-group member, additional research should be conducted to determine whether groupthink can be corrected by some mechanism used by persons outside the group. Such research could reveal whether any of a group's stakeholders, except in-group members, have any power or influence over a group suffering from groupthink. This research might offer a groupthink solution for concerned parties from outside the group, and, again, historical cases are useful subjects of study for such an investigation.

Continued examination of the courageous follower model is needed in order to continue to hone its applicability within contemporary organizations. As a result of the present study, at least four areas of potential research related to the courageous follower are indicated. First, there is a need to understand how the courageous followership model can be applied at a group level. The model itself is intrinsically focused on the development of an individual follower. The term *Courageous Collaboration* is tentatively offered as a means to reference the potential application of the courageous follower model within the collaborative context of a group. If a courageous collaboration model is to be developed, much conceptual research is needed to determine exactly how or if each of the seven courageous follower dimensions is applied in the group context and whether additional dimensions would need inclusion in the model. The idea of a courageous collaboration offers significant research potential. Second, research is needed to help understand whether the courageous follower model is the potential antidote to bad followership behaviors. Bad followership types and behaviors are identified in much of the literature as some application or combination of low engagement, low independent thinking, the tendency to conform, or the tendency to collude. Research could reveal whether persons equipped with bad followership tendencies could be retooled using the courageous follower model. It is not enough to simply identify the bad followership tendencies among some followers. A research need exists to help practitioners move bad followership into good or possibly courageous followership. Third, research is needed to provide a better understanding of how effective followership and/or courageous followership is impacted by dysfunctional, juvenile, or toxic leadership. As mentioned, followership is underrepresented in the literature, but the negative forms of leadership are also significantly underrepresented. As a result, little is known about the intersection of followership and poor leadership. Research in this vein could indicate whether followers are able to practice effective and/or courageous followership in an environment dominated by a toxic leader. Fourth, applied research should be conducted for the purpose of developing an organizational follower training program where members learn the courageous follower model and how to use the appropriate courage and when that courage should be manifested in action. It is not enough to simply encourage followers to be more courageous in the workplace or in their interactions with leaders. Followers need help in developing the practical skill and discernment for superior application of the courageous follower model. Although gaining some traction in the research literature, followership in general lags far behind leadership in empirical study whether in qualitative or quantitative form. Specifically advancing the research surrounding the courageous follower model would improve understanding of the model's application while simultaneously helping to bridge the gap between leadership and followership as related to levels of empirical research.

Chapter Take-Aways

There are five important takeaways worth noting from this chapter. First, Nicodemus can be understood as a courageous follower whose primary goal was in pursuit of his organization's original mission. Second, courageous followership can be understood as a mechanism for overcoming groupthink tendencies at the individual level. Third, senior organizational leaders should eliminate toxic behaviors among junior leaders, create a followership culture, and frequently assess those efforts. Fourth, organizational members (followers) must embrace their value to the organization, commit to the mission, provide an example of effective followership, and implement mental defenses against effective followership hazards. Fifth, groups within organizations should courageously work together and establish internal policing processes to deter negative group behaviors. Ultimately, this chapter demonstrates Nicodemus as an example of a courageous follower who conquered groupthink so that he could truly follow in the footsteps of Jesus.

Reflective Questions

- How might you experience groupthink differently when in the leader role as compared with when you are in the follower role?
- As an organizational leader, how could you go about creating organizational environments that encourage effective and courageous followership?
- As an organizational member, how do you work *with* your organizational leader instead of working *for* that leader?
- As a member of a group within an organization, what would be an effective method for deterring negative group behavior?
- Why are some organizational leaders afraid to encourage effective followership, and why are some followers fearful to implement the courageous follower model?

References

Badie, D. (2010). Groupthink, Iraq, and the war on terror: Explaining US policy shift toward Iraq. *Foreign Policy Analysis, 6*(4), 277. https://doi.org/10.1111/j.1743-8594.2010.00113.x

Bassler, J. (1989). Mixed signals: Nicodemus in the fourth gospel. *Journal of Biblical Literature, 108*(4), 635–646. https://doi.org/10.2307/3267184

Bell, R. M. (2016). First century groupthink: An exegetical case study. *Journal of Biblical Integration in Business, 19*(1), 26–37.

Burnette, J. L., Pollack, J. M., & Forsyth, D. R. (2011). Leadership in extreme contexts: A groupthink analysis of the May 1996 Mount Everest disaster. *Journal of Leadership Studies, 4*(4), 29–40. https://doi.org/10.1002/jls.20190

Chaleff, I. (2009). *The courageous follower: Standing up to & for our leaders* (3rd ed.). Berrett-Koehler.

Chaleff, I. (2011). Courageous followers. *Leadership Excellence, 28*(4), 19.

Chaleff, I. (2016). In praise of followership style assessments. *Journal of Leadership Studies, 10*(3), 45–48. https://doi.org/10.1002/jls.21490

Deffinbaugh, R. L. (2002). *That you might believe: A study of the Gospel of John.* Biblical Studies Press.

deSilva, D. A. (2004). *An introduction to the new testament: Contexts, methods & ministry formation.* InterVarsity Press.

Driscoll, J. F. (1911). Nicodemus. *The Catholic encyclopedia* (Vol. 11). Robert Appleton Company.

Farelly, N. (2013). An unexpected ally: Nicodemus's role within the plot of the Fourth Gospel. *Trinity Journal, 34*(1), 31–43.

Ford, D. F. (2013). Meeting Nicodemus: A case study in daring theological interpretation. *Scottish Journal of Theology, 66*(1), 1–17.

Harrison, E. F. (1946). The son of god among the sons of men. Jesus and Nicodemus. *Bibliotheca Sacra 103*(409), 50–56.

Henderson, C. (2015). *Toxic followership: A measure of followers associated with destructive leadership* (Doctoral dissertation). Available from ProQuest Dissertations and Theses Global database. (UMI No. 1759139102)

Hughes, P., & White, E. (2010). The space shuttle challenger disaster: A classic example of groupthink. *Ethics & Critical Thinking Journal, 2010*(3), 63–70.

Kellerman, B. (2005). How bad leadership happens. *Leader to Leader, 2005*(35), 41–46.

Kellerman, B. (2008). *Followership: How followers are creating change and changing leaders.* Harvard Business Press.

Kelley, R. E. (1988). In praise of followers. *Harvard Business Review, 66*(6), 142–148.

Kelley, R. E. (1992). *The power of followership: How to create leaders people want to follow and followers who lead themselves.* Doubleday.

Koonce, R., Bligh, M. C., Carsten, M. K., & Hurwitz, M. (Eds.). (2016). *Followership in action: Cases and commentaries.* Emerald Publishing.

Janis, I. L. (1982). *Groupthink: Psychological studies of policy decisions and fiascoes.* Houghton Mifflin.

Lavoie, B. B., Lavoie, G. R., Klutstein, D., & Regan, J. (1982). Jesus, the Turin shroud, and Jewish burial customs. *The Biblical Archaeologist, 45*(1), 5–6.

Malina, B. J. (2001). *The new testament world: Insights from cultural anthropology.* Westminster John Knox Press.

Padilla, A., Hogan, R., & Kaiser, R. B. (2007). The toxic triangle: Destructive leaders, susceptible followers, and conducive environments. *Leadership Quarterly, 18*(3), 176–194. https://doi.org/10.1016/j.leaqua.2007.03.001

Perrin, N., Brown, J. K., & Green, J. B. (2013). *Dictionary of Jesus and the Gospels.* IVP Academic.

Robbins, V. K. (1996a). *Exploring the texture of texts: A guide to socio-rhetorical interpretation.* Trinity Press International.

Robbins, V. K. (1996b). *The tapestry of early Christian discourse: Rhetoric, society, and ideology.* Routledge.

t Hart., P. (1991). Irving L. Janis' victims of groupthink. *Political Psychology, 12*(2), 247.

Thoroughgood, C. N., Padilla, A., Hunter, S. T., & Tate, B. W. (2012). The susceptible circle: A taxonomy of followers associated with destructive leadership. *Leadership Quarterly, 23*(5), 897–917.

Uhl-Bien, M., Riggio, R. E., Lowe, K. B., & Carsten, M. K. (2014). Followership theory: A review and research agenda. *The Leadership Quarterly, 25*(25th anniversary issue), 83–104. https://doi.org/10.1016/j.leaqua.2013.11.007
Whitenton, M. R. (2016). The dissembler of John 3: A cognitive and rhetorical approach to the characterization of Nicodemus. *Journal of Biblical Literature, 135*(1), 141–158.

CHAPTER 11

Apostle Jude: Jesus Said, "Follow Me"—The Power of Followership

Nestor L. Colls-Senaha

The Power of Followership

The chapter explores what type of follower Jude is in comparison to Chaleff (2009), Kellerman (2008), and Kelley's (1992, 2008) typologies. The purpose is not to prove or disprove the author of this epistle, date of penmanship, audience, or kinship to Jesus and James (deSilva, 2004; Nelson, 2019; Swindoll, n.d.); but demonstrate the similarities between effective follower and leader characteristics. Lanier (2012) surmised leaders and followers vacillate between roles depending on the situation, and both are mutually supportive. Consequently, followership exhibited by Jude can be used in today's workplace both trans-organizationally and cross-culturally.

The chapter outline is separated into three sections: a general overview of Jude's letter; the different followership approaches (Fairhurst & Grant, 2010; Katz & Kahn, 1978) and definitions (Carsten et al., 2018; Howell

N. L. Colls-Senaha (✉)
Regent University, Virginia Beach, VA, USA

D. J. Dean and R. B. Huizinga (eds.), *Followership and Faith at Work*, Christian Faith Perspectives in Leadership and Business,
https://doi.org/10.1007/978-3-030-90614-6_11

& Costley, 2005); and identifying specific areas of followership typology contributing to a praxis application of the follower-leader duality.

Overview of Jude's Letter

New Testament Epistles like Romans, Ephesians, and Galatians contribute heavily to concrete applications for followers and leaders alike; however, there is one seldom referenced, discussed, or addressed, the Epistle of Jude. Many biblical scholars concluded that Jude was the author and half-brother of Jesus Christ (deSilva, 2004; Nelson, 2019; Swindoll, n.d.). Neither the New Testament nor Christian history provided much information about Jude (Lea & Black, 2003). The New Testament mentions six individuals by Judas's name, translated Jude in English (Nelson, 2019): (1) Judas a brother of Jesus (Matt. 13:55, NASB), (2) Judas Iscariot, the infamous disciple who betrayed Jesus (Matt. 10:4), (3) Judas, the son of James (Luke 6:16), (4) Judas, Paul's host in Damascus (Acts 9:11), (5) Judas called Barsabbas, a leading Christian in Jerusalem and Paul's companion (Acts 15:22), and (6) Judas, a revolutionary leader (Acts 5:37); hence, the controversy surrounding the authorship. Jude was an unbeliever before Jesus' resurrection (John 7:5; Acts 1:4), becoming a follower post-resurrection (Acts 1:14), and believed to be the brother of James the Apostle (Jude 1:1, Matt. 13:55, Mark 6:3).

Dating the Epistle of Jude is arguable as he did not specify his intended audience, although some scholars believed the letter was written in the late first century (deSilva, 2004; Nelson, 2019; Swindoll, n.d.). The consensus of the first-century date is deducted from Jude 1:3, 17 due to the contextual references of faith (vs. 3), and the hearers being second-generation Christians because Jude reminds them of the apostles' words (vs. 17) (Brand et al., 2003, Holman's Bible Dictionary).

Overview of Followership

Approaches

Followership can be divided into two classifications: role-based and constructionist. A role-based approach (Katz & Kahn, 1978) is where followers exhibit certain behaviors while occupying an informal or formal position in a hierarchical system. For example, during the time of Jesus and Jude, the Roman Empire had a hierarchy of authority. Power flowed down from Caesar to the central administration, senate, and the provincial administration, and eventually to the Roman citizen (Wilson, 2011).

Conversely, the constructionist approach (Fairhurst & Grant, 2010) is a relational interaction between a leader and a follower that is not tied to a role, but a behavior (Uhl-Bien et al., 2014). An example of the constructionist approach is Jesus and His disciples. The leader taught the disciples, His followers, what they needed to know to accomplish shared goals in each situation. The leader–follower connection shared was an on-going, dynamic, relational process of give and take. This was accomplished by both the leader and follower acting ethically and morally by doing the right thing first and doing it the right way (Maroosis, 2008).

Jesus instituted a new paradigm of participatory organizational design by providing a spiritual leadership model where the disciples could aspire and engage the world (Wilson, 2011). He trained them by utilizing a program that incorporated three factors: institutional training, field assignments, and self-development actions (*AR 350–1*, 2017). In Matthew's book, institutional training was illustrated by Jesus going throughout Galilee teaching in their synagogues, preaching the good news, and healing the sick (Matt. 4:23). The disciples' intimate relationship began by believing in Him and accompanying Him to various special occasions and preaching events. Secondly, the field assignments were not given until later when Jesus sent the disciples and gave them authority to drive out evil spirits, heal every disease and sickness, and preach the good news of the kingdom of heaven (Matt. 10:1, 5–42). These twelve men were not just traveling companions, but co-workers trained through an intimate relationship, preparing them to preach in Jerusalem and, eventually, the world (Matt. 10:1–4). Self-development actions are reflected in Luke (11:2–5), when Jesus provides the disciples with the Lord's Prayer and the mandate, "anyone who wants to be first must be the very last, and the servant of all" (Mark 9:35).

Definition

Researchers introduced several definitions of "followership" into literature (Bjugstad et al., 2006; Chaleff, 2009; Fairhurst & Grant, 2010; Kellerman, 2008; R. E. Kelley, 1992). Carsten et al. (2010, p. 559) suggested, "Followership is a relational role in which followers can influence leaders and contribute to the improvement and attainment of the group and organizational objectives." Followership is also defined as "an interactive rather than a hierarchical approach to the relationship of leadership and followership roles" (Howell & Costley, 2005, p. 298), each being of equal value in achieving organizational performance and goals (Crossman & Crossman, 2011). Currently, despite the increased attention on followership, there is no generally accepted definition.

Being a significant follower involves risk because they adhere to the organization's mission by committing to serve the leader, challenge the leader, if necessary, and accept transformation when needed (Chaleff, 2008, pp. 72–73). The leader–follower exchange is a relationship that is intentionally resisting the status quo and providing the ability to respond effectively to changing situations (Maroosis, 2008).

The twelve disciples are the epitome of effective situational followers. Throughout the New Testament, the disciples serve their leader by assuming risk, ministering, challenging corrupt leaders, accepting, inducing transformation, and vacillating between assuming the roles of a leader and a follower. For example, Peter was one of the first to take the risk of becoming a disciple (Matt. 4:18) and walking on water (14:27). Also, Peter challenged Jesus when he explained His impending death, "Peter took Him aside and began to rebuke Him. "Never Lord!" he said. "This shall never happen to You!" (Matt. 16:22). After Pentecost, Peter's transformational shift initiates his move from follower/servant to leader/spiritual leader. Peter's Holy Spirit inspired vision, guides the change process from slavery to the law to freedom in the Spirit through his preaching, and 3,000 were saved (Acts 2:14, 41).

Followership Perspectives

Uhl-Bien et al. (2014) identified five followership perspectives. This section will address how each applies to Jude's book and will close with a praxis application of the follower-leader duality.

Followers Get the Job Done

Jude started his letter by suggesting he was initially going to write about salvation but abruptly changed to contend with something that required his readers' immediate attention and awareness (vs. 3). Simultaneously, it was a direct attack against the opponents of the Gospel (Brand et al., 2003). He felt strongly about supporting the leaders' policies and provided independent constructive criticism while displaying *exemplary follower* (Kelley, 1992) traits. Jude exposed those who were acting in opposition by championing a need for change, assuming responsibility for the common purpose, and taking a moral stand to prevent ethical abuses (Chaleff, 2008). Christian history illustrates that there will always be enmity against the church, and new threats will frequently arise (Gatiss, 2019).

Scriptures teach Jesus was a servant (Mark 10:45) and a spiritual leader (Fry & Egel, 2017). Likewise, Scripture identified Jude as a follower of Jesus (Jude 1:1) and a spiritual leader (Jude 1:3–4). Jude's effective followership arose from self-managing confidence, combined with his commitment, competence, and courage that is generally associated with leadership (Kelley, 2008). Applying his independent evaluation of the outcome, Jude offers recommendations or solutions to the situation, demonstrating how leaders and followers are closely intertwined. The interdependence between the leader and follower makes the roles more difficult to define in an organizational structure (Gobble, 2017). Also, Jude's awareness, attentiveness, supportiveness, independent thinking, self-development actions, and perseverance made him an *exemplar*.

Followers Work in the Best Interest of the Organization's Mission

Followers accomplish the mission by being proactive and placing the organizational goals ahead of the leaders. Jesus foresaw and warned His disciples/followers that because of the message they preach that people will go against them, throw them out of the synagogues, and eventually try to kill them, believing they were doing the will of God (John 16:1–4). In other words, He taught them to be vigilant and cognizant of the fact that there are people who will attempt to sabotage the organization. Jude remembered the warning and implemented a course of action to stop morally objectional behavior. Jude exposes the behaviors and characters of the "godless men, who changed the grace of our God into a license for immorality and denied Jesus Christ our only Sovereign and Lord" (v. Jude 1:4) to his followers. Jude challenged the "godless men" and exhibited the characteristics of a *partner* (Chaleff, 2009). He was not afraid to condemn these men who were perverting the Gospel and denying Jesus Christ. He compares them to Sodom and Gomorrah (Jude 1:7), "which likewise indulged in sexual immorality and pursued unnatural desire." He also compared them to Cain, Balaam, and Korah from the Old Testament (Gatiss, 2019). These men follow their dreams (verse 8) instead of the Holy Spirit and "defile the flesh, reject authority, and blaspheme the glorious ones."

Additionally, verse 16 states the men were "grumblers, malcontents, following their sinful desires," placing them as toxic leaders (Lipman-Blumen, 2008). The destructive behaviors and actions were counterintuitive to Jesus' teaching and undermining the integrity of the organization. Jude values the harmony within the organization and his relationship with his leader. He realizes the urgency of addressing and changing these behaviors by being "the primary defender of the toxic leaders" (Kelley, 2008, p. 14). Also, Jude's pro-activeness, vigilance, cognizant, initiative, integrity, harmonious, and defensive actions made him a *partner*.

Followers Challenge Leaders

Challenging leaders is not for the weak; therefore, an effective follower possessed three key elements: "(a) work-related knowledge, (b) good communication skills, and (c) motivation" (Yung & Tsai, 2013, p. 6). Judas displayed *work-related knowledge* by identifying the infiltrators as men who took part in the religious activities but were not part of the church. He highlights the fine line between real followers and the intruders, causing division and devoid of the Holy Spirit (Jude 1:19). Jude's behavior reflects Kellerman's typology of differentiating followers by a single attribute: *level of engagement* (Kellerman, 2008; Northouse, 2019). Kellerman (2008) describes followership at the lower end of the spectrum as an *isolate*, and at the opposite end as a *diehard*. The *isolate* is entirely unengaged, and the *diehard* is exceptionally engaged. Utilizing Kellerman's typology of a diehard, when it comes to toxic leaders, Jude was "ready to remove them from positions of power, authority, and influence by any means necessary" and "willing to risk life and limb" (Kellerman, 2008, p. 92). Jude's motivation, boldness, dedication, and commitment to the cause made him a true diehard. Also, Jude's communication, knowledge, skills, motivation, engagement, activeness, boldness, and commitment made him a *diehard*.

Followers Support the Leader

Balancing the duality of leadership, simultaneously leading while following, challenges the leader to obviate a person's title or position depending on the situation (Lanier, 2012). Jude demonstrated this by referring to his audience as dear friends and implored them to contend with the situation (verse 20). He continues by encouraging them to "build yourselves up in your most holy faith and pray in the Holy Spirit" (verse 21). Jude reiterates what he was taught as a follower/servant and now gives his followers the same instructions. Jude reminds them to be vigilant in their faith, call on the Holy Spirit, and not rely on their strengths to rectify the situation.

Jude exhibits *courageous follower* traits by supporting the leader (Chaleff, 2009). Jude reflects on his past experiences as a follower to better understand what to do in these circumstances as a leader, influencing a positive change in behavior. For example, instead of chastising the followers who were deceived by these ungodly men, Jude instructs his followers to "be merciful to those who doubt; snatch others from the fire and save them; to others show mercy, mixed with fear..." (1:22–23). He instructs them to be morally strong and strive to do the right thing despite the multitude of challenges surrounding them (Northouse, 2019). Jude recognizes them more as partners, or co-leaders, in the relationship than followers (Carsten et al., 2010). Also, Jude's vigilance, faithfulness, encouragement, awareness, supportiveness, and selflessness made him a *courageous follower*.

Followers Learn from Leaders

Leaders and followers are required for a "vision to be created, accepted, disseminated, and implemented" for an organization to be successful (Carsten & Bligh, 2008, p. 289). Skillfully and with discernment, a leader must possess the foresight to look at the current situation and envision future outcomes, as Jesus demonstrated (Heyler & Martin, 2018) and taught to His disciples. Therefore, *situational followership* requires a leading or a subservient role according to what is best for a situation (Colls-Senaha, 2018).

The vision must be communicated, motivate followers, and align organizational resources to support the vision (Kantabutra & Avery, 2010). Jesus expresses His vision to the disciples/followers by telling them about the Great Commission (Matt. 28:18–20). Jesus motivates them by explaining to His disciples that those who engage in the work of evangelism will receive great rewards in the future (Matt. 10:40–42). In Matthew, God's providence provides the necessary resources to accomplish the vision, initiating followers/leaders on earth.

In other words, the idea of a partnership involving the invisible leader solidifies the common purpose of defeating an invisible enemy (Maroosis, 2008). Jude concluded his letter with the doxology (1:24–25), which means "word of glory" (Newton, 2020). He intentionally and respectfully shifts the attention from himself to the only leader worthy of being praised, honored, and glorified (Jude 1:25). Also, Jude's discernment, foresightedness, flexibility, willingness, and ability to learn, teach, challenge, and serve made him a *situational follower*.

Practical Application

This section will use Uhl-Bien et al. (2014) five-followership perspectives to illustrate the similarities of Audie Murphy's and Jude's character traits required to be an exemplary, diehard, partner courageous follower.

Followers Get the Job Done

Audie Murphy was one of twelve children from humble beginnings. His father abandoned them, and his mother died when he was sixteen. He attempted to enlist in the U.S. Army, Marines, and Navy when he was seventeen but was rejected for being underweight and underage. Murphy eventually enlisted in the U.S. Army to support his family. He contended with a matter that was urgent and required his immediate attention, his siblings' safety, and welfare. Murphy completed his institutional training (basic training), field-assignment (advanced infantry training), and self-development training which was his subsequent deployment to Casa Blanca in French Morocco while assigned to the 15th Infantry Regiment, 3d Infantry Division (Grimsley, 2019). Murphy felt strongly about supporting the United States' foreign policies and acting in opposition to Germany and Japan. He championed the need for change, assumed responsibility for the common purpose, and took a moral stand (Chaleff, 2009). Also, Murphy's awareness, responsiveness, self-sufficiency, initiative, supportiveness, independent thinking, self-development actions, and perseverance made him an *exemplar*.

Followers Work in the Best Interest of the Organization's Mission

Audie Murphy accomplished the mission by being proactive and doing what was in the best interest of the organization's mission ahead of his safety by displaying *exemplar* follower traits (Kellerman, 2008). German soldiers attacked Murphy's platoon after landing on Yellow Beach during the Allied invasion of southern France. He advanced alone and eliminated several German positions and captured eleven prisoners. Similar to Jude, Murphy was not afraid to expose the enemy and place them in the category of *a toxic leader* (Lipman-Blumen, 2008). Murphy valued the harmony within the organization and his relationship with his leaders.

On two separate missions, within a month, at Montelimar and north-eastern France, Murphy was awarded the Presidential Unit Citation, Silver Star, and Purple Heart (Grimsley, 2019) for his actions. Murphy realized the urgency of addressing and changing these behaviors by being "the primary defender of a *toxic leader*" (R. Kelley, 2008, p. 14). Also, Murphy's proactiveness, independence, selflessness, bravery, fearlessness, aggressiveness, and defensiveness made him a *partner*.

Followers Challenge Leaders

Audie Murphy possessed three key elements that describe him as a *diehard* because he was intensely engaged (Kellerman, 2008). First, he displayed work-related knowledge by identifying the infiltrators. For example, Private Murphy demonstrated intense valor by single-handedly holding off two German reinforced companies for an hour and was one of the most-decorated American soldiers in World War II (Grimsley, 2019). Second, his communication skills were intense despite the fog of war and the deafening sounds of artillery, tanks, and machine guns. He was able to direct his men by climbing on a blazing tank and operating the machine gun. At one point, Murphy recalls a sergeant charging the German position approximately two hundred yards away and getting shot three separate times and getting up each time. Third, his bravery motivated him and his men to follow suit, which led to the Germans throwing down their weapons and surrendering (Britannica, 2020). Like Jude, Murphy was "ready to remove them from positions of power, authority, and influence by any means necessary" (Kellerman, 2008, p. 92). As a result of his combat actions, he was awarded several military combat award for valor (Grimsley, 2019). Also, Murphy's knowledge, skills, intensity, valorousness, knowledge, communication, delegation, motivation, engagement, boldness, initiation, bravery, and commitment made him a *diehard*.

Followers Support the Leader

Audie Murphy understood the duality of leadership. His actions earned him a battlefield commission to second lieutenant, which elevated him to platoon leader who could be upwards of 100–200 men. Murphy reflects on his past experiences as a follower to better understand what to do as a leader to influence a positive change in behavior. While traveling to Brouvelieures his platoon came under attack by a German sniper group. He captured two German soldiers and eliminated the third (Britannica, 2020). Like Jude, Murphy exhibited a courageous follower's traits by supporting his leaders (Chaleff, 2009). He not only instructed his soldiers but demonstrated how to be morally strong and strive to do the right thing despite the multitude of challenges surrounding them (Northouse, 2019). Also, Murphy's leadership, reflectiveness, influence, flexibility, supportiveness, morality, and selflessness made him a *courageous follower*.

Followers Learn from Leaders
Throughout his time in Europe, Audie Murphy's actions were so valorous, he eventually was awarded the Congressional Medal of Honor, the military's highest award. Later, Murphy was promoted to first lieutenant and moved from the front lines to Regimental Headquarters and made a liaison. First Lieutenant Murphy knew first-hand what it was to be a *situational follower,* which required a leading or a subservient role according to what was best for a situation (Colls-Senaha, 2018). After World War II, and after completing his time in the U.S. Army, Audie Murphy returned to Texas and continued his time in the Army National Guard. He was promoted to the rank of Major and completed his remaining time in the United States Army Reserves. Murphy eventually became a movie star making over 40 feature films and television series and wrote the book "To Hell and Back" about his World War II experiences. He died in a plane crash at the young age of 46 and was interred with full honors at Arlington National Cemetery (Britannica, 2020). Also, Murphy's discernment, valorousness, foresight, flexibility, willingness, ability to learn, teach, challenge, and serve made him a *situational follower*.

Chapter Takeaways

Followership is an untapped resource that is ready to be opened and explored. It has been around since the beginning of time, but people are still perplexed about what it is, what it does, or how to harness its power that is prevalent in all aspects of our daily lives. Societies have been built, destroyed, and rebuilt by followers, but we credit the handful of leaders. Time and time again we overlook the simple yet complex role a follower plays when deciding to adhere or refuse the directions of others. The military has the luxury of maintaining the status quo as a hierarchical bureaucracy because of the uniqueness of their mission, roles, and responsibilities. However, in these volatile times, the military must also devolve command responsibilities to lower-ranking individuals to exercise "complex leadership and management tasks" (Stringer, 2009, p. 88). Conversely, practitioners, scholars, and organizations alike must increase their focus on follower's traits and effectiveness in the workplace to be successful. Subsequently, an increasing number of writers argue that "exemplary," "courageous," and "star" followers are a precondition for high-performing organizations (Chaleff, 2009; Kellerman, 2008; Kelley, 2008; Northouse, 2019; Yung & Tsai, 2013) to name a few. Effective followers are an integral part in the positive change of an organization. Therefore, people at all levels must focus on changing culture through embedding a pro-followership mentality, utilizing every system and process to harness the power of followership, changing programs and systems to understand the positive influence fully, and influencing followers by reinforcing the new cultural focus (Colls-Senaha, 2018).

Reflective Questions

1. What additional personal character traits did you identify about Jude that made him an effective follower?
2. Can a follower truly be effective in a role-based organization?
3. How could organizations incorporate the three key elements of effective followership in their training and development programs?
4. What aspects of the five-followership perspectives can improve either a secular or Christian organization?
5. Describe the commonalities of followership and leadership as a means of improving the understanding of follower traits and their impact on organizational performance?

References

Army training and leader development. (2017). U.S. Government Printing Office. https://armypubs.army.mil/ProductMaps/PubForm/Details.aspx?PUB_ID=1002540

Bjugstad, K., Thach, E. C., Thompson, K. J., & Morris, A. (2006). A fresh look at followership: A model for matching followership and leadership styles. *Journal of Behavioral and Applied Management; Glendale*, *7*(3), 313–319.

Brand, C., Draper, C., & England, A. (2003). *Holman illustrated the bible dictionary—Liberty university*. https://liberty.alma.exlibrisgroup.com

Britannica. (2020, June 16). *Audie Murphy | Biography, films, & facts*. Encyclopedia Britannica. https://www.britannica.com/biography/Audie-Murphy

Carsten, M., & Bligh, M. (2008). Lead, follow and get out of the way: Involving, employees in the visionary process. In R. E. Riggio, I. Chaleff, & J. Blueman (Eds.), *The art of followershp: How great followers create great leaders and organizations* (pp. 277–290). San Francisco, CA: Jossey-Bass.

Carsten, M., Uhl-Bien, M., Wet, B., Paera, J., & McGregor, R. (2010). Exploring social constructions of followersip: A qualitative study. *The Leadership Quarterly, 21*(3), 543–562. https://doi.org/10.1016/j.leaqua.2010.03.015

Carsten, M. K., Uhl-Bien, M., & Huang, L. (2018). Leader perceptions and motivation as outcomes of followership role orientation and behavior. *Leadership, 14*(6), 731–756. https://doi.org/10.1177/1742715017720306

Chaleff, I. (2008). Creating new ways of following. In R. E. Riggio, I. Chaleff, & J. Lipman-Blumen (Eds.), *The art of followership: How great followers create great leaders and organizations* (pp. 67–87). Wiley. http://ebookcentral.proquest.com/lib/liberty/detail.action?docID=331447

Chaleff, I. (2009). *The courageous follower: Standing up to and for our leaders*. Berrett-Koehler Publishers. http://ebookcentral.proquest.com/lib/liberty/detail.action?docID=479212

Colls-Senaha, N. L. (2018). *A phenomenological study of different followership styles as perceived or experienced by officers and noncommissioned officers while serving on combat missions in Afghanistan or Iraq wars* (PhD dissertations). Regent University. http://search.proquest.com/pqdtglobal/docview/2151473851/abstract/592912EE07B54934PQ/1

Crossman, B., & Crossman, J. (2011). Conceptualising followership—A review of the literature. *Leadership, 7*(4), 481–497. https://doi.org/10.1177/1742715011416891

deSilva, D. (2004). *An introduction to the New Testament: Context, methods, and ministry formation*. InterVarsity Press.

Fairhurst, G. T., & Grant, D. (2010). The social construction of leadership: A sailing guide. *Management Communication Quarterly, 24*(2), 171–210. https://doi.org/10.1177/0893318909359697

Fry, L., & Egel, E. (2017). Spiritual leadership: Embedding sustainability in the triple bottom line. *Graziadio Business Report, 20*, 1–29.

Gatiss, L. (2019). Contending in the perpetual battle: Jude and the constant need to fight valiantly against heresy. *Foundations (Affinity), 77*, 6–14.

Gobble, M. M. (2017). The value of followership. *Research Technology Management; Arlington, 60*(4), 59–61. http://dx.doi.org.ezproxy.liberty.edu/10.1080/08956308.2017.1325695

Grimsley, M. (2019, November 7). Audie Murphy made a name for himself in battle and on the screen. *Military Times*. https://www.militarytimes.com/

military-honor/salute-veterans/2019/11/08/audie-murphy-made-a-name-for-himself-in-battle-and-on-the-screen/

Heyler, S. G., & Martin, J. A. (2018). Servant leadership theory: Opportunities for additional theoretical integration. *Journal of Managerial Issues, 30*(2), 230–243.

Howell, J. P., & Costley, D. L. (2005). *Understanding behaviors for effective leadership* (2nd ed.). Pearson.

Kantabutra, S., & Avery, G. C. (2010). The power of vision: Statements that resonate. *Journal of Business Strategy, 31*(1), 37–45. https://doi.org/10.1108/02756661011012769

Katz, D., & Kahn, R. L. (1978). *The social psychology of organizations* (2nd ed.). Wiley.

Kellerman, B. (2008). *Followership: How followers are creating change and changing leaders*. Harvard Business Review Press.

Kelley, R. E. (1992). *The power of followership*. Doubleday Business.

Kelley, R. (2008). Rethinking followership. In R. E. Riggio, I. Chaleff, & J. Lipman-Blumen (Eds.), *The art of followership: How great followers create great leaders and organizations* (pp. 5–24). Wiley. http://ebookcentral.proquest.com/lib/liberty/detail.action?docID=331447

Lanier, J. (2012). Situational dynamics of the leader-follower relationship. *Strategic Leadership Review, 2*(2), 36–41.

Lea, T., & Black, D. A. (2003). *The New Testament: Its background and message* (2nd ed.). B&H Academic.

Lipman-Blumen, J. (2008). Following toxic leaders: In search of posthumous praise. In R. E. Riggio, I. Chaleff, & J. Lipman-Blumen (Eds.), *The art of followership: How great followers create great leaders and organizations* (pp. 181–194). Wiley. http://ebookcentral.proquest.com/lib/liberty/detail.action?docID=331447

Maroosis, J. (2008). Leadership: A partnership in reciprocal following. In R. E. Riggio, I. Chaleff, & J. Lipman-Blumen (Eds.), *The art of followership: How great followers create great leaders and organizations* (pp. 17–24). Wiley. http://ebookcentral.proquest.com/lib/liberty/detail.action?docID=331447

Nelson, R. (2019, September 11). Who was Jude the Apostle? The beginner's guide. *OverviewBible*. https://overviewbible.com/jude-the-apostle/

Newton, C. (2020, September 25). Jude: Contending for the faith. *Sermons*. https://bcnewton.co/2020/09/25/judesdoxology-jude-24-25/

Northouse, P. G. (2019). *Leadership: Theory and practice* (8th ed.). Sage.

Stringer, K. (2009). Educating the strategic corporal: A paradigm shift. *Military Review, September–October*(1), 87–95. Retrieved from https://www.armyupress.army.ml/Military-Review/

Swindoll, C. (n.d.). *Book of Jude overview—Insight for living ministries*. The Bible Teaching Ministry of Pastor Chuck Swindoll. Retrieved August 28, 2020, from https://www.insight.org/resources/bible/the-general-epistles/jude

Uhl-Bien, M., Riggio, R. E., Lowe, K. B., & Carsten, M. K. (2014). Followership theory: A review and research agenda. *The Leadership Quarterly, 25*(1), 83–104. https://doi.org/10.1016/j.leaqua.2013.11.007

Wilson, J. H. (2011). *The serving organization: Jesus vs. Hierarchy in Matthew* 20:20–28. 2, 8.

Yung, C. T., & Tsai, K. C. (2013). Followership: An important partner of leadership. *Business and Management Horizons, 1*(2), 47. https://doi.org/10.5296/bmh.v1i2.4233

CHAPTER 12

Wholehearted and Committed Followership of Nathanael: How a Communicated Vision of Jesus Creates Buy-In

Oiseomokhai N. Imoukhuede

Introduction

The connection between leadership and vision shows vision as a vital component or factor for effective leadership (Bass, 1985; Dennis & Borcanea, 2005; Halle & Fields, 2007). According to LaFasto and Larson (2001), "leadership is about vision—having a vision, articulating the vision, inspiring a shared commitment to the vision" (p. 147). Leadership vision essentially encompasses how leaders interact with followers to influence and move followers toward a goal using imagery of the future goal, mission, or purpose (Kouzes & Posner, 1995).

It is no wonder that Scriptures often reflect the idea of a shared, clearly articulated vision, and how that vision creates a sense of motivation for

O. N. Imoukhuede (✉)
Regent University, Virginia Beach, VA, USA
e-mail: oiseimo@mail.regent.edu

D. J. Dean and R. B. Huizinga (eds.), *Followership and Faith at Work*, Christian Faith Perspectives in Leadership and Business,
https://doi.org/10.1007/978-3-030-90614-6_12

those who receive it—an excellent example in the book of Habakkuk. Habakkuk 2:2 states, "*And the LORD answered me, and said, Write the vision, and make it plain upon tables, that he may run that readeth it*" (NKJV). Habakkuk echoes the impact of vision clarity on those who receive it, creating motion, inspiring, and giving direction. What is written and subsequently visualized creates imagery that moves the recipients of that vision toward a shared goal. Nevertheless, while a shared and articulated vision leads to motivated responses from followership, it is also essential to examine followers' attitudes and perceptions when presented with this clearly articulated vision. The reason for this is that not all followers respond positively to a clearly articulated vision of the future, given that followers are individuals that reflect varying levels of comment and engagement (Kelley, 1992). Therefore, the extent to which followers accept the presented imagery will depend on the individual followers' will, self-awareness, psychological ownership, internalized moral perspectives, and requires wholehearted cooperation for tasks and ultimate goals' accomplishments (Kelley, 1992; Vanwhy, 2015; Bell, 2007).

With this in mind, stories found in the New Testament, especially in the Gospels (Matthew, Mark, Luke, and John), often reveal followership principles that highlight various responses to Christ's call for followership. From these stories, narratives, events, and parables, we are given glimpses into the way Christ's disciples approached his leadership style as well as their followership responses. By carefully studying these stories of the disciples from the New Testament, we can evaluate their expectations, approaches, actions, and responses to the admonitions and words of Christ, which often conjured up visions of a future goal, state, or achievement.

John 1:43:51 is an exciting story of a meeting between Jesus and his future disciple named Nathanael. Nathanael's encounter with Jesus provides an excellent backdrop to examine contemporary conceptual factors that impact followers as they engage in a shared vision. This chapter, therefore, highlights an excellent example of this dynamic in play, as found in John 1:43–51. Utilizing narrative criticism of the text in John 1:43–51, we learn how Jesus' perception, presentation, and portrayal of vision inspired internal and wholehearted followership and buy-in by Nathanael, who initially was noncommittal to accepting the invitation to follow Christ but later changed, radically becoming a staunch follower of the cause. This chapter also reviews Nathanael's background and some internal factors that may have encouraged positive responses to the words of Christ. Followership types, as espoused by Kelley (1992), Chaleff (2008), and Kellerman (2008), are utilized to describe Nathanael's followership style, thus applying followership principles to the text to extract the strengths and weaknesses of Nathaniel's followership styles. The chapter also reviews the applicability of vision clarity by leaders and how followers can best embrace vision within contemporary settings. The ultimate goal of this chapter is to leverage the leader-centric approach to studying the relationship that exists between leaders and followers by providing fresh follower-focused perspectives from the Biblical text in John that was written by followers, about followers to followers to address the lack of initial excitement and participation of followers toward a goal, vision, or task. This chapter will be most helpful for leaders within nonprofit spaces leading volunteers who may have some insight into an organization's activities but lack initial excitement and commitment to a goal, vision, or task.

Who Was Nathanael?

Not much is discussed about Nathaniel in the New Testament except for two instances recorded in John's book. The first instance is in John 1:43–51, which records Nathanael's initial meeting with Christ and subsequent conversion, and the second time in John 21, which identified Nathanael as one of the disciples who witnessed the resurrected Christ.

There is some disagreement about Nathanael's identity because Nathanael is not mentioned in any of the synoptic gospels but only in the book of John. Many authors have linked Nathanael's identity to other known apostles. For example, Hill (1998) supposes that Nathanael was also known as James, the son of Alphaeus. Beresford (2020) acknowledged a supposition that pointed out that Nathanael was also Stephen, one of the deacons mentioned in the book of Acts. Beresford further asserted that another likelihood around the cult following of Nathanael was that he was a prince who renounced his royal linage and wealth to become a humble fisherman. The generally accepted supposition, however, is that Nathaniel is the same person as Bartholomew, mentioned in synoptic gospels in Mathew 10:3, Mark 3:18, Luke 6:14, and in the book of Acts in Acts 1:13 (Beresford, 2020; Greenwood, 1828; Keener, 2012; Rose, 2009; Trump, 2017). Keener's (2012) commentary on the book of John explains that Bartholomew meaning the son of Tolmai would have likely been Nathanael's surname similar to Peter

BarJonah (son of Jonah). The association of Nathanael with Bartholomew is because of the association with Philip (Beresford, 2020). Beresford further asserted that all the synoptic gospels describe Bartholomew and Phillip in sequence, reflecting a similar relationship between Phillip and Nathanael in the book of John.

According to John 21:2, the birthplace of Nathanael is Cana of Galilee, which had a mix of Jewish and Greek residents. The meaning of Nathanael "Nathana –El," "God gives" suggests that he was Hebrew, especially when compared to other disciple's names like Philip or Andrew, who had Greek names (Westcott, 2004). It is also likely that his name underscores the way Jesus perceives him as a true Israelite (Sarmiento, 2019). However, there is sparse discussion in the New Testament about Nathanael's missionary work except for details in the book of Acts listing Bartholomew with the apostles in the book of Acts. Rose (2009) points to traditions that suggest that Bartholomew ministered in Asia Minor and took the Gospel to India. Traditions also suggest that a cult of Bartholomew developed because of the way historical accounts described his death. According to traditions as posited by Rose, Nathanael died by being flayed alive and crucified upside down. The sheer violence of his death and the execution's viciousness revealed Nathanael's overall commitment to the Gospel and willingness to lose his life in such a painful way in order to advance the vision.

Examining the Text

John 1:43–51 is part of a larger narrative from the book of John 1 to chapter 12 called the "Book of Signs" (Sarmiento, 2019). This text, John 1:43–51, comes after a prologue that shows Christ as the eternal Word and the testimony of John the Baptist about Jesus as the Messiah. John the Baptist's testimony of Jesus sparks interest among his hearers, one of whom is the Apostle Andrew. Andrew's call, followed by Peter's as highlighted in verses 35 to 42, precedes the text. According to Trump (2017) and Sarmiento (2019), the events occurring within John 1:43–51 occurred over a four to six-day period. However, it is unclear whether the events occur in sequence or parallel with verses 35–42 (Sarmiento, 2019; Trump, 2017). Although the story of the conversion of Nathanael recorded in John 1:43–51 is not recorded in any of the synoptic gospels, Schreiber (1998) argued that the text is worthy of distinct focus and study as a single literary unit as themes within the text reveal the legitimacy of

Christ as the Messiah and the subsequent impact this revelation has on those involved in the narratives.

Verse 43 begins the text on a day following the day of the call of Peter. On this day, Jesus proactively goes to Galilee and finds Phillip in the process. Jesus calls on Philip, who is also from Bethsaida, similar to Andrew and Peter, to follow him. Phillip, intrigued by Jesus and convinced that Jesus is the Messiah, looks for his friend Nathanael in verse 45. Philip finds Nathanael and tells him that the person Moses and the Prophets wrote about had been found. Sarmiento (2019) suggested that this choice of words by the implied writer reflects a prophetic expectation fulfilled by this meeting. Nathanael, in verse 46, shows strong skepticism when he realizes that Jesus is from Nazareth. He questions the validity of Philip's assessment because nothing good comes from Nazareth. Nathanael does not accept the claim readily and easily as the other disciples. Nathanael is different. He questions everything. It is uncertain whether Nathanael's skepticism was because of prior knowledge of Jesus' background or that the Jews generally believed that Nazareth was not the birthplace of the Messiah (Sarmiento, 2019; Vanier, 2004). However, Philip encourages Nathanael to test his hypothesis by checking Jesus out himself by reassuring Nathanael to "come and see." Jesus meets Nathanael in verse 47, and as he approaches Jesus, Jesus preempts the conversation by affirming the origin and authenticity of Nathanael by declaring him as a genuine son of Israel and a man of integrity. In verse 48, Nathanael is surprised by this affirmation and questions how Jesus knew him. Jesus reveals that he had seen Nathanael under a fig tree even before Philip did. Jesus' comments trigger excitement in Nathanael, who declares Jesus as a Rabbi and the Messiah. In verses 50 and 51, Jesus paints an image or a vision of future events and experiences by stating that Nathanael was going to experience heavenly and angelic encounters that would reinforce Jesus' confirmation of Nathanael's personality.

Vision in the Text

The use of symbolism within the text reveals imagery that creates a vision for the participants in the narrative. For example, the frequent use of the word "see" or "to seek" plays into the concept that vision or imagery must be seen or experienced first before believing (Sarmiento, 2019). While this assertion may go against the idea of faith not based on what we see, the use of the word "see" reinforces the impact vision has on our faith. Also, this idea that Jesus was proactively looking, as posited by Trump (2017) and Sarmiento (2019), engages the faculties of sight. There is a proactive search by Christ and a responsive search by Nathanael fueled by an image of future hope; both parties are looking to make a connection, it seems, as revealed in verse 43.

Collins (1991) confirms this by positing that the idea behind the word "to seek" in the text suggests that individuals are looking for something more than they are experiencing. Furthermore, the implied writer's use of the word "found" when describing Phillip's initial conversation with Nathanael also suggests this common theme that involves the faculties of sight. Phillip's call to Nathanael also suggests that these individuals are looking to make a connection. The text reveals that both Nathanael and Phillip hold on to an image of a future sourced by Old Testament prophesy. Phillip comments in the text that he had found the one that Moses and the Prophets have written about, and Nathanael's response showed that these men understood the Scriptures and revealed Nathanael's ultimate goal to experience the manifestation of the vision foretold in the Old Testament. Jesus continues this concept of casting a vision by telling Nathanael that he had seen him under a fig tree. Although great detail of the significance and symbolism of the fig tree will not be discussed in this chapter since it is beyond the scope of this chapter, it is essential to note that Jesus' preemptive affirmation of a vision of Nathanael under a tree sparked a connection with Jesus. According to Dennis and Borcarnea (2005), vision is an integral factor in servant leadership, and a central component of vision has to do with the extent to which a follower's vision aligns and connects with the larger vision of the leader. Somehow Nathanael saw himself in the large scheme of things as Jesus saw him when no one was looking and affirmed him. Jesus tells Nathanael that the ideals of a hoped future were attainable by the interaction with higher dimensions of spirituality, which Jesus' words that Nathanael would see more extraordinary things in the future confirmed. Again, the implied author's word "you will see greater things" in verse 50 reveals Jesus as the source of the vision. While it is true that the vision of the future, in this case, the revelation of the Messiah, inspired Nathanael to follow, it is also safe to say that there was inherently an innate desire within Nathanael as well to seek, recognize, and affirm the vision albeit, through a vetting process that involved severe questioning. Nathanael was looking to connect with the Messiah; connecting the dots from the imagery and words presented was crucial to deciding to proceed in followership. Followers who question what is presented either via a vision, a task, or a goal's impact on their everyday existence are, in most cases, trying to find themselves within that large imagery or vision. When that connection is inaccurate or weak, followers tend to be disengaged and non-committed (Kelley, 1992).

Followership

The way a follow perceives inclusivity, participation, self-awareness, and engagement determines a follower's level of commitment and response to a vision (Baker, 2006). Agreement, alignment, and unity of focus are essential; however, to better understand this connection, a balanced view of this relationship is warranted by looking at a leader's perception of those they lead and the followers' perception of who is leading them. In essence, leadership and followership styles matter when it comes to the way both groups share and respond to a vision. It is essential to look at various followership styles and their characteristics to see how followers perceive their leaders. Several followership frameworks understand the types of followers and their characteristics. However, as stated earlier, we will review Nathanael's characteristics as revealed within the text in John alongside followership typologies by Kelley's (1992), Chaleff's (2008), and Kellerman's (2008) to see how these characteristics reveal the type of follower Nathanael was and whether or not those characteristics may have contributed to his acceptance of his buy-in to Christ's call for followership.

R.E. Kelley

Kelley's (1992) initial work titled "*In Praise of Followers*" in the Harvard Business Review focused on a follower-centric approach to observing followers' behavior. The initial work in 1988 revealed several factors that distinguish exemplary followers from ineffective followers. Kelley explored what it meant to be a good follower, positing that followers were not mindless subordinates without the ability to participate and think critically but highly essential for the success and growth of an entity. After identifying factors such as enthusiasm, intelligence, self-reliance, motivations, perceptions, and participation without self-promotion in the accomplishment of an organizational goal as factors that distinguish exemplary followers from ineffective followers, Kelly (1992) developed a followership framework based on a 20-item questionnaire categorized under two primary behaviors. According to Kelley, the first category for determining the type of follower is independent critical thinking match with dependent uncritical thinking ranked on a passive or aggressive scale. Kelley (1992) maintained that "the best followers are described as individuals who 'think for themselves,' 'give constructive criticism,' 'are their person,' and are 'innovative and creative'" (p. 93). On the other side of the scale (on the passive side) are individuals who cannot think for themselves and do not think critically (Kelley, 1992).

The second category is active engagement. According to Kelley (1992), followers actively engage, take the initiative, assume ownership, are self-starters, go above and beyond, and participate actively. On this scale, activity and passivity reflect the degree of participation by the follower. According to Kelley (1992), five types of followers emerge when we examine these two categories (critical thinking and active engagement) together. Based on this, we get the following followership types.

Alienated Followers

Alienated followers are very high independent thinkers but passive in active engagement. According to Kelley (1992), alienated followers see themselves as mavericks with healthy skepticism and stick up for the "little guy." They are also troublesome, cynical, and pessimistic. According to Kelley, alienated followers "see themselves as victims who unfairly got the short end of the stick" (p. 100). It is most unlikely that Nathanael was an alienated follower based on the above assessment. Nathanael may have shown some level of skepticism when he meets Jesus, but his quest to make a connection overrides that skepticism. According to Kelley (1992), alienated followers often find solace in isolation and are generally not looking to connect positively with those who lead them.

Additionally, Nathanael actively engages in critical thinking by questioning the validity of Christ. According to Kelley, alienated followers are usually too detached to seek answers to questions they may have. Nathanael's probing questions and Christ's subsequent answers create this opportunity to make a connection.

Conformists

Conformists are the second type of follower based on Kelley's (1992) framework. Conformists show low levels of independent critical thinking and very high levels of active engagement. Conformists accept assignments easily, trust, and avoid conflict when possible. Conformists are non-threatening to the leaders but also have difficulty in generating ideas, unwilling to be unpopular with their leaders, and are beholden to the establishment instead of outcomes (Kelley, 1992). In relating these behaviors to Nathanael, it is safe to conclude that Nathanael was not a conformist in the sense that he was not what Kelley describes as a "yes man." Although the text shows Nathanael as an individual willing to explore the possibilities in knowing who Jesus was as he accepted Phillips's invitation to "come and see," his exploration was balanced by his keen sense of critical Scriptural evaluation. Kelley supports this assertion by stating that conformists do not possess "informed intellect" (p. 112), a trait displayed by Nathanael as he processed who Christ was. Informed intellect, in this case, Scriptural evaluation reveals this innate sense of finding common ground from what already exists. For example, Nathaniel uses Scriptures as a foundation to see if there is integrity between the written Word from the past, what Nathanael is currently experiencing, and the future imagery. Conformists do not have this investigative ability because conformists usually only respond to what the leader prescribes instead of measuring responses by other factors such as a standard moral or established construct.

Passive Follower

Based on Kelley's framework, the third type of follower is passive. According to Kelley (1992), the passive follower shows very little independent thinking and very low or passive engagement. Passive followers act when inspired, motivated, or prompted by the leader. Passive followers do the barest minimum and spend the least time on a task. Kelley further states that passive followers lack initiative and are at the opposite end of the spectrum of exemplary or effective followers. Nathanael did not show passive behavior from the text in John. His desire for truth spurred the action to question the validity of Christ. The admission of Christ that Nathanael was a man of integrity reflected an individual that balanced intentional curiosity with the flexibility to explore critically.

Pragmatic Follower

Kelley (1992) discussed the fourth type of follower, the pragmatic follower. Pragmatic followers exhibit just the right amount of active engagement and independent critical thinking. Pragmatists, according to Kelley, are familiar with the system, know how to function in environments of uncertainty, and do just enough to keep things moving along. Pragmatic followers are survivors and individuals who do not want to ruffle feathers even though they may have some issues with what is going on. Kelley (1992) posited that pragmatists usually engage in a transactional relationship with their leaders. It is tempting to categorize Nathanael as a pragmatic follower especially given his initial hesitation to commit to Christ's call. This pushback may suggest that Nathanael's approach to Christ is reasonably cautious and filled with sensibility. One could also argue that Nathanael's approach toward accepting Jesus was transactional especially given that he seemed to change his mind rather quickly after Jesus had shown some detailed attention to him by stating He had seen Nathanael under a fig tree. However, Nathanael, it seemed from the text, was identified by Christ as a true Israelite, one in whom there is no deceit or guile. This description contradicts Kelley's (1992) pragmatic followers, skilled in playing political games with their leaders. Even when things are not going well, authenticity is not a pragmatic follower's "go-to" character, as pragmatic followers seek survival first before authenticity (Kelley, 1992).

Exemplary Follower

The fifth type of follower discussed by Kelley (1992) is an exemplary follower. According to Kelley, exemplary followers show high levels of active engagement and independent critical thinking. Individuals that fall into this category are self-starters, think independently of their leaders, add value to the leadership, are focused, committed to the cause, take the initiative, and engage actively regardless of the situation (Kelley, 1992). Kelley posited that exemplary followers could balance the mutually exclusive independent thinking and engagement categories. They know that their feedback and input matter; they are confident in their assessment of the situation but yet willing to engage in constructive discussions with their leaders. Nathanael showed measured skepticism about Jesus when Philip first approached him. This measured skepticism revealed that

Nathanael was thinking for himself and not just about himself. Phillip's reasoning did not easily sway Nathanael that the Messiah was from Nazareth and further clarified the claims brought before him. Collins (1991) revealed that the symbolism of Nathanael under a fig tree represented a seeker looking through the Scriptures for the truth. Neyrey (2007) posited that "Nathanael was a student of the writings of Moses and the Prophets" (p. 58) so much so that he could employ them against claims for Jesus. However, when Jesus tells him that he "saw him under the fig tree," he recants his earlier reading of the Scriptures and now acclaims Jesus of Nazareth as the improbable "Son of God and King of Israel" (p. 58). Nathanael's self-awareness and awareness of Scripture display competence, focus, and courage to explore further. Based on this analysis, all these factors point to a followership style that is more exemplary than pragmatic, conformist, passive, or alienated.

Barbara Kellerman

Kellerman's (2008) book, *Followership: How Followers Are Creating Change and Changing Leaders,* is the basis for the second followership analysis. Kellerman posited that followership reveals a relationship based on rank and behaviors in the book. According to Kellerman (2008), a proper understanding of followership involves evaluating the relationship between leaders and followers' rank and followers' response to the leader's influence. Kellerman asserts that followers without influence are just as consequential in the leadership construct as the leaders and that there are often roles or behavioral reversals between leaders and followers depending on the situation. In describing the different types of followers, Kellerman (2008) affirms some similarities with other followership frameworks like Kelley (1992) and Chaleff (2008) but finalized followership types based on one single metric, which is the level of engagement. According to Kellerman, the continuum for engagement ranges from doing absolutely nothing to being incredibly passionate and committed to the leader. According to Kellerman, five different followership types emerge based on this single metric.

Isolate

The first type of follower based on Kellerman's framework is the isolate. According to Kellerman (2008), isolates are detached and not engaged with the leader. Kellerman asserts that isolates do not know or care about their leaders. According to Kellerman, trust is not a significant factor in establishing commitment from an isolate. There is no commitment period because of the lack of concern for the leaders. Kellerman (2008) also noted that isolates are not only disengaged, but they are also uninformed and unmotivated with the process. Judging from these descriptions of isolates by Kellerman, Nathanael would not be considered an isolated follower due to his active engagement in the process of discovery. Initially, his initial response to the invitation to accept Jesus as the Messiah was skeptical, but it did not result in disinterested and unmotivated behavior. On the contrary, Nathanael is motivated and well-informed about who and where the Messiah comes from, as discussed earlier.

Bystander

The second type of follower described by Kellerman (2008) is the bystander. Bystanders, according to Kellerman, do nothing even when the stakes are not costly. They leave the decision-making to the group, and although they are well-informed, they deliberately disengage from the process to maintain their status quo. Bystanders wait to see the outcome of their decision instead of preempting the outcome due to their participation. Their lack of engagement makes them complacent, especially when the results are detrimental to others. Kellerman (2008) asserted that bystanders cede influence to those in power when they deliberately reject their responsibility to engage. Relating this type of follower to Nathanael poses some challenges given that the text in John 1:43–51 does not occur with the context of genocide which was the primary bias of Kellerman's book. However, Israel was under Roman rule, and the idea of a Messiah coming to rescue Israel from oppression was not only appealing but also welcomed by many. Nathanael's desire to seek after the Messiah, even though some initial skepticism points to an engaged individual whose desire to know prompts a deliberate reaction to follow and not abstain. So Nathanael would not be associated as a bystander because he exhibits a measured yet significant level of interest and activity to the revealed personality of Christ.

Participants

Kellerman (2008) discussed participants as another type of follower. Kellerman posits that participants are somewhat engaged in the process, put their money where their mouth is, and either view their leaders as favorable or not. Kellerman discusses the participant from the context of very highly skilled subordinates who can influence decisions or make changes that impact the overall perception of leadership. Kellerman stressed that these "knowledge workers" can change the cause of events if not adequately monitored or checked. Again, Kellerman's context of Merck's pharmaceutical company makes it difficult to evaluate whether Nathanael was a participant. Kellerman (2008) writes that certain highly skilled workers in Merck were responsible for pushing the Vioxx into the market against the knowledge of the public. This drug, according to Kellerman, had side effects that the public did not know. Kellerman asserted that participants with little oversight by their leaders were responsible for this. In essence, Kellerman's participants are "experts who, as a result of the expertise, worked independently and ultimately without sufficient oversight from the man supposedly in charge" (p. 126). Based on this context, Nathanael is not a participant. However, Nathanael's reaction to Phillips saying that Jesus was from Nazareth showed that Nathanael had a vast knowledge of Scripture, as noted by Sarmiento (2019). Nathanael's knowledge of Scripture also showed skill in interpreting and applying Old Testament text to the context of the day when the event occurred. While we can argue that Nathanael's later life and behavior reveal participatory tendencies, this classification as a participant is to the extent that Nathanael's followership of Jesus occurred once convinced of Jesus' identity and that followership leads to a life of discipleship.

Activist

Kellerman's (2008) fourth followership type is the activist; activists feel strongly about their leader and act accordingly. They invest their time and resources into the leader's agenda or idea. According to Kellerman, activists are passionate, committed, and act in favor or against a leader. This ability to positively or negatively impact leaders makes activists assets to those they are committed to or a significant pain to those they are against (Kellerman, 2008). Activists care a lot about their leaders, are engaged with the people and the process. That is what makes them an intriguing group, according to Kellerman. Activists take the lead and are change agents, making them somewhat polarizing either negatively or positively. The text in John 1:43–51 does not entirely show Nathanael as a polarizing figure or change agent per se. However, we can surmise that Nathanael does show some activist behavior in John 1:43–51 because Nathanael shows passion and commitment to the faith and Christ, which extended to his eventual martyrdom in Asia Minor. However, it is not easy to completely distinguish whether Nathanael's impact as a minister in Asia Minor, as posited by Rose (2009), was sole because Nathanael was an activist or because of his faith in Christ.

Diehard

The diehard is the last category of followers Kellerman (2008) discussed. Diehards die for a cause, idea, leader, or vision. On a reverse application, diehards remove anything that goes against their values, including leaders by any means necessary. This intense determination, according to Kellerman, makes the diehards extremely dedicated, passionate, and willing to risk everything for the accomplishment of the goal, vision, individual, or cause. Rose (2009) discusses a phenomenon referred to as the cult of Bartholomew, which centers on Nathanael's commitment and willingness to lose his life for the Gospel. According to traditions, Nathanael died a violent life, flayed alive, which means he was skinned alive and later crucified because of his faith. It is doubtful that an individual sentenced to die in such a way would not have prepared themselves if such a fate would occur. John 1:49 alludes to this mindset as Nathanael declares Christ as Lord and King of Israel. This statement on the surface may seem like the overwhelmed confession of a new believer, but as Sarmiento (2019) put it, "full of conviction, Nathanael wants to defend his long search for the Messiah as being a student of the Law of Moses. He is seeking whom the fulfillment of God's promise will be accomplished" (p. 40).

Ira Chaleff

Chaleff's (2008) work discusses the virtues of courage when it comes to followership. This pioneering work by Chaleff on followership development reveals varying levels of courage that a follower should have.

Followers, according to Chaleff, must have the courage to take responsibility, the courage to serve, the courage to challenge, the courage to participate in transformation, the courage to take moral action, and the courage to speak to the hierarchy.

According to Chaleff (2008), followership styles fall within two dimensions, namely the degree of support a follower gives a leader (high and low) and the degree to which the follower is willing to challenge the leader's behavior or policies (high and low). When these two dimensions are combined, it results in four followership styles.

Implementers

Implementers lie in quadrant 2 of Chaleff's followership-style quadrant and represent followers who show high support for their leader but are low in challenging leadership. Implementers do not dare to challenge but love to serve. According to Kellerman (2008), implementers are the most common followership type, especially in large organizations, because leaders rely on their subordinates to get the job done. Implementers are like the worker bees that get the job done but do not necessarily want to be involved in the details regarding leadership perceptions and actions. Based on this and from the review of John 1:43–51, Nathanael is more engaged yet also courageous to question the status quo (Sarmiento, 2019). A respectful inquisitiveness emanates from Nathanael that undermines the implementer's behavior. In summary, Nathanael would not fall into the category of an implementer for the same reasons he does not fall under Kellerman's (2008).

Resource

Resource lies in quadrant 4 of Chaleff's followership style. They are low in support for their leaders and low in challenging leadership. Resources do not go above the minimum expected and are available to their leaders but not committed to them. Nathanael shows commitment to Christ after it is revealed to him that Jesus is the Messiah. Resources share similar behavioral traits with Kelley's (1992) passive and pragmatics followers, and as mentioned earlier, Nathanael does not exhibit characteristics of a resource based on Chaleff's (2008) descriptions.

Individualists

Individualists are in quadrant 3 of Chaleff's (2008) followership framework and show low support for their leaders but are very high in challenging leadership. Individualists are "independent, self-assured, and forthright" (Kellerman, 2008; p. 84). They share similar behavioral traits with Kelley's (1992) alienated followers, and as noted earlier, Nathanael's behavior as described in John 1: 43–51 does not reveal him as an individualist even though Nathanael expressed independent thinking and skepticism when meeting Jesus.

Partners

Partners are in quadrant 1 of Chaleff's (2008) framework. Partners are high in participation and high in challenging leadership. According to Chaleff (2008), partners are goal getters and take risks to accomplish the organization's goals. Partners have a sense of ownership because they have a vested interest presented to them by their leaders. Partners exhibit similar characteristics to Kelley's (1992) exemplary followers, who dare to engage in transformational behavior. Nathanael's commitment to knowledge, his ability to question the status quo, and his response to vision make Chaleff's (2008) partner a more appropriate followership type for Nathanael.

Classifying Nathaniel's Followership

Nathanael exhibits wholehearted and sincere followership. Although Nathanael has some reservations at first, his commitment, authenticity, and critical thinking shine through, as discussed earlier. The text in John 1:43–51 is a good reminder about what true discipleship and followership mean and that genuine followership is not void of critical thinking and even skepticism. Jesus' interaction and use of vision further accentuate Nathanael's followership style as we see Nathanael's sudden transformation from skeptic to a student of Christ. Followers do not just become exemplary right away in some cases. This gradual transformation confirms Kelley's (1992) observation that followership behavior is not static, with followers moving from one followership level to another based on specific situations and contexts. In essence, followers can be groomed, taught, positioned, or influenced to advance their followership, moving from one level of the continuum to another (Blackshear, 2003). The reality is that Nathanael's initial skepticism is not a bad trait but one that reveals Nathanael as a true Israelite, authentic, self-aware, skilled, and highly knowledgeable about the context and the implication of Scriptures to his immediate situation. Nathanael not only questions his friend Phillip on the authenticity of his proclamation that Jesus was the Messiah but also questioned Jesus about how Jesus was aware of his position physically and otherwise. Nathanael's unique approach makes him stand out and highlights authenticity and the role of vision.

Therefore, based on the evaluation of Kelley's (1992), Kellerman's (2008), and Chaleff's (2008) framework, Nathanael would identify as a diehard partner with exemplary characteristics. In essence, Nathanael's commitment, wholehearted dedication to Jesus, and a strong passion for the manifestation of Scriptures as revealed in the text show how dimensions of critical thinking, active engagement, as well as courage all intermingle to produce a committed, wholehearted, and sincere follower to spread the Gospel even at the risk of losing one's life as noted by Rose (2009). Nathanael's exemplary behavior accounts for his ability to accept the vision or imagery as presented by Jesus concerning Nathanael's present and future situation. Nathanael took ownership regarding his initial skepticism and was willing to adapt, risking his future for the end goal.

Chapter Take Away

Let us look at some lessons and contemporary applications extrapolated from this chapter.

The Power of Vision Concerning the Present and Future

The first has to do with the impact of vision. The writer of John utilizes symbolism that shows Jesus painting an accurate picture of Nathanael's present and future. When Jesus first notices Nathanael, Nathanael is under a fig tree; what Nathanael is doing under the tree is not as relevant as the fact that Jesus notices Nathanael there. Jesus' attention to this simple detail surprises Nathanael and creates an "aha" moment for the disciple. Leaders are often so preoccupied with the future that they fail to see the present. Leaders must simultaneously handle current day-to-day events and identify with the follower's current needs while focusing on a clear-cut vision. Leaders must learn to cast vision and investigate their followers' current mental, physical, and psychological position.

The Power of Vision and Buy-In

Another point is that Jesus' encounter with Nathanael paints a picture of the interrelationship between leaders and followers and how leadership and followership behavior encourage buy-in. Nathanael, the main character in John 1:43–51, has his reservations at first about the description of this Nazarene Messiah. His skepticism, though somewhat legitimate, is eased by Jesus' approach and declaration of what Nathanael represented. Servant, authentic, and transformational leaders have a way of diffusing skepticism by identifying and declaring imagery that fortifies a follower's self-awareness (Vanwhy, 2015). Jesus' image of the future aligned with Nathanael's present perception of his place in the future. To this point, it is essential to note that vision and value alignment plays a crucial role in accomplishing a shared goal. Kelley (1992) affirmed this and stated that exemplary followers respond positively to leaders' vision clarity and intrinsic connectivity.

The Power of Vision and Self-Discovery

Collins (1991) posited that Nathanael is the disciple that sees and preempts Nathanael to embark on a quest for discovery. Nathanael was able to see value in who Jesus was and what he brought to the table. The acknowledgment that Jesus was the Lord and King of the Israelites by Nathanael served as a pledge of allegiance to the mission of Christ and showed Nathanael's commitment to go on a journey of self-discovery. The reality is that it took a leader like Jesus to understand this quest to identify with this value, connect, and show a path for the future. While many applaud the power of leaders to cast a vision for the accomplishment of shared goals, that step by followers to accomplish organizational goals will often begin with the intrinsic self-discovery by followers. In practice, leaders must identify the current state of their followers by connecting with them on their level.

The Power of Vision that Connects the Dots

The last aspect has to do with connecting the dots. Jesus meets Nathanael where he is, paints a picture of the future, and connects the dots meaning he describes how it will take place in verses 50 and 51. Although leadership occurs under varying levels of uncertainty, the extent to which leaders take time to map out clear strategies to get their followers from point A to B creates trust, a sense of security, and wholehearted followership. According to Winston and Patterson (2006), a leader's role is to identify gaps between the prophetic vision and the status quo and "utilize critical thinking skills, insight, and intuition to allow followers to move through ambiguity toward clarity of understanding and shared insight" (p. 7).

Practical Applications

On the other hand, followers have to open up and be sincere about their current walk in the organizational process. This self-awareness by followers is crucial for followership development. Another practical application is that leaders must lead. Leaders can utilize follower evaluations, informal meetings, and creative ways to connect with followers to achieve this. Jesus leads by painting a picture of Nathanael's future; Jesus engages Nathanael with a proposition and sells the idea that the best is yet to come. Winston and Patterson (2006) suggest that active listening and positive discourse by leaders facilitate and draw forth the opinions and beliefs of the followers. While this may be true, the opinions and beliefs must reflect accurate and precise steps of the how. Jesus's assessment of the future is accurate, which is why Nathanael keys into it. Accurate assessment of what comes next in the leadership-followership relationship regardless of the engagement level of the follower type tends to create an atmosphere of security and protection for the followers (Winston & Patterson, 2006).

Conclusion

Wholehearted and committed followership is not always automatic; it requires focus and the engagement of both leaders and followers. Most of all, it requires some time for some form of development. When this development is slow, leaders must not panic but seek ways to engage their followers in active discussion while patiently walking through challenges and follower skepticism. Followers must also show courage, self-awareness about their ability to learn more, show flexibility to change, especially when presented with an alternative picture of their present situation. Although the length of time needed for this may vary, the idea is to observe both leaders and followers and determine the factors that might expedite this process. While leaders are the sources for influence and inspiration for vision, the text in John 1 showed that a follower's response to a very well articulated and clear vision may not always be positive initially but possesses the power to contract between the present and future, power to followership self-discovery, and the power to provide steps for the accomplishment of goals.

Reflective Questions

1. How does faith or belief in a cause, idea, or mission affect followership styles?
2. Why did Nathanael follow? Was it because he was exemplary or because of Jesus' influence? How much of it is attributed to Jesus, and how much is attributed to Nathanael?
3. What type of leadership style would produce wholehearted or sincere followership?
4. How do leaders and followers ensure that sincere connectivity is maintained?
5. Being a diehard follower and working in faith seems opposed; how does faith impact being a diehard follower?

References

Bass, B. M. (1985). *Leadership and performance beyond expectations*. The Free Press.

Baker, S. D. (2006). *The effect of the leader-follower agreement on team effectiveness*. The George Washington University.

Bell, D. (2007). *Followers' preferences for leaders' behavioral characteristics: A case study of franchise restaurants*. Capella University.

Blackshear, P. B. (2003). The followership continuum: A model for fine tuning the workforce: A seasoned public manager draws on her experience at the federal and local levels and offers a case illustration from Anne Arundel County, MD, on how to identify opportunities for improving organizational performance. *The Public Manager, 32*(2), 25.

Beresford, A. M. (2020). Hagiographic tradition and the transformation of identity: The origin and evolution of the cult of St. Bartholomew. In *Sacred skin: The legend of St. Bartholomew in Spanish art and literature* (pp. 1–44). Brill.

Collins, R. F. (1991). *John and his witness*. Liturgical Press.

Chaleff, I. (2008). *The courageous follower. Standing up to and for our leaders* (3rd ed.). Barrett.

Dennis, R. S., & Bocarnea, M. (2005). Development of the servant leadership assessment instrument. *Leadership & Organization Development Journal, 26*(8), 600–615.

Greenwood, F. W. P. (1828). *Lives of the twelve apostles: With explanatory notes*. Hilliard, Gray, Little, and Wilkins.

Hale, J. R., & Fields, D. L. (2007). Exploring servant leadership across cultures: A study of followers in Ghana and the USA. *Leadership, 2*, 397–417.

Hill, C. E. (1998). The identity of John's Nathanael. *Journal for the Study of the New Testament, 20*(67), 45–61.

Keener, C. S. (2012). *The gospel of John. A commentary* (Vol. 2). Baker Academic.

Kellerman, B. (2008). *Followership: How followers are creating change and changing leaders*. Harvard Business School Press.

Kelley, R. E. (1992). *The power of followership: How to create leaders people want to follow and followers who lead themselves*. Broadway Business.

Kouzes, J. M., & Posner, B. Z. (1995). *The leadership challenge: How to keep getting extraordinary things done in organizations*. Jossey-Bass Publishers.

LaFasto, F. J., & Larson, C. E. (2001). *When teams work best: 6,000 team members and leaders tell what it takes to succeed*. Sage.

Neyrey, J. H. (2007). *The Gospel of John*. Cambridge University Press.

Rose, H. G. E. (2009). Chapter two. Bartholomew: Apostle against idols. In *Ritual memory* (pp. 79–123). Brill.

Russell, R. F., & Gregory Stone, A. (2002). A review of servant leadership attributes: Developing a practical model. *Leadership & Organization Development Journal, 23*(3), 145–157. https://doi.org/10.1108/01437730210424

Schreiber, S. (1998). Die Jüngerberufungsszene Joh 1, 43–51 als literarische Einheit.

Sarmiento, P. J. D. (2019). Nathanael—The true disciple under the fig tree: A narrative criticism of John 1: 43–51 and its implications to discipleship. *International Journal of Religion & Spirituality in Society, 9*(2).

Trump, M. L. (2017). *The first thing Andrew did'[John 1: 41]: Readers As witnesses in the fourth gospel.*

Vanier, J. (2004). *Drawn into the mystery of Jesus through the gospel of John*. Paulist Press.

VanWhy, L. P. (2015). *Development of the Authentic Followership Profile (AFP) test instrument* (Doctoral dissertation), Regent University.

Westcott, B. F. (2004). *The gospel according to St The Greek text with introduction and notes*. Wipf and Stock Publishers.

Winston, B. E., & Patterson, K. (2006). An integrative definition of leadership. *International Journal of Leadership Studies, 1*(2), 6–66.

CHAPTER 13

Judas Iscariot: Follower? Yes. Courageous Follower? No.

R. Lewis Steinhoff

Introduction

So, who exactly was Judas Iscariot? Judas was an apostle of Christ. He was one of the twelve Jesus personally chose to follow him. And we know from the Biblical narrative that he did indeed follow Jesus Christ. But he will forever be known only as the one who betrayed Christ.

How could any good come from a study of Judas Iscariot? The Holy Bible—both Old and New Testaments—provides valuable insights into the conflicted apostle that can help us evaluate ourselves to see where we might improve our commitment to the Lord. A study of Judas helps peel away layers of our own walk so that we can see more clearly "the plank in *our* own eye" (Luke 6:42, NIV) that we first must remove before we can even consider being courageous followers of Christ.

R. L. Steinhoff (✉)
Regent University, Virginia Beach, VA, USA

D. J. Dean and R. B. Huizinga (eds.), *Followership and Faith at Work*, Christian Faith Perspectives in Leadership and Business,
https://doi.org/10.1007/978-3-030-90614-6_13

Our examination of Judas begins with a Bible study. We will examine the facts as found in the New Testament. This will be followed by examining a section of Old Testament scripture that describes a very similar story of betrayal ending in the suicide of the betrayer. Next, we will examine opinion and conjecture surrounding Judas Iscariot to see if there is any relevance or connection to the Gospel passages. Down through the centuries, the Gnostic gospels and early writings created a foundation upon which much of the opinion and conjecture is based. Last, the experiences Judas witnessed and the events he participated in during the three-year ministry of Jesus Christ are examined. In this section a case study involving a mission trip Judas and the other disciples participated in where he is given powers to preach and to heal. We will see a sorrowful but unrepentant Judas who ultimately decides to hang himself. Some reflective questions will be posited throughout the chapter and at the end to contemplate as we examine our own walk with Christ.

What the Bible Has to Say About Judas Iscariot

The Holy Bible, made up of the Old Testament and the New Testament, reveals a few details about Judas that are factual and some presumed based on the specific author of the book. In case of the Old Testament—specifically the two Psalms that talk about betrayal—more is gleaned about the type of man Judas was. The New Testament of course provides sordid comments about Judas' presumed approach to life. By discussing the New Testament facts and opinions, and the Old Testament prophecy, we will have a good foundation to look further into this complex character and extract some traits, some good and some bad, about followership.

New Testament Facts

There are four facts about Judas Iscariot mentioned in the New Testament. First, he carried the bag (John 12:6). This means he was the treasurer for Jesus and the disciples. Second, he was the son of Simon Iscariot (John 6:71, John 13:2, and John 13:26). Many have tried to associate this fact with a possible hometown connection between him and Jesus, but there is nothing to substantiate that. Third, and most recognizable, he was the betrayer of Christ (many verses). Fourth, he is referred to as a traitor in Luke 6:16 and John 18:5, and a thief in John 12:6. Despite these traits, Judas Iscariot will forever be known for only one thing and that is that he is the one who betrayed Jesus Christ. There is one more fact about Judas, he hanged himself (Matt 27:5). This event punctuates the raw emotion of Judas' flawed character and links back to the Old Testament prophecy discussed later in this chapter. Ballantine (1889) suggests, "The sum of the testimony is that Judas was from the first to the last a monster of cool and devilish wickedness" (p. 100).

But was he?

The interpretation of what some including Jesus had to say about Judas appears to back this up. Take John for instance. The beloved disciple said this about Judas when he saw what Mary did for Jesus during his visit with Mary, Martha, and Lazarus.

> Then Mary took about a pint of pure nard, an expensive perfume; she poured it on Jesus' feet and wiped his feet with her hair. And the house was filled with the fragrance of the perfume. But one of his disciples, Judas Iscariot, who was later to betray him, objected, 'Why wasn't this perfume sold and the money given to the poor? It was worth a year's wages.' He did not say this because he cared about the poor but because he was a thief; as keeper of the money bag, he used to help himself to what was put into it. (John 12:4–6, NIV)

John does not hold anything back here about his personal feelings for Judas. In fact, this episode does say a lot about Judas' state of mind. His focus does not seem to be on the adoration Mary is showing Jesus but rather the value of the ointment. Ballantine (1889) adds the word liar in describing how John felt about Judas perhaps because the ending of the verse says Judas used to help himself to the treasury.

Jesus himself had some choice words to describe Judas as seen below. With emphasis he added.

> Then Jesus replied, "Have I not chosen you, the Twelve? Yet one of you is a devil!". (John 6:70, NIV)

> While I was with them in the world, I kept them in thy name: those that thou gavest me I have kept, and none of them is lost, but the son of perdition; that the scripture might be fulfilled. (John 17:12, KJV)

> The Son of Man is to go [to the cross], just as it is written [in Scripture] of Him; but woe (judgment is coming) to that man by whom the Son of

> Man is betrayed! It would have been good for that man if he had never been born. (Matt 26:24, AMP)

Jesus recognized Judas for what he was. A devil, a son of perdition, and someone who should never have been born. These statements fit with an event at the last supper involving Jesus and Judas. John writes…

> Jesus answered, "It is the one to whom I will give this piece of bread when I have dipped it in the dish." Then, dipping the piece of bread, he gave it to Judas, the son of Simon Iscariot. As soon as Judas took the bread, Satan entered into him". (John 13:26, NIV)

If there was ever any doubt as to whether Judas was a true follower of Christ, this verse makes it clear he was not. He was in fact a child of the devil.

What does the suicide tell us? The scripture tells us that once he realized Christ had been condemned to death, he felt remorse and tried to give the money back to the high priests.

> Judas, the one who betrayed him, realized that Jesus was doomed. Overcome with remorse, he gave back the thirty silver coins to the high priests, saying, 'I've sinned. I've betrayed an innocent man.' They said, 'What do we care? That's your problem!'
>
> Judas threw the silver coins into the Temple and left. Then he went out and hung himself. (Matt 27:3–5, MSG)

We see remorse but not necessarily repentance. Ballantine (1889) posits, the suicide "was the crowning act of petulance, unbelief and selfishness…and…was a gross insult to the divine love…and a cruel unfaithfulness to the interests of all mankind" (p. 101). His internal battle between flesh and spirit was like a veil that blinded him from the works of Christ.

Next we'll look at Old Testament prophesy.

Old Testament Prophecy

Judas is not specifically mentioned in the Old Testament but in the book of Psalms we find two chapters that discuss the betrayal of King David by his close friend and counselor, Ahithophel. In Psalm 41:9, we see David state,

> Even my close friend, someone I trusted, one who shared my bread, has turned against me. (Psalm 41:9, NIV)

This verse is stated at a time when David is under great anguish due to his son Absalom's take-over attempt. We see in 2 Samuel,

> Now David had been told, 'Ahithophel is among the conspirators with Absalom.' So David prayed, 'Lord, turn Ahithophel's counsel into foolishness'. (2 Sam 15:31, NIV)

These verses provide us with a few nuggets that play into the Judas Iscariot story. Ahithophel is a close friend. He is also described as one who David trusted. Pentiuc (n.d.) posits that the original Hebrew idiom states, "colleague, comrade, companion" and he adds "it connotes a specific deep bond of shared intimacy" (p. 2/7). So, we sense real pain on David's part because this was not just a friend, but a very close trusted friend. In fact, if we consider the breaking of bread together, the Hebrew text phrases as "the one who was eating my bread" and further implies that this was a continuous or habitual activity. Pentiuc (n.d.) states some scholars have suggested the sharing of bread here was a covenantal meal "in order to consecrate the friendship of David and Ahithophel" (p. 3/7). Again, there are parallels to the last supper here. We do not have any proof that Jesus specifically prayed about Judas' betrayal but the fact that David prayed Ahithophel's counsel would become foolishness seems to plant that seed.

The next Psalm where the Ahithophel betrayal is discussed is Psalm 55. We see in this Psalm Ahithophel described as David's equal.

> If an enemy were insulting me, I could endure it; if a foe were rising against me, I could hide. But it is you, a man like myself, my companion, my close friend, with whom I once enjoyed sweet fellowship at the house of God, as we walked about among the worshipers. (Psalm 55:12–14, NIV)

There is one more very important part of the Ahithophel betrayal of David story. And, as we will see, it too is prophetic. We see God answered David's prayer about making Ahithophel's counsel foolishness and after David successfully defended his throne, this follows:

> When Ahithophel saw that his advice had not been followed, he saddled his donkey and set out for his house in his hometown. He put his house in order and then hanged himself. (2 Sam 17:23, NIV)

We have examined a story of betrayal in the Old Testament that could be considered a prophetic proclamation of the Messiah's betrayal. The betrayer, Ahithophel, was a trusted friend who ate with David, later betrayed David, then went out and hanged himself.

We have identified who Judas was as stated in the New Testament by the disciples themselves. He was a liar, thief, betrayer, traitor, petulant, selfish, and unfaithful. Why then was he selected to be part of the Twelve? Neither the Old Testament nor New Testament states anything about the selection criteria Jesus used to form his team. Several theologians and researchers have attempted to explain things about Judas that simply cannot be validated. It is opinion and conjecture, but for the sake of completeness, we will discuss a few of these now.

Opinion and Conjecture

The existing accepted Canon we call The Holy Bible made up of the Old Testament and the New Testament does not include the books of the apocrypha nor the gnostic gospels. However, these documents are unreliable as they provide an alternative story of deception that in no way relates to what is in the Holy Bible. For example, in *The Gospel of Judas*, Judas is elevated from the Twelve and after hearing secrets that none of the others know about, he becomes the catalyst to help Jesus escape from his human body. As a matter of fact, Jesus asks him to do it. The translators state in their closing remarks, "Judas is described not as a betrayer, but as a special, obedient assistant who worked with Jesus to bring about the crucifixion and the larger plan of God" (Kassar et al., 2006, p. 7).

Cane (2000), in his work *Contested Meanings of the Name 'Judas Iscariot,'* offers an analysis of the name Iscariot and concludes, "Iscariot, as being derived from a Hebrew form meaning 'man of Kerioth'" (p. 44). The only reason this may be of significance is that there are two cities noted in the Old Testament that have this name. In Joshua 15:25, Kerioth-Hezron is identified as one of the cities of Judah. Unfortunately, Jeremiah 48:24 identifies a Moabite city named Kerioth. Thus, one location would identify him as a Jew from a Jewish land while the other would place him from a land outside Judah and Israel. We will revisit this when we analyze Judas' follower characteristics.

In another Cane (1998) work titled, *Judas Iscariot, Bishop Roderick Wright and the Testing of Eucharistic Boundaries*, the topics of scapegoating, foot washing, and the proper boundaries of the eucharis are discussed. In the upper room scene, Jesus is there with all twelve disciples. He washes their feet and breaks bread with them...all of them. Cane (1998) shares arguments that essentially un-validate Judas' participation in the feeding of the bread by attaching it to the foot washing.

> 'No,' said Peter, 'you shall never wash my feet.' Jesus answered, 'Unless I wash you, you have no part with me.' 'Then, Lord,' Simon Peter replied, 'not just my feet but my hands and my head as well!' Jesus answered, 'Those who have had a bath need only to wash their feet; their whole body is clean. And you are clean, though not every one of you.' For he knew who was going to betray him, and that was why he said not every one was clean. (John 13:8–10, NIV)

The point of this twelfth-century argument is that Judas, even though Jesus had cleaned his feet, was unclean and therefore did not actually receive the bread Jesus gave him as stated later.

> Jesus answered, 'It is the one to whom I will give this piece of bread when I have dipped it in the dish.' Then, dipping the piece of bread, he gave it to Judas, the son of Simon Iscariot. As soon as Judas took the bread, Satan entered into him. (John 13:26–27a, NIV)

Obviously, Judas did receive it but as Cane (1998) points out, it is an issue of how it was received given Jesus had already singled him out and immediately Satan stepped in. We cannot help but assume Judas was already feeling left out. Cane (1998) concludes, "Fallible Christians (and whom does that not include?) should be grateful that their tradition indicates that Judas did so receive, and that imperfect human beings can be channels for the grace of God" (p. 123). So true.

I would last like to discuss the *Psychology of Judas Iscariot*. Uraguchi (1918) noted,

> Some have regarded him as a most inhuman devil. According to their simple logic, as a Chinese proverb says, 'The worst form of ingratitude is to betray one's teacher, while it is still worse to betray one's master.'

> Others have rejected the whole story of this man of Kerioth as a myth, saying, 'Judas is a Christian fiction to represent the treacherous Judaism which put Jesus to death, and no one among the Twelve was really guilty of this enormity.' (p. 345)

Uraguchi (1918), in making his case against the three prejudices usually associated with Judas, dismisses them as follows:

- Judas was not the last and least of the Twelve just because he is always mentioned last.
- He was a man of considerable business talent because he quickly determined the value of ointment Mary poured on Jesus's feet.
- He was not necessarily of an avaricious character just because one apostle, John, called him a thief.

Probably the most important thing to consider about the psychology of Judas Iscariot is historically driven. And, unfortunately this history is found in the apocryphal books not included in the accepted Canon of the Holy Bible. Uraguchi (1918) offers a brief review of where Jews were at during the time of Christ. Summarizing,

- During their exile to Babylon, the people of Israel had been deprived of their power as an independent nation because their country had been destroyed first by the Greek armies then by Roman soldiers.
- They only had the hope of a Messiah and with that, national sovereignty, which led to their "national consciousness" being made stronger and stronger.
- Now in the eyes of these people, the crucifixion of Jesus undermined the fundamental qualification of the Messiah himself.

As Uraguchi (1918) states, "The disciples were then conscious of a revolution in their own minds. It shook the very ground upon which they were standing. As one of these men, Judas Iscariot suffered much from this unsettled state of mind" (p. 349). Many believe this solely was the reason Judas betrayed Jesus. When he realized Jesus was going to die, he mentally disconnected.

Following

We are now ready to look at Judas as a follower of Jesus. We will do this by examining what the literature says about followership and then check that against Judas' experiential opportunities as an apostle of Christ. The literature examined is that of Robert E. Kelley, Barbara Kellerman, and Ira Chaleff; all have done pioneering work in the field of followership.

Robert E. Kelley

A follower, according to Merriam-Webster (2020), is one in the service of another, one that follows the opinions or teachings of another and one that imitates another. Kelley (2008), one of the first to dive into the study of followership notes, "The word follower has its etymological roots in Old High German *follaziohan*, which meant 'to assist, help, succor, or minister to'" (p. 181). Basically, followers assisted in taking care of the leaders. Kelley later notes this definition parallels the root of *leader* in Old High German, which meant "to undergo, suffer, or endure" (p. 181). He describes the relationship between leader and follower as symbiotic.

In his first work on followership, Kelley (1988) initiated a discourse on effective followers versus ineffective followers. He posits, "What distinguishes an effective from ineffective follower is enthusiastic, intelligent, and self-reliant participation – without star billing – in the pursuit of an organizational goal" (p. 143). Already we might be tempted to juxtapose these traits against Judas Iscariot but that might not be a fair analysis given the possibility of some of the other apostles wrestling with the same challenges, for example, Thomas and his doubting. Kelley later defines a clear list of qualities of effective followers. He notes:

- Manage themselves well;
- Are committed to the organization and to a purpose, principle, or person outside themselves;
- Build their competence and focus their efforts for maximum impact; and
- Are courageous, honest, and credible (Kelley, 1988, p. 144).

When we think of Judas Iscariot, especially given the discussed above, it is difficult to think of him in these ways. However, Jesus did choose him. In Jesus' mind, he must have been qualified to do the job.

Kelley (2008) over the years honed his followership research into styles that are determined by how a person performs in two behavioral dimensions where the first is independent critical thinking and the second is an active-positive, passive-negative scale. He adds, "Depending on a person's performance, he or she will fall into one of five separate styles of followership" (p. 182) as shown below.

- Alienated Followers—Independent/Critical Thinking and Negative Energy/Passive
- Sheep/Passive Followers—Dependent/Uncritical Thinking and Negative Energy/Passive
- Star/Exemplary Followers—Independent/Critical Thinking and Positive Energy/Active
- Yes Person/Conformist Followers—Dependent/Uncritical Thinking and Positive Energy/Active
- Pragmatic Followers—"Avoid taking a strong position that crosses powerful people. They are constantly monitoring the wind direction, and their motto is 'better safe than sorry.' They keep conflict to a minimum and always have a ready excuse with a corresponding paper trail for any failure" (Kelley, 2008, p. 183).

Judas strikes me as someone focused on self-preservation and that would connect with Kelley's Pragmatic.

Barbara Kellerman

Kellerman (2007) argues that presently, cultural, organizational, and technological changes are what determine the superior-subordinate relationship. She adds though, "leader–follower relationships, no matter the situation, culture, or era in which they are embedded, are more similar than they are different" (p. 87). She posits, "knowledge workers often care as much if not more about intrinsic factors – the quality of their interpersonal relationships with their superiors, for instance, or their passion for the organization's mission – than about extrinsic rewards such as salary, titles, and other benefits" (p. 87). From what we discussed earlier about Judas; it is unclear but highly likely he may have been more interested in what he could get out of being on Jesus' team.

Kellerman introduced a new typology for followership based on a single factor; level of engagement. Kellerman (2007) claims, based on her research, there are five types of followers:

- Isolates—Completely detached. Not aware of what is going on and really does not care about their leaders.
- Bystanders—As the name implies, they observe what is going on but do not participate. They may participate if in their best interest.
- Participants—They care enough to invest some of what they have (time or money, for example) to try to make an impact.
- Activists—They feel strongly about their leaders and organizations, and they act accordingly (for or against their leaders).
- Diehards—They are prepared to go down for their cause—whether it is an individual, an idea, or both (Kellerman, 2007, pp. 88–90).

As we will see later, Judas probably fit into a couple of these categories and perhaps where he fit evolved over time.

Ira Chaleff

Chaleff (2009) has made an important distinction in followership by introducing the term "Courageous Follower." His contribution to the genre of followership has evolved with time and has been updated recently to reflect generational and environmental changes. He notes in his latest edition of *Courageous Followership*, that there are two major reasons for the update. First "is the emerging power of electronically connected networks of people who form 'communities of interest' to share information and organize for action" (p. xiv). Second "the upper levels of hierarchies in large and global institutions are often more impermeable…senior leaders are struggling to stay on top of the punishing pace of change" (p. xiv). With these facts, the stage is set for twenty-first-century courageous followership.

Chaleff (2009) defines seven dimensions of courageous followership; five original and two new ones. They are:

- Courage to Assume Responsibility;
- Courage to Serve;
- Courage to Challenge;
- Courage to Participate;
- Courage to Take Moral Action;
- Courage to Speak to the Hierarchy; and
- Courage to Listen to Followers (Chaleff, 2009, pp. 6–8).

Chaleff explores each of these concepts in detail but as you can see from the first word of the first six, it takes action on the part of the follower. The last one is clearly for the leader. Judas clearly had a problem with several of these. For example, under responsibility, Chaleff includes things like self-assessment, eliciting feedback, taking care of ourselves, passion, initiative, breaking the rules, breaking the mindset, and testing your ideas as well as others. Judas certainly had a focus on taking care of himself and perhaps breaking the rules but lacked woefully in the areas of passion and initiative.

Perhaps Judas' biggest hurdle was courage to serve. Chaleff includes things like acquiring access and responsibilities of a gatekeeper. Clearly, he did these things but to the detriment of the leader, Jesus Christ. Chaleff also includes giving the leader feedback, giving the leader input, avoiding knee-jerk rejection, THE DUTY TO OBEY, challenging abuse early, arrogance, personal issues, and several others. Judas had issues with obedience and arrogance and if the truth were known, perhaps even giving the leader input.

Regarding courage to challenge, Chaleff posits, "Courageous followers give voice to the discomfort they feel when behaviors or policies of the leader or group conflict with their sense of what is right" (p. 7). He adds, they "value organizational harmony and their relationship with the leader, but not at the expense of the common purpose and their integrity" (p. 7). It would perhaps be unfair to comment assertively on whether Judas sought organizational harmony with the apostles and Jesus because he could have at the beginning of the three-year ministry. From the little we know of Judas; this was probably not likely.

The courage to participate involved participation in transformation. This is what Jesus' ministry was all about. Transforming lives. He came to seek and to save that which was lost (Luke 19:10, KJV). There were occasions where Judas possessed powers given to him by the Holy Spirit and possibly "transformed" lives but he himself was never really transformed. Chaleff (2009) describes this courage as, "They champion the need for change and stay with the leader and group while they mutually struggle with the difficulty of real change" (p. 7). He notes they become full participants.

The courage to take moral action involves taking a stand that is different from the leader's. Correctly, Chaleff notes that these kinds of actions involve personal risk. The question to ask here is, what were Judas' morals like. Was this another case of evolving morals—probably better to say devolving morals? Chaleff notes, "they are answering to a higher set of values" (p. 7). What could be higher than his lord at the time; the Lord Jesus Christ?

The last of the follower specific courage is the courage to speak to the hierarchy. Obviously, Judas had no problem with this unless you consider which hierarchy. Did he pray? Did he approach Peter about certain things troubling him? The literature casts Judas and Jesus as close friends. If the hierarchy includes Jesus himself, how comfortable was Judas approaching him? Of course, we do not know these answers. Chaleff (2009) posits, "Courageous followers give careful thought to application of courageous follower principles in these contexts and develop the sensitivities and strategies required to speak effectively to the hierarchy" (p. 8).

The final courage is the one for the leader. The courage to listen to followers. This involves the leader's "responsibility to support the conditions of courageous followership and to respond productively to acts of courageous followership...when done well, it offers powerful paybacks for the leader and the organization" (p. 8). One can only imagine the dialogue between Jesus and Judas on a good day. Did Jesus give him his undivided attention? Did Jesus cast aside some of his divine powers to think more humanly about what his disciples were bringing to his attention? Again, we may never really know.

In the next section—The Practicum—we will conduct a case study involving Judas Iscariot and the other disciples. This case study deals with the first mission trip assigned to the Twelve, not the second one involving the 72 disciples. The case study walks through the instruction by Jesus given to the disciples just prior to sending them out two by two on the mission trip. That trip was the experiential learning part of their three-year ministry with Jesus.

The Practicum

Jesus trained his disciples by talking with them, speaking parables, letting them witness healings, and letting them simply be part of his Twelve. One additional thing he did was experiential in that they were sent out on a mission trip to the lost sheep of Israel. Matthew's accounting of the event in Chapter 10 is long and detailed. It is important to examine this passage however to glean a good understanding of what Judas was asked to do by Jesus.

> Jesus called his twelve disciples to him and gave them authority to drive out impure spirits and to heal every disease and sickness.
>
> 2These are the names of the twelve apostles: first, Simon (who is called Peter) and his brother Andrew; James son of Zebedee, and his brother
> John; 3Philip and Bartholomew; Thomas and Matthew the tax collector;
> James son of Alphaeus, and Thaddaeus; 4Simon the Zealot and Judas Iscariot, who betrayed him.
>
> 5These twelve Jesus sent out with the following instructions: "Do not go among the Gentiles or enter any town of the Samaritans. 6Go rather to the
> lost sheep of Israel. 7As you go, proclaim this message: 'The kingdom of
> heaven has come near.' 8Heal the sick, raise the dead, cleanse those who have leprosy,[a] drive out demons. Freely you have received; freely give.
>
> 9 "Do not get any gold or silver or copper to take with you in your belts—
> 10no bag for the journey or extra shirt or sandals or a staff, for the worker
> is worth his keep. 11Whatever town or village you enter, search there for
> some worthy person and stay at their house until you leave. 12As you
> enter the home, give it your greeting. 13If the home is deserving, let your
> peace rest on it; if it is not, let your peace return to you. 14If anyone will
> not welcome you or listen to your words, leave that home or town and
> shake the dust off your feet.15Truly I tell you, it will be more bearable for Sodom and Gomorrah on the day of judgment than for that town. (Matt 10:1–15, NIV)

If we examine each of these paragraphs, it will give us greater appreciation of the opportunity Judas was given as a follower of Christ. We see in the first paragraph (verse 1) that Jesus calls his twelve and equips and empowers them. They have been granted the ability to drive out evil spirits and to heal the sick. If I am Judas and I am already feeling somewhat out of place then suddenly I feel the Holy Spirit filling me that could have been life changing. He had seen Jesus do these things but now he would be able to do them! Perhaps Kelley's (2008) "*Build their competence and focus their efforts for maximum impact*" would be the pertinent follower quality or perhaps Kellerman's (2007) participative follower could describe Judas at this stage because participants *"care enough to invest some of what they have (time or money, for example) to try to make an impact."* Chaleff's (2009) *Courage to Serve* might be applicable at this point in the ministry, presumably toward the beginning part of the ministry, and he may have indeed felt that "Duty to Obey."

The second paragraph above (verses 2–4) just identifies the Twelve Disciples. The two things to note here are that Jesus sent them two by two which is a common practice used by churches during visitation and door knocking. It does not elaborate on who is paired up with who and Matthew is the only Gospel of the three that mention this mission trip that identifies the men by name. But as explained earlier, Judas Iscariot is always mentioned last. If we assume the pairings were by order listed, Judas was paired with Simon the Zealot. The Zealots of that day were "members of a first-century political movement among Judean Jews who sought to overthrow the occupying Roman government. The word *zealot* derives from the Greek *zelotes*, meaning 'emulator or (zealous) follower'" (GotQuestions.org). As discussed earlier, it is very possible Judas Iscariot too was one of these supporters. Potentially this pairing was the most zealous and perhaps through their experiences was the most humbled. Again, we have no way of proving that.

The third paragraph (verses 5–8) is when the assignment is made clear. It is also when more detail is provided on just what powers they will have. Do not go to the gentiles. The gentile mission would come later with Peter first followed by Paul. Do not go to the Samaritans. Jesus himself would take the gospel to the Samaritans when he shared the Gospel with the woman at the well. No, this mission was to one people group; the lost sheep of Israel. Why? They were the ones who had been promised the Messiah and had waited hundreds of years for his arrival. In fact, Jesus instructed them to proclaim the message, "*The kingdom of heaven has come near.*" Consider how these two zealots must have felt to be given this opportunity. I liken this to Kellerman's (2007) *Diehard* followers as "*They are prepared to go down for their cause.*" The next part of this paragraph is powerful because it deals with the equipping of Jesus' soldiers. They were given the power to heal the sick, raise the dead, cleanse those who have leprosy, and drive out demons. At this point, Satan had not entered Judas so this was entirely possible especially if the zeal was focused in the right Christ-centered direction. This is equivalent to Chaleff's (2009) *Courage to Participate* because "*They champion the need for change and stay with the leader and group while they mutually struggle with the difficulty of real change.*"

The fourth paragraph is all about provision. Jesus stresses you are to do this mission without taking any food or money or even an extra set of clothes. He is teaching them to rely on God to take care of them. He explains how this will be done utilizing the accommodations of people that offer them accommodations. He backs this up with a statement that lets them know, he has their back. Simon the Zealot and Judas Iscariot knew all about what happened to Sodom and Gomorrah so that promise from Jesus probably gave them even more zeal. Now, the hard part of this section would be the money part for Judas. If even part of what we learned earlier was true, Judas had a love for money. It is not clear whether he oversaw the bag yet, but the thought of going on this journey without money probably tore at his inner being. Was it possible Judas might be trying to muster the courage to challenge? As Chaleff (2009) explains; *"Courageous followers give voice to the discomfort they feel when behaviors or policies of the leader or group conflict with their sense of what is right."*

Matthew Chapter 10 goes on for 27 more verses and in those verses, Jesus is giving them even more specifics on the mission and what they are to do if certain things happen. He even tells them in verses 19 and 20, "*But when they arrest you, do not worry about what to say or how to say it. At that time you will be given what to say, for it will not be you speaking, but the Spirit of your Father speaking through you*" (Matt 10:19,20, NIV). Matthew 10 is all about reliance on God. Remember, Judas was there. After the disciples return, the feeding of the five thousand occurs. The disciples participate in distributing the bread and fish. There are twelve baskets full of leftovers. Judas was there. Later, the twelve disciples are in a boat being tossed by the waves and then they see Jesus walking on water. Judas was there. The feeding of the four thousand follows sometime later and the disciples once again help with the distribution of bread and fish. It does not state specify all twelve disciples are there, but it is highly likely Judas was there. And one "what if" scenario involves Jesus sending two of the disciples to fetch a donkey and her colt. One of those disciples could have been Judas.

Data and Analysis

As you can see in Table 13.1, the types of followers are listed based on the research of Kelley (2008), Kellerman (2007), and Chaleff (2009) along with a simple evaluation of how Judas Iscariot lines up with those types. It is clear based on the simple analysis of the facts we know of Judas Iscariot and the experiential data from the mission trip case study, that Judas Iscariot at best was a follower of Jesus but not a courageous follower.

Table 13.1 Summary of types of followership and applicability to Judas Iscariot

Source	*Type of follower*	*Comments*
Robert E. Kelly (2008)	Alienated	Yes, due to him being the outsider
	Sheep/Passive	Yes, due to negative energy
	Star/Exemplary	No
	Yes Person/ Conformist	No
	Pragmatic	Yes, constantly monitoring the wind direction
Barbara Kellerman (2007)	Isolates	No
	Bystanders	No
	Participants	Yes
	Activists	No
	Diehards	No
Ira Chaleff (2009)	Courage to Assume Responsibility	No. Lacked in the areas of passion and initiative
	Courage to Serve	No. Trouble with obedience & arrogance
	Courage to Challenge	Yes, as seen with ointment event but for personal concern, not for concern of the Jesus
	Courage to Participate in Transformation	No. He participated but was not transformed
	Courage to take Moral Action	No
	Courage to Speak to Hierarchy	Yes, initially to Peter & Jesus and later with the priests when he decided to betray Jesus
	Courage to Listen [as the leader] to Followers	No. He was not the leader

He lacked the transformative spirit and the concept of obedience and support for his master. Diving down one more level in the analysis, we see that in the areas where a "Yes" is indicated, it is always in a negative way. For example, yes, he had the courage to challenge in the case of the ointment Mary poured on Jesus, but his heart was not on Jesus; it was rather on the value of the ointment. Another example, yes, he had the courage to speak to the hierarchy (the priests) when he turned Jesus over to the authorities, but it was a selfish reason of greed.

Despite all the opportunities Judas had to be a Star/Exemplary follower given all he had seen and personally experienced, he put pride, selfishness, and arrogance above love in his following Christ. Jesus said, "Whoever wants to be my disciple must deny themselves and take up their cross daily and follow me" (Luke 9:23, NIV). Judas did not do this.

Chapter Take-Aways

Was Judas Iscariot a courageous follower of Jesus Christ? No. He was at best a follower but as we have seen lacked in some basic areas of normal followership. The only areas of courage were in areas that best suited his interests. Alternatively, as Dr. Richard Harrell notes, "Is Judas any different in his betrayal of Jesus than Thomas or Peter? Especially Peter, who denied Jesus three times in public. He showed remorse but was there repentance? Judas showed remorse and attempted to correct as he stated, 'his sin' but was their repentance?" Harrell (2020) adds, "It appears that all of the disciples betrayed Jesus in some form or fashion but were forgiven. It remains to be seen in eternity if Judas fell into that category."

As we look at the current century we are living in, we have chaos all around us. Crime is rampant in our big cities and we are battling a pandemic that has killed thousands. We hear the solution is to educate people on the problems we face such as prejudice, police brutality, violence toward elderly and disabled people, with the hope they will then change. But isn't it really a heart issue? All through the Bible in both the Old Testament and New Testament, God is more concerned about the heart than on the process. For someone to become a courageous follower of Jesus and, if inclined, a courageous leader of Jesus, they need to take up their cross daily and do this with love.

Dr. Teman Knight (2020), notes, "We don't like to think about him [Judas] too much because he reminds us too much of ourselves." Knight adds that he was always intrigued by Contemporary Christian singer Michael Card's song titled, Traitor's Look. The third stanza of the song is...

Now Judas don't you come too close
I fear that I might see
That traitor's look upon your face
Might look too much like me
Cause just like you I've sold the Lord
And often for much less
And like a retched traitor
I betrayed Him with a kiss. (Card, 2017)

Reflective Questions

1. Was Judas Iscariot a troubled soul? If so, do you believe this hindered him in his allegiance to Jesus?
2. Did the other disciples betray Jesus at one time or another?
3. By Judas admitting he had sinned, could that be considered repentance? If so, does that or would that potentially change the narrative about Judas?
4. Do you see any of yourself in Judas?
5. When comparing Judas with Peter, can we make a clear distinction between who is a follower and who is a courageous follower?

References

Ballantine, W. G. (1889). Judas iscariot. *The Old and New Testament Student, 9*(2), 100–102. Retrieved 17 May 2020 from www.jstor.org/stable/3157725

Cane, A. (1998). Judas Iscariot, Bishop Roderick wright and the testing of Eucharistic boundaries. *Theology, 101*(800), 119–124.

Cane, A. (2000). Contested meanings of the name 'Judas Iscariot.' *The Expository times, 112*(2), 44–45.

Card, M. (2017). Traitor's look. *Songlyrics Know the Words*. Retrieved on 22 August 2020 from http://www.songlyrics.com/card-michael/traitor-s-look-lyrics/

Chaleff, I. (2009). *The courageous follower: Standing up to & for our leaders*. Berrett-Koehler Publishers.

Harrell, R. (2020). Communication with Dr. Lew Steinhoff via email dated August 9, 2020.

Kasser, R., Meyer, M., & Wurshttp, G. (2006). *The gospel of Judas*. Retrieved on 17 May 2020 from www.scriptural-truth.com/PDF_Apocrypha/The%20Gospel%20of%20Judas.pdf .

Kellerman, B. (2007). What every leader needs to know about followers. *Harvard Business Review, 85*(12), 84.

Kelley, R. E. (1988). *In praise of followers* (pp. 142–148). Harvard Business Review Case Services.

Kelley, R. E. (2008). Followership. In G. E. Hickman (Ed.), *Leading Organizations: Perspectives for a New Era* (2nd ed.). Sage.

Knight, T. (2020). Communication with Dr. Lew Steinhoff via email dated August 12, 2020.

Merriam-Webster Dictionary. (2020). https://www.merriam-webster.com/dictionary/follower

Pentiuc, E. (n.d.). Judas' profile in the psalms: Meditation on the holy week. *Greek Orthodox Archdioceses of America*. Retrieved on 17 May 2020 from https://www.goarch.org/-/judas-profile-in-the-psalms-meditation-on-the-holy-wednesday

Uraguchi, B. (1918). The psychology of Judas Iscariot. *The Biblical World, 51*(6), 345–360.

CHAPTER 14

Following in the Footsteps of Jesus: Conclusion

Debra J. Dean and Robert B. Huizinga

This book has examined faith perspectives in followership by focusing on Ananias, Andrew, Apollos, Aquilla, John, Judas, Jude, Mary of Magdala, Nathanael, Nicodemus, Peter, Philip, Priscilla, and Stephen. Each disciple was exegetically examined to understand how they followed Jesus and if their style matched those of Kelley, Chaleff, and Kellerman. Ananias was considered an exemplary follower, as well as a follower of the Way and a transient follower. John was metaphorically considered an open vessel and flowing water. Mary of Magdala was considered a faithful

D. J. Dean (✉) · R. B. Huizinga
Regent University, Virginia Beach, VA, USA
e-mail: debrdea@regent.edu; drdebra@drdebradean.com

R. B. Huizinga
e-mail: rhuizinga@auriniapharma.com; robehui@mail.regent.edu

R. B. Huizinga
North Saanich , BC, Canada

D. J. Dean and R. B. Huizinga (eds.), *Followership and Faith at Work*, Christian Faith Perspectives in Leadership and Business,
https://doi.org/10.1007/978-3-030-90614-6_14

follower, servant follower, and devoted follower. Peter's followership style had passion and loyalty. Stephen was full of faith and the Holy Spirit. He had wisdom, grace, power, peace, joy, and boldness. These early church followers provide followers in the twenty-first century with examples of how one can practically integrate their faith at work and in all areas of life.

Theoretically speaking, this book extends the examination of followership by focusing on the disciples of Jesus. Leadership and followership are intertwined, united in a common cause, which is the health of the organization. But for followers, it is more than just being in an organization. We are called into following Christ, through the church and our individual lives. Jesus' first and last commands to the disciple Peter were to "follow me" (Mark 1:17; John 21:21). And so this book, using the examples of various early disciples, explored followership from a Christian perspective.

Caullton (2021) notes that the church is the oldest continually operating organization in the world. Ricketson (2009) tells us that a church, which is an organized group of followers with specific responsibilities, should utilize a *Follower First* philosophy. This means that the modern church should empower followers such that they are held responsible for the growth of the church. We then have a responsibility therefore to act in a manner that strengthens and expands that organization. Phillips (2021) stated: "Followership is being a presence that strengthens." And so it is: Christ followers strengthen others.

As we have seen throughout the chapters, there are key elements of followership that resonate throughout this text. Bonnet and Henson (2021) speak to exemplary followership using Kelley's definitions. Kelley (1992) states that exemplary followers are independent, enthusiastic and use their intellect to support organizational objectives. Bonnet & Hansen (2021) call these followers the "go-to person" or the "right-hand person" through which positive followership is enabled. The fruits of the Holy Spirit (Galatians 5), living within these exemplary followers, are therefore displayed: love, joy, peace, patience, kindness, goodness, faithfulness, gentleness, and self-control. Pastors fall into the effective follower category and are seen to be as active and having positive energy. While not always agreeing with the leader (for example, their church board), effective followers offer constructive alternatives to what the leader is suggesting.

Toulassi (2021), using Andrew as an example, speaks to followers who do not care for their own fame: "Isn't follower achievement more important than title or structural position?" Rather than chase position, these humble followers perceive what the leaders need for the good of the organization. This can be seen as a spiritual gift, perceiving (Gr: propheteia).

Steinhoff (2021) brings in Chaleff's definition of courageous followership and notes that the impact of courageous followership is immediate. Using Judas as an example, he notes that simple followership can betray the leaders or the organization. Courageous followers on the other hand invoke change. Courageous followership conquers groupthink (Bell, 2021) in a bottom-up approach. While followership can be collective, it can be a lonely exercise in similar fashion to leadership.

Finally, followership may be invisible yet the impact is felt in the organization. We focus on the visible impacts of leadership or followership and use these as examples to propel future leaders/followers. Yet, we should be content with followership that remains out of the spotlight. In the same way where Jesus left the crowd to pray (Mark 1, Luke 5), he exhorts his followers to conduct themselves in similar fashion in Matthew 6. He tells His disciples (and us) how to follow:

- To not practice righteousness in front of others (vs. 1).
- To give to the needy in private (vs. 2–4).
- To pray in private (vs. 5–8).

These verses appear to tell us that we should be willing to practice followership, not in a manner that shows off how well we follow, but in a manner where we simply put the needs of our organization and our church above ourselves. The disciples of Christ were effective in their followership, and in doing so they changed not only the world but each of us personally. May we be followers who change the lives of others!

References

Bell, R. M. (2021). Nicodemus: An example of courageous followership conquering groupthin. In D. J. Dean & R. B. Huizinga (Eds.), *Followership and faith at work*. Palgrave Macmillan.

Bonnet, C., & Henson, J. D. (2021). "Follow me!"—The story of followership through the eyes of the Apostle Peter. In D. J. Dean & R. B. Huizinga (Eds.), *Followership and faith at work*. Palgrave Macmillan.

Caullton, J. (2021). Come, see, do: Igniting the spark that energizes followers. In D. J. Dean & R. B. Huizinga (Eds.), *Followership and faith at work*. Palgrave Macmillan.

Kelley, R. E. (1992). *The power of followership: How to create leaders people want to follow, and followers who lead themselves*. Doubleday/Currency.

Phillips, L. D. (2021). Implicit followership traditions in the new testament: Priscilla, Aquila, and Apollos. In D. J. Dean & R. B. Huizinga (Eds.), *Followership and faith at work*. Palgrave Macmillan.

Ricketson, R. (2009). *Follower first: Rethinking leading in the church*. Heartworks Publications.

Steinhoff, R. L. (2021). Stephen: Deacon, Martyr and agent of change. In D. Dean & R. B. Huizinga (Eds.), *Followership and faith at work*. Palgrave Macmillan.

Toulassi, B. (2021). Reading your leader: Essence of followership. In D. J. Dean & R. B. Huizinga (Eds.), *Followership and faith at work*. Palgrave Macmillan.

Index

D. Dean et al. (eds.), *Followership and Faith at Work*, Christian Faith Perspectives in Leadership and Business,
https://doi.org/10.1007/978-3-030-90614-6

G

H

www.ingramcontent.com/pod-product-compliance
Lightning Source LLC
Chambersburg PA
CBHW062142200726
48454CB00005BB/361
9783030906139